AT HOME
with the WORD®
2018

Sunday Scriptures and Scripture Insights

YEAR B

Catherine A. Cory, PHD

Rev. Patrick J. Hartin

Ed Langlois

Tanya Rybarczyk, MA, MAPM

ALSO AVAILABLE IN A LARGE PRINT EDITION

LTP

LITURGY
TRAINING
PUBLICATIONS

Nihil Obstat
Very Reverend Daniel A. Smilanic, JCD
Vicar for Canonical Services
Archdiocese of Chicago
February 8, 2017

Imprimatur
Very Reverend Ronald A. Hicks
Vicar General
Archdiocese of Chicago
February 8, 2017

Prayers in the introductions to each liturgical time are adapted from *Prayers for Sundays and Seasons, Year B* by Peter Scagnelli, Chicago: Liturgy Training Publications, 1996.

AT HOME WITH THE WORD® 2018 © 2017 Archdiocese of Chicago: Liturgy Training Publications, 3949 South Racine Avenue, Chicago, IL 60609; 800-933-1800; fax 800-933-7094; e-mail: orders@ltp.org; website: www.LTP.org. All rights reserved.

This book was edited by Lorie Simmons. Michael A. Dodd was the production editor, Anna Manhart was the designer, and Kari Nicholls was the production artist.

The cover for this year's *At Home with the Word*® is by Cody F. Miller. The interior art is by Kathy Ann Sullivan.

Printed in the United States of America.

ISBN 978-1-61671-321-8

AHW18

Welcome to At Home with the Word® 2018

The Authors of the Introductions

Marielle Frigge, osb, taught Scripture and theology for thirty-three years at Mount Marty College in Yankton, South Dakota, and is now formation director for Sacred Heart Monastery. Michael Cameron teaches Scripture and history of Christianity in the theology department at the University of Portland in Oregon.

Scripture Readings

For each Sunday, you will find the three readings and Responsorial Psalm from the *Lectionary for Mass*, from which readings are proclaimed in Roman Catholic churches in the United States.

Scripture Insights

Two authors have written Scripture Insights for 2018. Catherine Cory is associate professor of theology at the University of St. Thomas in St. Paul, Minnesota. She received her doctoral degree in Christianity and Judaism in antiquity from the University of Notre Dame, and has taught at the undergraduate and graduate level since 1991. She is coeditor of *The Christian Theological Tradition* (Routledge, 2008) and authored some of its chapters. She is also the author of *Revelation* (Liturgical Press, 2006) and other works on the New Testament. Dr. Cory wrote Scripture Insights from the First Sunday of Advent through the Seventh Sunday of Easter.

Fr. Patrick Hartin, a priest of the Diocese of Spokane, Washington, taught New Testament studies and Christian spirituality at Gonzaga University from 1995 to 2016. His doctorate in New Testament is from the University of South Africa (Pretoria). His books include *James,* in the Sacra Pagina Series (2003), *Exploring the Spirituality of the Gospels* (2010), and *A Window into the Spirituality of Paul* (2015), all from Liturgical Press. Fr. Hartin has written Scripture Insights from Pentecost Sunday through the end of the liturgical year.

Dennis Hamm, sj, contributed to Scripture Insights for the Fifth Sunday of Lent.

Practice of Faith, Hope, Charity

Two authors wrote the Practice of Faith, Hope, or Charity. Ed Langlois is managing editor of the *Catholic Sentinel* in the Archdiocese of Portland, Oregon. He has a bachelor's degree in English (Colorado College) and a master of arts in pastoral ministry from the University of Portland. Ed's practices appear from the Seventh Sunday of Easter through the end of the liturgical year. Tanya Rybarczyk holds master's degrees in pastoral ministry (University of Portland) and English (Binghamton University, New York). She is a Catholic adult faith formation educator, and her writing has been featured in *America* magazine. She has written practices from the First Sunday of Advent through the Ascension of the Lord.

Additional Downloadable Questions and Activities

Download additional questions and activities for families, Christian initiation groups, and other adult groups. Follow this link to the product supplements page on the LTP website: http://www.ltp.org/t-productsupplements.aspx. Scroll to the icon of the cover of *At Home with the Word*® and click on one of the three audiences listed below it.

Weekday Readings

See the opening of each liturgical time for a list of weekday Mass readings.

Art for 2018

On the cover, Cody Miller, an artist from Columbus, Ohio, has used paint and cut paper to imagine the scene in Genesis 15:1–6, when God forms a covenant with Abraham. Abraham and Sarah look up at the stars that represent the many future descendants promised by God. We hear this Scripture proclaimed on the Feast of the Holy Family, January 31. This is the second of several scenes from salvation history to appear on the covers of *At Home with the Word*® in coming years. Kathy Ann Sullivan uses a scratch board technique in the interior designs to evoke the liturgical seasons. She lives in Colorado Springs, Colorado.

Table of Contents

The Lectionary

by Marielle Frigge, OSB

WHAT IS A LECTIONARY?

The word *lectionary* comes from the Latin word *legere*, "to read," and names a collection of Scripture readings from both the Old and New Testaments that are proclaimed throughout the liturgical year in a particular order. Christian lectionaries were in use already in the fourth century, but before the invention of the printing press in the mid-fifteenth century, readings differed from place to place. Printing allowed for a more standardized lectionary, so that Catholics around the world could hear the same Bible readings at Mass on any given day.

However, in the four centuries before the Second Vatican Council (1963–65), the lectionary had a somewhat limited ability to touch the faith lives of Catholics. Most could not understand what was read because Scripture readings as well as the prayers of the Mass were proclaimed in Latin. Further, because the lectionary of that time used only particular selections from the Bible repeated year after year, Catholics received a restricted exposure to the riches of Scripture.

GIFTS OF THE SECOND VATICAN COUNCIL

After the Second Vatican Council, not only were the biblical readings made available in the language of the people, but the structure of the lectionary was expanded as well. These changes resulted from a fresh understanding of the role of Scripture in the liturgy. Returning to the ancient understanding that Christ is present in the Scriptures, the Council Fathers further emphasized that the Eucharist nourishes God's people at two tables: the proclaimed Word of God and the Eucharistic banquet. For this reason, the revised Lectionary includes much more Scripture. Rather than repeating a yearly pattern, it includes a three-year cycle for Sundays and a two-year cycle for weekdays. Through this expanded array of selections, it aims to present the broad sweep of the salvation story, arranged purposefully around the liturgical year with the four major liturgical seasons of Advent, Christmas Time, Lent, and Easter Time punctuating the many weeks of Ordinary Time.

These great liturgical seasons instruct the faithful in the most significant aspects of salvation history. The liturgical year begins with Advent, expressing the ancient longing and hope of God's covenant people for redemption. Christmas Time celebrates the Incarnation of the Lord, God's Word of salvation fully present and active in the world, made flesh in Jesus the Christ. During Lent, the Scripture readings call Christians to deeper conversion: to amend their ways of failing to respond to God's saving Word, to cultivate greater intimacy with God, and to rejoice that he never ceases to offer life-changing mercy. These Scriptures about conversion speak powerfully to those preparing for initiation. Easter Time proclaims the Paschal Mystery, the redeeming Death and Resurrection of Jesus Christ. That mystery leads us into life in divine Spirit, poured out upon all the faithful at Pentecost, sending us out to serve. In addition to highlighting the liturgical seasons, the Lectionary illuminates other key mysteries of Catholic faith in solemnities such as the Most Holy Trinity, the Most Holy Body and Blood of Christ, the Assumption of the Blessed Virgin Mary, and in feasts such as the Presentation of the Lord and the Exaltation of the Holy Cross.

FOUR SUNDAY SCRIPTURE SELECTIONS

At Home with the Word® provides all four Scripture passages of each Sunday: a selection from the Old Testament (except during Easter Time when we hear from Acts of the Apostles); a Responsorial Psalm or canticle; a New Testament reading from one of the letters, Acts of the Apostles, or Revelation; and, most important, a Gospel passage. Each year of the three-year cycle draws from a particular Gospel account: Matthew in Year A, Mark in Year B, and Luke in Year C. The Gospel of John, so highly symbolic and profound, is heard in the liturgical seasons. The Lectionary includes readings from John on several Sundays of Lent, during the sacred Triduum, and most Sundays of Easter Time. Because Mark is the shortest Gospel account, some Sundays of Ordinary Time in Year B use passages from John.

The pattern of today's Catholic Lectionary has served as a model for lectionaries of several other Christian churches. As a result, Catholics and many Protestants hear the same Scripture passages proclaimed on Sundays. The biblical Word of God thus draws them closer.

Understanding how the four Scripture passages of each Sunday are related can help us appreciate how the Lectionary invites Christians to understand, ponder, and integrate the message of God's Word. The First Reading from the Old Testament usually bears some connection to the Gospel passage, often by means of a significant person, event, or image. Rooted in the ancient practice of the Jewish synagogue, the Responsorial, which follows the First Reading, is usually from a psalm and represents the people's response to God's Word in the First Reading. In this way the first two Scripture passages mirror a theme woven throughout the Bible: God always takes the initiative to address humankind, speaking a Word that invites a response from God's people. The Responsorial may also illustrate or clarify what the First Reading proclaims, or may be related to the liturgical season, and thus is intended to foster meditation on the Word of God.

Frequently the Second Reading, always from the New Testament, follows the ancient practice of *lectio continua* (Latin for "continuous reading"), so that on each Sunday we hear important selections in order from a particular book. For example, the Second Reading is often an excerpt from one of the letters of Saint Paul, and by continuous reading over several Sundays, the Lectionary presents some of his major theological insights in a particular letter.

During Ordinary Time the Lectionary presents continuous reading in the Gospels also, allowing us to see each evangelist's distinctive way of unfolding the Gospel story. For example, in Year A, from the Fourteenth Sunday of Ordinary Time to the end of the liturgical year in November, we hear the Gospel of Matthew from chapter 11 through chapter 25. Not every verse of Matthew is included, and occasionally a Sunday solemnity or feast requires a reading from a different Gospel, but continuous reading relates major aspects of Matthew's narrative, just as it does for Mark's in Year B and Luke's in Year C. Over time, through continuous reading, we can become familiar with the particular content and qualities of each Gospel account.

THE LECTIONARY AS A VISUAL SIGN

The Lectionary nourishes us with its words proclaimed in the liturgy—the Lord's own voice speaking to his people. It also nourishes us as a visual sign of the Lord's presence among us. The United States' Conference of Catholic Bishops reminds Catholics that gestures and physical objects used in liturgy are "signs by which Christians express and deepen their relationship to God" (*Built of Living Stones: Art, Architecture, and Worship,* 23). Although the Lectionary's proper place during the liturgy is on the ambo (the special podium from which readings are proclaimed), a part of the Lectionary—the Gospel readings—has been made into a separate Book of the Gospels. That book, often richly decorated, may be carried in the entrance procession on Sundays and holy days. It is placed on the altar at the beginning of Mass and then, when the assembly rises to sing the Alleluia, the Gospel reader may processes with the book to the ambo, accompanied by servers holding candles. In response to the deacon or priest's introduction to the Gospel Reading, the people respond, signing their forehead, lips, and heart with a small cross. Observing such signs and ceremonies, one could not miss the special reverence we give to the Word of God—especially in the Gospel.

In the bishops' teaching about the ambo, from which the Scriptures are proclaimed, we find an apt crystallization of the Church's conviction about the role of Scripture in the Mass. Urging that the ambo should be of a size and placement that draws attention to the sacred Word, the document says, "Here the Christian community encounters the living Lord in the word of God and prepares itself for the 'breaking of the bread' and the mission to live the word that will be proclaimed" (*Built of Living Stones,* 61).

Introduction to the Gospel according to Mark

by Michael Cameron

In the late 60s of the first century, nearly forty years since the Resurrection and Ascension of the Lord, he had not yet returned. Jerusalem was under siege by the Romans, and the persecution of Christians in Rome itself was intensifying after the fire of 64. Peter and Paul had died, and few eye witnesses to Jesus' ministry were left. Christians had told and retold the stories of Jesus' ministry, Death, and Resurrection over the years, but Christians began to feel the need for written instruction.

In these years, Mark, leaning on the teachings of Peter and others, wrote his Gospel, the earliest one we have. It is likely that he wrote for his suffering community in the environs of Rome. His main concern was to record the basic facts and stay faithful to the tradition, and Mark wrote with a flair for the dramatic and a rich theological sense.

Suffering had thrown Mark's community into a spiritual crisis. The crisis came not because of weak faith, but through a strong faith too focused on the privileges and glory of being the community of the Resurrection: Being disciples meant enjoying the benefits of Jesus' victory (see 10:35–45). As a counterweight to this, Mark refocused on Jesus' Death as the foundation of discipleship (8:31–35). Mark's primary themes of the Kingdom of God, the identity of Jesus, and the call to discipleship each undergo dramatic development in the Gospel in light of the Cross. For Mark, everything, even Jesus' glorious return, stands in the shadow of his Crucifixion. The German New Testament scholar Martin Kähler aptly called the Gospel according to Mark "a passion narrative with an extended introduction."

JESUS PROCLAIMS THE KINGDOM

In Mark's first chapters, Jesus is a messianic figure on the move, proclaiming the nearness of God's Kingdom in his words and works. As the Spirit "drove" Jesus into the wilderness after his baptism (1:12), so Jesus charges the early pages of Mark with divine power and urgency. The synagogue exorcism in 1:21–28 demonstrates Jesus' mastery of the spiritual world; the healings that follow in

1:29—2:10 reveal that the Kingdom's power lies in redemptive service. Jesus never defines the Kingdom of God, but the parables of chapter 4 describe its characteristics. Irresistibly it comes, grows, changes everything, feeds everyone. It heals bodies, repairs hearts, defeats evil, creates community. Nothing stops its relentless coming; not sin (2:7), disease (1:40–45), calamity (4:35–41), or demonic forces (3:22–27). The Kingdom emerges as a result of God's action, not humanity's.

The unfeeling religious leaders fail to receive the message (3:1–6). They lack the spiritual eyes and ears to perceive the new in-breaking of God's love in Jesus' ministry and the new turning to God's love that this requires. Paradoxically Jesus does find this among tax collectors (2:15–17), the sick (1:29–34), and the wretched (5:1–20).

BECOMING DISCIPLES OF JESUS

Initial faith through the miracles is only a first step. The disciples struggle to fulfill the Master's hopes for them. "Do you not yet have faith?" Jesus asks early on (4:40). After Jesus feeds the five thousand, he cares for the disciples by walking to them on the water during their midnight struggle. They merely become frightened, Mark comments, "They had not understood the incident of the loaves. On the contrary, their hearts were hardened" (6:52). Jesus tries again by feeding the four thousand, but their minds are fixed on literal bread. "Do you still not understand?" Jesus asks (8:21).

Peter confesses that Jesus is the Messiah (8:29). But his awareness is only partial, for he needs Jesus to fit his expectations, which definitively exclude suffering. Jesus calls the idea satanic (8:33). Eventually one disciple betrays him, another denies him, and all desert him. Some readers think that Mark's telling of the disciples' failures is his way of disparaging "official" Christian leadership. But the disciples were later reconciled to the Lord after his Resurrection and lived to prove their faith. It is more likely that Mark is encouraging Jesus' followers to take heart from the disciples' example of recovery from failure. With Peter's

martyrdom still a recent memory, the story of him denying the Lord would have special power.

CHRIST THE SUFFERING SERVANT

The Son of God has a rich, deep humanity in this Gospel. Mark's Greek word for Jesus' reaction to the plight of the leper in 1:41 might be translated "his heart melted with compassion," the same word used for Jesus' compassion on the crowds.

Jesus insists that his divinity should not be made known (1:44; 3:12; 5:43; 7:36; 8:26, 30), a motif known as the messianic secret. He refuses to be the political messiah that people expected. He reinterpreted honors in terms of his mission as suffering servant, processing into Jerusalem on a humble little donkey (11:1–10), not a horse, as a conquering king would. He is anointed by an anonymous woman, not for enthronement but for burial (14:3–9). He wears royal attire and receives homage from the Gentiles, but in mockery (15:16–20). Jesus establishes the new covenant of Jeremiah 31 by becoming the Suffering Servant of Isaiah 53: "This is my blood of the covenant poured out for many" (14:24).

From the beginning the reader knows that Jesus is the Son of God (1:1). Throughout the Gospel the only voices to confess his true identity come from God (1:11; 9:7) and demons (1:24; 3:11; 5:7). Meanwhile, religious leaders call him demon-possessed (3:22), his family thinks he's a lunatic (3:21), and village neighbors complain he's pretentious (6:2–3). To their credit the disciples do begin to wonder, "Who then is this?" (4:41). But no human lips confess his true identity—until the end. Stripped of his dignity, his disciples, his life, destitute and utterly alone, Jesus draws his last breath. But at this precise moment the long-awaited confession comes from a Roman centurion: "Truly this man was the Son of God!" (15:39). Jesus' Death reveals the identity of God's Son, a living tableau of the disciples' calling to live the Way of the Cross. The Resurrection is proclaimed by disciples who have received a new life after they have lost their lives "for my sake and that of the gospel" (8:35).

Introduction to the Gospel according to John

by Michael Cameron

This Gospel has no year of its own in the Lectionary's three-year cycle, but it is strongly represented *every* year during Christmas, Lent, and Easter Time; it also appears in Ordinary Time in Mark for Year B, Sundays 17–21. John shares some features of the first three Gospels (called "synoptic" for "seeing together"). Some stories overlap, characters seen in the Synoptics reappear, and John clearly voices the evangelistic, instructional purpose of all the Gospels: that you may believe and receive life in Jesus' name (20:31).

But its vision stands majestically apart, like the eagle that became this Gospel's symbol. It is rooted in the teaching of a mysterious unnamed figure, the "disciple whom Jesus loved" (13:23; 19:26; 20:2; 21:7, 20), who authenticates this Gospel's "testimony" (19:35; 21:24). It uniquely portrays the divine Word acting with God and as God to create all things (1:1–5), taking human flesh to reveal the Father's glory (1:1, 14–18).

John communicates in distinctive ways. The Synoptics tell Jesus' story in compact vignettes; John constructs chapter-long dramas (see especially chapters 4, 9, and 11). The first three Gospels contain pithy, memorable sayings about God's Kingdom; John's Jesus speaks hypnotically repetitive discourses focused on eternal life (for example, 6:22–59; 10:1–18; chapters 14–17). The Synoptics' homespun parables pique curiosity about Jesus' message; the Johannine Jesus poetically develops elements like water (4:7–15), bread (6:25–35), and light (3:19–21; 9:4–5; 12:35–36) into metaphors for contemplating divine truth.

John tells unique stories about Jesus: He changes water into wine (2:1–11), disputes with Nicodemus (3:1–21), engages the Samaritan woman at the well (4:4–26), heals a man born blind (9:1–41), raises dead Lazarus (11:1–45), chides the doubting Thomas (20:24–29), and cooks post-Easter breakfast for the disciples (21:1–14). John also varies details from some familiar synoptic stories, among which Jesus "cleanses the Temple" early in his ministry rather than late

(2:13–22); the Synoptics' Passover meal ("the Last Supper") is a meal *before* Passover where Jesus washes the disciples' feet (13:4–15); the synoptic Jesus anguishes before death, but in John goes to the Cross with serenity (12:27; 18:11); and unlike the Synoptics, John has Jesus die on the day of preparation for Passover when the Passover lambs are sacrificed. These repeated references to Passover heighten the sacrificial symbolism of Jesus' Death. Likewise, a strong liturgical symbolism makes Jesus' Death the true Passover lamb sacrifice (1:29), his risen body the true Temple (2:21), and his sacramental Body and Blood the true food and drink of Israel's wilderness journey (6:53–58).

John's hallmark strategies of indirectness and double meanings entice characters to move from surface earthly meanings to encoded heavenly meanings. Some catch on, like the woman at the well (4:4–26), but others miss the point, like Nicodemus, (3:3–10), the crowds (7:32–36), and Pilate (18:33–38). This indirectness separates truly committed disciples from the half-hearted window shoppers (2:23–25). Jesus performs "signs" (not "miracles") that lure people up the new ladder of Jacob arching from earth's pictures to heaven's glory (1:51; Genesis 28:12). This imagery of signs ends in a plain revelation about Jesus' divinity not found in the Synoptic Gospels. His seven solemn "I AM" statements (6:35; 8:12; 10:7; 10:11; 11:25; 14:6; 15:1) recall God's revelation to Moses as "I AM" (Exodus 3:14) and testify to Jesus as the only source of life. So the inner truth of the blind man seeing is, "I am the light of the world" (9:5), and of the dead man rising, "I am the resurrection and the life" (11:25).

Jesus' signs hint at his divine glory (2:11) to be fully revealed at his "hour" (2:4; 7:30; 8:20; 13:1). Like the disciples, readers put things together only after the Resurrection (2:22); then we realize that as Jesus was "lifted up" for crucifixion by the Romans, he was lifted up to glory by his Father (3:14; 8:28; 12:32). He mounted his Cross like a king ascending his throne, as Pilate's placard unwittingly proclaimed (19:19–22). The Son's mission was to reunite the world to its source of eternal life in God (3:16; 4:34; 17:4). He died with satisfaction that this work was accomplished, and announced, "It is finished!" (19:30).

In the Gospel according to John, God the Father is unseen and mostly silent, but pervasively present. The Father sent the Son, loves him (5:20; 15:9), bears him witness (5:37; 8:18), glorifies him (8:54), and dwells with him (14:11). The Father grants the Son to have life in himself, to judge the world, and to raise the dead (5:19–30). Father and Son together gave life to the world at creation (1:1–2), and continue to do so (5:17). God the Son in human flesh has "explained" the Father, literally "brought God into the open" (1:18). The Son does this so completely that Jesus says, "Whoever has seen me has seen the Father" (14:9; 12:45).

But divine life emanates from a third mysterious presence, "the Spirit of truth" (14:17). The Father and the Son together send the Spirit (15:26), who teaches the disciples about what Jesus said and who he was (14:26; 16:13). By the Spirit's indwelling, divine life flows through them like a river (7:38–39; 14:17).

John depicts the disciples as fruitful vine branches that the Father lovingly tends (15:1–5). Omitting all other ethical instruction, this Gospel says that the only measure of the disciples' fruitfulness is their love for one another (13:34–35; 15:12–17).

True to character, this Gospel is sometimes one-sided. John's sense of Jesus' real humanity is relatively weak; and though teaching that "salvation is from the Jews" (4:22), it can be hostile toward Judaism (8:21–26, 37–59). John must be balanced by the rest of the New Testament and the Church's later teaching. But its profound spiritual theology of the Word made flesh (1:14) has decisively shaped Christian theology, spirituality, and art, ever since it was written in the late first century.

Introduction to St. Paul and His Letters

by Michael Cameron

PAUL'S CONVERSION

Saul of Tarsus was born about the same time as Jesus, to a pious Jewish family in Tarsus, in the Roman province of Cilicia (modern eastern Turkey). Well-educated and extremely religious, this son of Roman citizens was a member of the strict Pharisees (Philippians 3:5–6). In Christianity's earliest days, he says, "I persecuted the church of God beyond measure and even tried to destroy it" (Galatians 1:14–15). But then came the sudden turning point of his life: just outside Damascus, a brilliant flash of light blinded his eyes, buckled his legs, and altered his mind about God's design for human salvation (Acts 9:1–19). Christ's last known post-Resurrection appearance suddenly brought the Pharisee to birth as an Apostle, as "one born abnormally" (1 Corinthians 15:8).

Since Moses had said that anyone hanged on a tree was cursed by God, the crucified Christ had been a stumbling block to Saul, the Jew. But God revealed to Paul (Saul's Greek name) the awesome truth that this crucified man was God's power and wisdom (1 Corinthians 1:24). Christ's Death and Resurrection had turned the page of world history and unleashed the powers and blessings of the Age to Come. In that knowledge, Paul discounted everything that went before in his life as "rubbish" in comparison to knowing Christ, even his prized Jewish pedigree. Paul's blockbuster insight was that, for Jews and Gentiles alike, saving faith in Jesus Christ alone, not the works of Moses' Law, made one a part of God's people (Philippians 3:5–10).

PAUL'S MISSION AND TEACHINGS

That insight released a mighty energy in Paul to announce Christ to the whole world. So began Paul's thirty-plus-year missionary ministry. He suffered beatings, imprisonments, and repeated brushes with death, but by the mid-60s of the first century, he had planted a network of vibrant Christian communities throughout the eastern Mediterranean basin. Concerned to stay in touch with his churches, to feed them with sound teaching, and to protect them from poachers, he wrote letters that eventually became part of our New Testament. Their profound theology, breathless style, and stirring imagery have kindled and rekindled Christian faith ever since.

Paul never knew the earthly Jesus, and he speaks little of stories familiar to us from the Gospels (though he knew Peter and the Apostles personally, used their traditions, and quotes Jesus' words at the first Eucharist). Paul's thinking flows almost exclusively from the reality of the Lord's Death and Resurrection—the moment when God's power decisively defeated sin and inaugurated the Age to Come.

Paul explains that event with an outpouring of vivid metaphors. His imagery of "justification" imagines a scene at the Judgment Day when Christ's Death acquits us of breaking the Law of Mount Sinai (Romans 3:21–31). His liturgical concept of "sanctification" pictures Christ giving believers the holiness needed to approach God in purity (1 Corinthians 6:11). Paul connects to economic imagery when he speaks of "redemption," portraying Christ's costly Death buying us back from slavery to sin (Romans 3:24; 1 Corinthians 6:20). His political-military picture envisions humanity's ancient and chronic warfare with God brought to an end in "reconciliation" (Romans 5:10–11). He evokes the family with his "adoption" image, conveying our change of status when Christ made us over from slaves to children of God (Romans 8:14–15; Galatians 4:4–7).

Christians behave not according to external laws, Paul teaches, but by the force of the Holy Spirit, who produces in believers the many fruits of the new life (Galatians 5:22–23), the greatest of which is love (1 Corinthians 13:13). The same love of God displayed in Christ's Death pours forth into our hearts through the Holy Spirit (Romans 5:5–8). The Spirit remakes us in the image of Christ: "all of us, gazing with unveiled face on the glory of the Lord, are being transformed into the same image from glory to glory, as from the Lord who is the Spirit" (2 Corinthians 3:18).

Christ somehow joined us to himself at his Cross so that when he died, we died (2 Corinthians 5:14). Christians "baptized into Christ's death" die to their old selves and rise to newness of life (Romans 6:3–4). In this new humanity, which leaves behind old identities, the oneness of Christ knows "neither Jew nor Greek, slave nor free, male nor female" (Galatians 3:28). All drink of the same Spirit who makes them the mystical "Body of Christ" (1 Corinthians 12:12–27), the Church, whose members offer worship to God while humbly serving one another. In Christ we are "the new creation: the old things have passed away; behold, the new things have come" (2 Corinthians 5:17).

But the new life emerging in Christians conflicts with the world as it is. Paul leaves social change to God while urging Christians to live patiently within the structures of society as they stand until the new age takes over. So slaves do not seek freedom, the unmarried do not seek marriage, and Gentiles do not seek circumcision, because "the world in its present form is passing away" (1 Corinthians 7:17–31).

For the time being we see God, the world, and ourselves in a blur, but one day we will understand everything (1 Corinthians 13:12). Bodily death is pure gain: we depart to "be with Christ" (Philippians 1:23)—Paul does not say more—and await the resurrection of the body, when Christ "will change our lowly body to conform with his glorious body" (Philippians 3:21). We will be radically different, but somehow still ourselves, just as wheat stalks are both different from, and the same as, the tiny seeds they come from (1 Corinthians 15:36–49). When that moment comes, Christ's work will be done, and God will be "all in all" (1 Corinthians 15:28).

But for Paul and his readers, including us, the present remains the time for work. With the hope of the Resurrection constantly drawing us on, Paul says, we must "be firm, steadfast, always fully devoted to the work of the Lord, knowing that in the Lord your labor is not in vain" (1 Corinthians 15:58).

Studying and Praying Scripture

by Michael Cameron

A recent study claimed that only 22 percent of American Catholics read the Bible regularly, and just 8 percent are involved in Scripture groups. Not many know how profoundly biblical the Roman Catholic Church has been from her very roots, having "always venerated the divine scriptures as she venerates the Body of the Lord" (*Dei Verbum* [*Dogmatic Constitution on Divine Revelation*], 21). How may Catholics learn to read Scripture? This essay sketches a path for seekers.

PREPARING TO READ

Become an apprentice to the Bible. Ordinary people can reach a good level of understanding, but at a cost: the Bible yields its riches to those who give themselves to the search for understanding. Start by reading daily, even if only for a few minutes. Join a group that reads and discusses Scripture together.

You will need tools. Think of yourself as a prospector for the Bible's gold. Nuggets on the ground are easily picked up, but the really rich veins lie beneath the surface. Digging requires study, commitment, and skills.

Invest in tools that reap the harvest of others' labors. Buy a study Bible with introductions, explanatory notes, and maps. Use another translation for devotional reading and comparison. Get access to a Bible dictionary with detailed information on biblical books, concepts, geography, outlines, customs, and so forth. Bible concordances will help you find all occurrences of particular words. A dictionary of biblical theology will give guidance on major theological ideas. A Bible atlas will give a sense of the locations and movements in the biblical stories. Recent Church documents on the Bible offer rich instruction to seekers.

READING FOR KNOWLEDGE

Get to know historical contexts suggested by a passage. Learn all you can about the Bible's basic story line, its "salvation history," beginning with Israel and continuing in the Church. Salvation by God's grace, obedience to God's will, and judgment on

sin are basic to both Old and New Testaments. Learn about the covenants with Abraham and David that emphasize God's grace. The covenant with Moses presumes God's grace and emphasizes obedience. Both covenant traditions reemerge and are fulfilled in the New Covenant in Jesus, who pours out his life to save all people (grace) but is extremely demanding of his disciples (obedience).

Read entire books of the Bible in order to gain a sense of the "whole cloth" from which the snippets of the Sunday Lectionary are cut. Try to imagine what the books meant for their original authors and audiences. Ask how and why a book was put together: What is its structure, outline, main themes, literary forms, overall purpose?

Get to know the Old Testament narratives and psalms, but learn the Gospel accounts especially. The Lectionary's yearly focus on Matthew, Mark, or Luke offers an opportunity to learn each one. John is the focus during the Church's special seasons.

READING FOR WISDOM

Read as one who seeks God, like the writer of Psalm 119. Ask what the text is asking you to believe, do, or hope for. Jesus' powerful proclamation in Mark 1:15 gives a strong framework: "This is the time of fulfillment" (now is the time to be attentive and ready to act); "the kingdom of God is at hand" (God is about to speak and act); "repent" (be willing to change your mind and move with fresh direction); "believe in the gospel" (embrace the grace that has already embraced you).

Read books straight through, a self-contained section at a time, carefully, slowly, and meditatively. Stop where natural breaks occur at the end of stories or sequences of thought.

Beware the sense that you already know what a text is going to say. Read attentively, asking what God is teaching you through this text at this minute about your life or about your communities—family, church, work, neighborhood, nation. Trust the Holy Spirit to guide you to what you need.

READING FOR WORSHIP

The goal of reading the Bible is not learning new facts or getting merely private inspiration for living, but entering into deeper communion with God. Allow the Bible to teach you to pray by giving you the words to use in prayer. The psalms are especially apt for this, but any part of the Bible may be prayed. This practice, dating back more than fifteen hundred years, is called *lectio divina*, Latin for "sacred reading."

Read Scripture in relation to the Eucharist. The Bible both prepares for Jesus' real presence and helps us understand it. The same Jesus who healed the lepers, stilled the storm, and embraced the children is present to us in the Word and in the Sacrament.

The Bible is a library of spiritual treasures waiting to be discovered. The Church intends that this treasury be "wide open to the Christian faithful" (*Dei Verbum* [*Dogmatic Constitution on Divine Revelation*], 22).

RESOURCES

Brown, Raymond E., ss. *101 Questions and Answers on the Bible*. Mahwah, NJ: Paulist Press, 2003.

Casey, Michael. *Sacred Reading: The Ancient Art of Lectio Divina*. Liguori, MS: Liguori, 1997.

Frigge, Marielle, osb. *Beginning Biblical Studies*. Winona, MN: Anselm Academic, 2013.

Hahn, Scott. *Catholic Bible Dictionary*. New York: Doubleday, 2009.

Magrassi, Mariano. *Praying the Bible*. Collegeville, MN: Liturgical Press, 1998.

New Collegeville Bible Commentary Series. Collegeville, MN: Liturgical Press. (Short books on individual books of the Bible, various dates.)

Paprocki, Joe. *The Bible Blueprint, A Catholic's Guide to Understanding and Embracing God's Word*. Chicago: Loyola Press, 2009.

The Bible Documents: A Parish Resource. Chicago: Liturgy Training Publications, 2001.

The Catholic Study Bible, 3rd Edition. General editor, Donald Senior, cp. New York: Oxford, 2016.

Advent

Prayer before Reading the Word

O God,
whose Word is comfort
and whose promise is a new creation,
prepare the way in the wilderness of our world.

Speak today to the inmost heart of your people,
that by lives of holiness and service
we may hasten the coming of that day
and be found at peace when at last it dawns.

We ask this through our Lord Jesus Christ,
who was, who is, and who is to come,
your Son, who lives and reigns with you
in the unity of the Holy Spirit,
one God, for ever and ever. Amen.

Prayer after Reading the Word

Great and merciful God,
from among this world's lowly and humble,
you choose your servants
and call them to work with you
to fulfill your loving plan of salvation.

By the power of your Spirit,
make your Church fertile and fruitful,
that, imitating the obedient faith of Mary,
the Church may welcome your Word of life
and so become the joyful mother of
                countless offspring,
a great and holy posterity of children
destined for undying life.

We ask this through our Lord Jesus Christ,
your Son, who lives and reigns with you
in the unity of the Holy Spirit,
one God, for ever and ever. Amen.

Weekday Readings

December 4: *Isaiah 2:1–5; Matthew 8:5–11*
December 5: *Isaiah 11:1–10; Luke 10:21–24*
December 6: *Isaiah 25:6–10a; Matthew 15:29–37*
December 7: *Isaiah 26:1–6; Matthew 7:21, 24–27*
**December 8: Solemnity of the Immaculate Conception
   of the Blessed Virgin Mary
   Genesis 3:9–15, 20; Ephesians 1:3–6, 11–12;
   Luke 1:26–38**
December 9: *Isaiah 30:19–21, 23–26;
   Matthew 9:35—10:1, 5a, 6–8*

December 11: *Isaiah 35:1–10; Luke 5:17–26*
**December 12: Feast of Our Lady of Guadalupe
   Zechariah 2:14–17; Luke 1:26–38**
December 13: *Isaiah 40:25–31; Matthew 11:28–30*
December 14: *Isaiah 41:13–20; Matthew 11:11–15*
December 15: *Isaiah 48:17–19; Matthew 11:11–15*
December 16: *Sirach 48:1–4, 9–11; Matthew 17:9a, 10–13*

December 18: *Jeremiah 23:5–8; Matthew 1:18–25*
December 19: *Judges 13:2–7, 24–25a; Luke 1:5–25*
December 20: *Isaiah 7:10–14; Luke 1:26–38*
December 21: *Song of Songs 2:8–14 or Zephaniah 3:14–8a;
   Luke 1:39–45*
December 22: *1 Samuel 1:24–28; Luke 1:46–56*
December 23: *Malachi 3:1–4, 23–24; Luke 1:57–66*

READING I
Isaiah 63:16b–17, 19b; 64:2–7

You, LORD, are our father,
    our redeemer you are named forever.
Why do you let us wander,
        O LORD, from your ways,
    and harden our hearts so that we fear
        you not?
Return for the sake of your servants,
    the tribes of your heritage.
Oh, that you would rend the
        heavens and come down,
    with the mountains quaking before you,
while you wrought awesome
        deeds we could not hope for,
    such as they had not heard of from
        of old.
No ear has ever heard, no eye ever
        seen, any God but you
    doing such deeds for those who wait
        for him.
Would that you might meet us doing right,
    that we were mindful of you in
        our ways!
Behold, you are angry, and we are sinful;
    all of us have become like unclean people,
    all our good deeds are like polluted rags;
we have all withered like leaves,
    and our guilt carries us away like
        the wind.
There is none who calls upon your name,
    who rouses himself to cling to you;
for you have hidden your face from us
    and have delivered us up to our guilt.
Yet, O LORD, you are our father;
    we are the clay and you the potter:
    we are all the work of your hands.

RESPONSORIAL PSALM
Psalm 80:2–3, 15–16, 18–19 (4)

R. Lord, make us turn to you; let us see your face
        and we shall be saved.

O shepherd of Israel, hearken,
    from your throne upon the cherubim,
        shine forth.

Rouse your power,
    and come to save us. R.

Once again, O LORD of hosts,
    look down from heaven, and see;
take care of this vine,
    and protect what your right hand has planted,
    the son of man whom you yourself
        made strong. R.

May your help be with the man of your right hand,
    with the son of man whom you yourself
        made strong.
Then we will no more withdraw from you;
    give us new life, and we will call upon
        your name. R.

READING II 1 Corinthians 1:3–9

Brothers and sisters: Grace to you and peace from God our Father and the Lord Jesus Christ.

I give thanks to my God always on your account for the grace of God bestowed on you in Christ Jesus, that in him you were enriched in every way, with all discourse and all knowledge, as the testimony to Christ was confirmed among you, so that you are not lacking in any spiritual gift as you wait for the revelation of our Lord Jesus Christ. He will keep you firm to the end, irreproachable on the day of our Lord Jesus Christ. God is faithful, and by him you were called to fellowship with his Son, Jesus Christ our Lord.

GOSPEL Mark 13:33–37

Jesus said to his disciples: "Be watchful! Be alert! You do not know when the time will come. It is like a man traveling abroad. He leaves home and places his servants in charge, each with his own work, and orders the gatekeeper to be on the watch. Watch, therefore; you do not know when the lord of the house is coming, whether in the evening, or at midnight, or at cockcrow, or in the morning. May he not come suddenly and find you sleeping. What I say to you, I say to all: 'Watch!'"

Practice of Faith

Why must we wait when people around us are already celebrating Christmas? We know how the story ends: Jesus is born and lain in a manger! We wait because Advent isn't simply about celebrating Christ's birth centuries ago, but about connecting with our own soul's longing for Christ's Kingdom to come. We wait and keep watch this Advent, praying for our Lord to be born anew in our hearts, our communities, and our world. ◆ Listen to "Waiting in Silence" at https://www.youtube.com/watch?v=bg8XCxUtKec. Meditate on these questions: What does your heart hope for this Advent? How might God speak to this hope? ◆ Create a Jesse Tree, on which, each day, you can hang a Scripture-based ornament that recalls the events leading to Jesus' birth. Find instructions on various websites: The website Catholic Icing offers ideas for making a Jesse tree with young children and provides links to free printable ornaments at http://www.catholicicing.com/jesse-tree-readings-ornaments-and-free-printables/. Another source is this website: http://www.myjessetree.com/p/the-ultimate-guide-to-making-jesse-tree.html#header. Purchase a Jesse Tree Activity Kit from Abby Press at http://www.abbeytrade.com/product.asp_Q_pn_E_73132#.Vm8sxb8-Pf4 or Paulist Press at http://www.paulistpressbookcenter.com/product/58272/jesse-tree-activity-kit. Find free daily Jesse tree readings at the Loyola Press site: http://www.loyolapress.com/the-jesse-tree-for-the-first-week-of-advent.htm. ◆ On this First Sunday of Advent, when the family is gathered for prayer, light the first violet candle of your Advent wreath. If you don't have an Advent wreath, you can create a simple one with three violet candles and one rose candle (any size or shape) placed in candle holders and arranged in a circle. Place evergreens around their bases. On the Second, Third, and Fourth Sundays of Advent, light an additional candle, using the pink one for the Third Sunday of Advent. Consider also hiding the baby Jesus apart from the nativity scene until Christmas morning.

Download more questions and activities for families, Christian initiation groups, and other adult groups at http://www.ltp.org/t-productsupplements.aspx.

Scripture Insights

The readings on this First Sunday of Advent express well the meaning of the season. The Latin word *adventus* means "a coming" or "an arrival." Theologians use its Greek equivalent, *parousia*, to refer to the Second Coming of Christ. This season of the liturgical year is not only about getting ready to celebrate Jesus' birth, but also about anticipating the arrival of God's Kingdom in fullness at the end time.

The First Reading, from Isaiah, is part of a long lament that began at Isaiah 63 and extends to the middle of Isaiah 66. As the Judeans returned to Jerusalem from exile in Babylon, they found their Temple destroyed and felt that God had abandoned them. Here the prophet prays that God will come to them in a more wondrous way than he did at Sinai. Despite his sadness over the past and the recognition that God has a right to punish the people for their failure to keep covenant, the prophet ends on a note of hope for the future: "We are all the work of your hands!" (Isaiah 64:7).

Today's Gospel comes from a passage sometimes called Mark's "Little Apocalypse," a teaching about preparing for the Second Coming of Christ. These lines were written shortly before the Second Temple in Jerusalem was destroyed in AD 70 and before a time of persecution began. The parable that Jesus uses to demonstrate our need to be watchful is compelling! It suggests that we are not in charge of the comings and goings of the Lord of the house. Instead, we are the gatekeepers, waiting to welcome the coming Kingdom of God. Will you be ready?

◆ Do a careful reading of today's Gospel. What question is Jesus addressing with the parable of the gate keeper? What does that image mean for you?

◆ Select a phrase from today's Responsorial Psalm and reflect on how it speaks to you about the compassion and generosity that accompanies God's coming.

◆ When have you felt yourself being shaped like clay in God's hands? Did you or do you now experience it as a time of hope for the future?

December 10, 2017

READING I *Isaiah 40:1–5, 9–11*

Comfort, give comfort to my people,
    says your God.
Speak tenderly to Jerusalem, and proclaim
        to her
    that her service is at an end,
    her guilt is expiated;
indeed, she has received
        from the hand of the LORD
    double for all her sins.

    A voice cries out:
In the desert prepare the way of the LORD!
    Make straight in the wasteland
        a highway for our God!
Every valley shall be filled in,
    every mountain and hill shall be
        made low;
the rugged land shall be made a plain,
    the rough country, a broad valley.
Then the glory of the LORD shall be revealed,
    and all people shall see it together;
    for the mouth of the LORD has spoken.

Go up onto a high mountain,
    Zion, herald of glad tidings;
cry out at the top of your voice,
    Jerusalem, herald of good news!
Fear not to cry out
    and say to the cities of Judah:
    Here is your God!
Here comes with power
    the Lord GOD,
    who rules by his strong arm;
here is his reward with him,
    his recompense before him.
Like a shepherd he feeds his flock;
    in his arms he gathers the lambs,
carrying them in his bosom,
    and leading the ewes with care.

RESPONSORIAL PSALM
Psalm 85:9–10, 11–12, 13–14 (8)

R. Lord, let us see your kindness,
        and grant us your salvation.

I will hear what God proclaims;
    the LORD—for he proclaims peace to
        his people.
Near indeed is his salvation to those who
        fear him,
    glory dwelling in our land. R.

Kindness and truth shall meet;
    justice and peace shall kiss.
Truth shall spring out of the earth,
    and justice shall look down from heaven. R.

The LORD himself will give his benefits;
    our land shall yield its increase.
Justice shall walk before him,
    and prepare the way of his steps. R.

READING II *2 Peter 3:8–14*

Do not ignore this one fact, beloved, that with the Lord one day is like a thousand years and a thousand years like one day. The Lord does not delay his promise, as some regard "delay," but he is patient with you, not wishing that any should perish but that all should come to repentance. But the day of the Lord will come like a thief, and then the heavens will pass away with a mighty roar and the elements will be dissolved by fire, and the earth and everything done on it will be found out.

Since everything is to be dissolved in this way, what sort of persons ought you to be, conducting yourselves in holiness and devotion, waiting for and hastening the coming of the day of God, because of which the heavens will be dissolved in flames and the elements melted by fire. But according to his promise we await new heavens and a new earth in which righteousness dwells. Therefore, beloved, since you await these things, be eager to be found without spot or blemish before him, at peace.

GOSPEL Mark 1:1–8

The beginning of the gospel of Jesus Christ the Son of God.

As it is written in Isaiah the prophet:

Behold, I am sending my messenger ahead
of you;
he will prepare your way.
A voice of one crying out in the desert:
"Prepare the way of the Lord,
make straight his paths."

John the Baptist appeared in the desert proclaiming a baptism of repentance for the forgiveness of sins. People of the whole Judean countryside and all the inhabitants of Jerusalem were going out to him and were being baptized by him in the Jordan River as they acknowledged their sins. John was clothed in camel's hair, with a leather belt around his waist. He fed on locusts and wild honey. And this is what he proclaimed: "One mightier than I is coming after me. I am not worthy to stoop and loosen the thongs of his sandals. I have baptized you with water; he will baptize you with the Holy Spirit."

Practice of Charity

Let us "make way" for Christ by serving him in the poor and vulnerable of our community. ◆ The lyrics of "Ready the Way" by Curtis Stephan are based on today's reading from Isaiah. Listen at https://www.youtube.com/watch?v=uxyKS7f W8ug. ◆ Help your children create a "kindness chain" to hang on the tree, adding a link for every kind thing they do for someone between now and Christmas. ◆ Catholic social teaching guides us in working toward the Kingdom of God by creating a more just and merciful society. For a concise summary of these teachings, visit http://www. usccb.org/beliefs-and-teachings/what-we -believe/catholic-social-teaching/seven-themes -of-catholic-social-teaching.cfm.

Download more questions and activities for families, Christian initiation groups, and other adult groups at http://www.ltp.org/t-productsupplements.aspx.

Scripture Insights

Perhaps you can recall making preparations for a big event, a wedding or anniversary. There were invitations to send, menus to prepare, decorations to make, and party clothes to purchase. Today's readings are about preparing for an even bigger event, the coming of God's Chosen One.

The Gospel begins with a proclamation of the "good news" of (or about) Jesus Christ. Mark apparently believes that his community already received a "Save the Date" notice for this celebration in the words of the prophet Isaiah, words which are also part of our First Reading.

The historical context for Isaiah's oracle is the Babylonian Exile, a time of great sadness for the Jewish people. But the prophet's message is one of tenderness and consolation. A straight path is being prepared for God's coming. God's glory (the Hebrew word *kavod*, meaning "splendor" or "honor") will again be revealed to the people, and Jerusalem can shout from the mountain top, "Here is our God!"

But Mark goes a step further by identifying John the Baptist as the one called to deliver the invitation for the great event of God's coming. He even dresses John for the occasion, making him look like the prophet Elijah (2 Kings 1:8). The baptism (literally "dunking") that John proclaims is not Christian Baptism, but rather a commitment to a change of heart that makes it possible for us to receive God's coming Kingdom.

The Second Reading, from a letter attributed to Peter, continues this theme of preparing for the coming of God's Kingdom. We are reminded that cultivating a disposition that leads to good action is another important way to prepare for this party.

◆ Carefully read today's Gospel. What does it say about the nature of John's baptism? Who is called to this baptism?

◆ As you reflect on the Second Reading, ask yourself how you might better prepare for God's coming Kingdom.

◆ Describe how the First Reading and the Responsorial Psalm can be sources of encouragement for us as we prepare for the manifestation of God's reign.

READING I *Isaiah 61:1–2a, 10–11*

The spirit of the Lord GOD is upon me,
 because the LORD has anointed me;
he has sent me to bring glad tidings to the poor,
 to heal the brokenhearted,
to proclaim liberty to the captives
 and release to the prisoners,
to announce a year of favor from the LORD
 and a day of vindication by our God.

I rejoice heartily in the LORD,
 in my God is the joy of my soul;
for he has clothed me with a robe of salvation
 and wrapped me in a mantle of justice,
like a bridegroom adorned with a diadem,
 like a bride bedecked with her jewels.
As the earth brings forth its plants,
 and a garden makes its growth spring up,
so will the Lord GOD make justice and praise
 spring up before all the nations.

RESPONSORIAL PSALM *Luke 1:46–48, 49–50, 53–54 (Isaiah 61:10b)*

R. My soul rejoices in my God.

My soul proclaims the greatness of the LORD;
 my spirit rejoices in God my Savior,
for he has looked upon his lowly servant.
 From this day all generations will call
 me blessed. R.

The Almighty has done great things for me,
 and holy is his Name.
He has mercy on those who fear him
 in every generation. R.

He has filled the hungry with good things,
 and the rich he has sent away empty.
He has come to the help of his servant Israel
 for he has remembered his promise
 of mercy. R.

READING II *1 Thessalonians 5:16–24*

Brothers and sisters: Rejoice always. Pray without ceasing. In all circumstances give thanks, for this is the will of God for you in Christ Jesus. Do not quench the Spirit. Do not despise prophetic utterances. Test everything; retain what is good. Refrain from every kind of evil.

May the God of peace make you perfectly holy and may you entirely, spirit, soul, and body, be preserved blameless for the coming of our Lord Jesus Christ. The one who calls you is faithful, and he will also accomplish it.

GOSPEL *John 1:6–8, 19–28*

A man named John was sent from God. He came for testimony, to testify to the light, so that all might believe through him. He was not the light, but came to testify to the light.

And this is the testimony of John. When the Jews from Jerusalem sent priests and Levites to him to ask him, "Who are you?" he admitted and did not deny it, but admitted, "I am not the Christ." So they asked him, "What are you then? Are you Elijah?" And he said, "I am not." "Are you the Prophet?" He answered, "No." So they said to him, "Who are you, so we can give an answer to those who sent us? What do you have to say for yourself?" He said:

 "I am *the voice of one crying out in the desert,*
 'make straight the way of the Lord,'

as Isaiah the prophet said." Some Pharisees were also sent. They asked him, "Why then do you baptize if you are not the Christ or Elijah or the Prophet?" John answered them, "I baptize with water; but there is one among you whom you do not recognize, the one who is coming after me, whose sandal strap I am not worthy to untie." This happened in Bethany across the Jordan, where John was baptizing.

Practice of Hope

"My soul proclaims the greatness of the LORD; / my spirit rejoices in God my Savior," sings the mother of our Lord. *Gaudete* means "Rejoice!" Today, Gaudete Sunday, we pause in our more solemn preparations to rejoice with Mary in the promise of God's coming. At Mass we mark the day with rose-colored vestments and at home, with a rose-colored candle in the Advent wreath. Christ is our first and greatest gift, source of our hope and joy! ♦ Whenever you decorate your Christmas tree, gather the household to bless it, with your own prayer or with this one from the website of the United States Conference of Catholic Bishops: http://www.usccb.org/prayer-and-worship/sac raments-and-sacramentals/sacramentals-blessings /objects/blessing-of-a-christmas-tree.cfm. Afterward, share in Mary and Joseph's journey of hope. Watch the film, *The Nativity Story* (2006; rated G; with Keisha Castle-Hughes). ♦ At Christmas time, opportunities abound to spread the hope of Christ. Invite someone to your home for Christmas dinner who might otherwise be alone, or volunteer at a local soup kitchen over the holidays. Reflect on your experience and consider extending yourself in this way on a more regular basis. ♦ For an unusual and energetic musical experience, listen to the Choir of Clare College Cambridge perform the centuries-old Latin Advent carol "Gaudete" at https://www.youtube. com/watch?v=l1NgHonWNE0.

Download more questions and activities for families, Christian initiation groups, and other adult groups at http://www.ltp.org/t-productsupplements.aspx.

Scripture Insights

Today's readings continue the preparation theme we heard in the previous two weeks of Advent. But now the focus shifts somewhat to the joy that awaits us in God's coming Kingdom. This Sunday is Gaudete (Latin, "rejoice") Sunday or, as Pope Francis calls it, the Sunday of Joy.

In today's First Reading, the prophet writes about the mission conferred upon him by God—to bring glad tidings to the lowly and to heal the broken hearted—and about the joy he experiences in God who clothes him in justice and salvation. Early Christians appropriated this text to describe Jesus' mission (see Luke 4:18–19). By virtue of our Baptism in Christ, this ought to be our mission as well. As the prophet suggests, there is no greater joy than doing God's work.

The Gospel presents John the Baptist as the one who testifies or gives witness to the Light who is coming into the world (John 1:8). We can rejoice because he is the Light that darkness cannot overcome! As the story unfolds, we see John testifying on Jesus' behalf before the priests and Levites of Jerusalem and declaring that Jesus is already among them, though they do not recognize him. John declares he is lower than the lowest household servant by comparison to Jesus, the revealer of God. This is cause for great joy!

On the theme of joy, the Church has wisely paired these two readings with a reading from Paul's First Letter to the Thessalonians. Paul admonishes us to always live in joy, praying and giving thanks, because this is God's will for us. Everything we do and say should be inspired by this Spirit as we await the coming of our Lord Jesus Christ.

♦ Carefully read and reflect on today's First Reading. What makes the prophet's call to mission and the work it demands a source of joy? How does this reading relate to your own sense of mission?

♦ Where do you see Jesus already in our midst today? Describe the joy that this knowledge brings to you.

♦ What does it mean to you to always live in joy?

READING I
2 Samuel 7:1–5, 8b–12, 14a, 16

When King David was settled in his palace, and the LORD had given him rest from his enemies on every side, he said to Nathan the prophet, "Here I am living in a house of cedar, while the ark of God dwells in a tent!" Nathan answered the king, "Go, do whatever you have in mind, for the LORD is with you." But that night the LORD spoke to Nathan and said: "Go, tell my servant David, 'Thus says the LORD: Should you build me a house to dwell in?

"'It was I who took you from the pasture and from the care of the flock to be commander of my people Israel. I have been with you wherever you went, and I have destroyed all your enemies before you. And I will make you famous like the great ones of the earth. I will fix a place for my people Israel; I will plant them so that they may dwell in their place without further disturbance. Neither shall the wicked continue to afflict them as they did of old, since the time I first appointed judges over my people Israel. I will give you rest from all your enemies. The LORD also reveals to you that he will establish a house for you. And when your time comes and you rest with your ancestors, I will raise up your heir after you, sprung from your loins, and I will make his kingdom firm. I will be a father to him, and he shall be a son to me. Your house and your kingdom shall endure forever before me; your throne shall stand firm forever.'"

RESPONSORIAL PSALM
Psalm 89:2–3, 4–5, 27, 29 (2a)

R. For ever I will sing the goodness of the Lord.

The promises of the LORD I will sing forever;
    through all generations my mouth shall
        proclaim your faithfulness.
For you have said, "My kindness is
        established forever";
    in heaven you have confirmed your
        faithfulness. R.

"I have made a covenant with my chosen one,
    I have sworn to David my servant:
forever will I confirm your posterity
    and establish your throne
        for all generations." R.

"He shall say of me, 'You are my father,
    my God, the Rock, my savior.'
Forever I will maintain my kindness toward him,
    and my covenant with him stands firm." R.

READING II   *Romans 16:25–27*

Brothers and sisters: To him who can strengthen you, according to my gospel and the proclamation of Jesus Christ, according to the revelation of the mystery kept secret for long ages but now manifested through the prophetic writings and, according to the command of the eternal God, made known to all nations to bring about the obedience of faith, to the only wise God, through Jesus Christ be glory forever and ever. Amen.

GOSPEL   *Luke 1:26–38*

The angel Gabriel was sent from God to a town of Galilee called Nazareth, to a virgin betrothed to a man named Joseph, of the house of David, and the virgin's name was Mary. And coming to her, he said, "Hail, full of grace! The Lord is with you." But she was greatly troubled at what was said and pondered what sort of greeting this might be. Then the angel said to her, "Do not be afraid, Mary, for you have found favor with God.

"Behold, you will conceive in your womb and bear a son, and you shall name him Jesus. He will be great and will be called Son of the Most High, and the Lord God will give him the throne of David his father, and he will rule over the house of Jacob forever, and of his kingdom there will be no end." But Mary said to the angel, "How can this be, since I have no relations with a man?" And the angel said to her in reply, "The Holy Spirit will come upon you, and the power of the Most High will overshadow you. Therefore the child to be born will be called holy, the Son of God." And behold, Elizabeth, your relative, has also conceived a son in her old age, and this is the sixth month for her who was called barren; for nothing will be impossible for God." Mary said, "Behold, I am the handmaid of the Lord. May it be done to me according to your word." Then the angel departed from her.

Practice of Faith

When Mary is told she will bear the Christ child, she trusts—not in her own reality, but in God's. Obediently she proclaims herself the handmaid of the Lord; her trust makes her fearless and fills her with joy. Full of faith, she tells Elizabeth, "From now on will all ages call me blessed." ◆ Celebrate Mary's yes by listening to "Ave Maria" performed by Andrea Bocelli at the Roman Coliseum: https://www.youtube.com/watch?v=pwp1CH5R-w4. ◆ Take some time in prayer today. Is God asking you to say yes to something? Or is there a challenge, burden, or hurt that you could offer God in faithful trust? Write your answer on a Christmas tag and hang it on the tree as your gift of faith. ◆ Use the decorations of the season to focus your family on the true meaning of Christmas. Lights symbolize Jesus, the light of the world, the tree recalls the Cross, which is our tree of life, and gifts remind us of God's gift to us in Jesus. All together they fill us with joy!

Download more questions and activities for families, Christian initiation groups, and other adult groups at http://www.ltp.org/t-productsupplements.aspx.

Scripture Insights

Not until 2023 will Christmas Eve again fall on the Fourth Sunday of Advent. The proximity of these two solemnities highlights the theme of today's readings—the revelation of God's mystery. The biblical word "mystery" is not about a puzzle to be solved or something impossible to understand. Rather it concerns a magnificent thing that will now be revealed in the last days to those who have faith.

In the First Reading, David desires to build a house for God, but through the prophet Nathan, God tells David that he never asked for a house and plans always to dwell among the people as he did during their desert wanderings. At the same time, God promises to build a house (or a dynasty) for David and to give him a son who will be an everlasting king and whom God will treat like his own son. What astonishing favor David receives from God!

The Gospel builds upon the imagery of this David story. The angel Gabriel tells Mary that she is God's favored one and that she will give birth to a son who "will be called Son of the Most High" and who will be given "the throne of David his father" (Luke 1:32). How utterly confused this young girl must have been! Yet she quickly gives her *fiat* (Latin for "let it happen") to the angel's words.

In the Second Reading, we are invited to join in a doxology, a prayer of praise to God that celebrates God's hidden plan for humanity. This plan is gradually revealed through the prophets and the covenants and is fully manifest in the person of Jesus. That manifestation is what we celebrate at Christmas.

◆ Carefully read today's Gospel and First Reading. Locate the connections between the two readings. Why do you think Luke relied so heavily on the themes of the David story to tell us about Jesus' conception?

◆ How does the theme of the revelation of God's mystery relate to today's Responsorial Psalm and Second Reading?

◆ What is your reaction to the story of Mary's fiat? How does this story relate to your own life?

Christmas Time

Prayer before Reading the Word

While all the world, Lord God,
lay wrapped in deepest silence,
and night had reached its midpoint,
your all-powerful Word came down.

Enlighten us to know the glorious hope to which
        you have called us;
upon the deep darkness of our world,
shine the light of your countenance,
that our hearts may exult and sing for joy at the
        Savior's coming,
with angels and shepherds, with Mary and Joseph,
and with all people of good will who long for
        your peace.

We ask this through our Lord Jesus Christ,
Emmanuel, God-with-us,
your Son, who lives and reigns with you
in the unity of the Holy Spirit,
one God, for ever and ever. Amen.

Prayer after Reading the Word

With a star's radiance, O God, you guided the
        nations to the Light;
in a prophet's words you revealed the mystery of
        the Messiah's coming;
through the magi's gifts you unfolded the
        richness of the Savior's mission.

Give us words inspired enough to make known
the mercy that has touched our lives,
deeds loving enough to bear witness
to the treasure you have bestowed,
and hearts simple enough to ponder
the mystery of your gracious and abiding love.

We ask this through our Lord Jesus Christ,
Emmanuel, God-with-us,
your Son, who lives and reigns with you
in the unity of the Holy Spirit,
one God, for ever and ever. Amen.

Weekday Readings

December 26: Feast of St. Stephen
Acts 6:8–10; 7:54–59; Matthew 10:17–22

December 27: Feast of St. John
1 John 1:1–4; John 20:1a, 2–8

December 28: Feast of the Holy Innocents
1 John 1:5—2:2; Matthew 2:13–18

December 29: Fifth Day in the Octave of the Nativity of the Lord
1 John 2:3–11; Luke 2:22–35

December 30: Sixth Day in the Octave of the Nativity of the Lord
1 John 2:12–17; Luke 2:36–40

January 1: Solemnity of Mary, the Holy Mother of God
Numbers 6:22–27; Galatians 4:4–7; Luke 2:16–21

January 2: *1 John 2:22–28; John 1:19–28*

January 3: *1 John 2:29—3:6; John 1:29–34*

January 4: *1 John 3:7–10; John 1:35–42*

January 5: *1 John 3:11–21; John 1:43–51*

January 6: *1 John 5:5–13; Mark 1:7–11 or Lune 3:23–38 or 3:23, 31–34, 36, 38*

January 8: Feast of the Baptism of the Lord
Isaiah 42:1–4, 6–7 or Isaiah 55:1–11 or Acts of the Apostles 10:34–38 or 1 John 5:1–9; Mark 1:7–11

READING I *Isaiah 62:1–5*

For Zion's sake I will not be silent,
    for Jerusalem's sake I will not be quiet,
until her vindication shines forth like the dawn
    and her victory like a burning torch.

Nations shall behold your vindication,
    and all the kings your glory;
you shall be called by a new name
    pronounced by the mouth of the LORD.
You shall be a glorious crown in the hand
      of the LORD,
    a royal diadem held by your God.
No more shall people call you "Forsaken,"
    or your land "Desolate,"
but you shall be called "My Delight,"
    and your land "Espoused."
For the LORD delights in you
    and makes your land his spouse.
As a young man marries a virgin,
    your Builder shall marry you;
and as a bridegroom rejoices in his bride
    so shall your God rejoice in you.

RESPONSORIAL PSALM
Psalm 89:4–5, 16–17, 27, 29 (2a)

R. For ever I will sing the goodness of the LORD.

I have made a covenant with my chosen one,
    I have sworn to David my servant:
forever will I confirm your posterity
    and establish your throne for all
        generations. R.

Blessed the people who know the joyful shout;
    in the light of your countenance, O LORD,
      they walk.
At your name they rejoice all the day,
    and through your justice they are exalted. R.

He shall say of me, "You are my father,
    my God, the rock, my savior."
Forever I will maintain my kindness toward him,
    and my covenant with him stands firm. R.

READING II *Acts 13:16–17, 22–25*

When Paul reached Antioch in Pisidia and entered the synagogue, he stood up, motioned with his hand, and said, "Fellow Israelites and you others who are God-fearing, listen. The God of this people Israel chose our ancestors and exalted the people during their sojourn in the land of Egypt. With uplifted arm he led them out of it. Then he removed Saul and raised up David as king; of him he testified, 'I have found David, son of Jesse, a man after my own heart; he will carry out my every wish. From this man's descendants God, according to his promise, has brought to Israel a savior, Jesus. John heralded his coming by proclaiming a baptism of repentance to all the people of Israel; and as John was completing his course, he would say, 'What do you suppose that I am? I am not he. Behold, one is coming after me; I am not worthy to unfasten the sandals of his feet.'"

GOSPEL *Matthew 1:18–25*

Longer: Matthew 1:1–25

This is how the birth of Jesus Christ came about. When his mother Mary was betrothed to Joseph, but before they lived together, she was found with child through the Holy Spirit. Joseph her husband, since he was a righteous man, yet unwilling to expose her to shame, decided to divorce her quietly. Such was his intention when, behold, the angel of the Lord appeared to him in a dream and said, "Joseph, son of David, do not be afraid to take Mary your wife into your home. For it is through the Holy Spirit that this child has been conceived in her. She will bear a son and you are to name him Jesus, because he will save his people from their sins." All this took place to fulfill what the Lord had said through the prophet:

Behold, the virgin shall conceive and bear a son,
    and they shall name him Emmanuel,

which means "God is with us." When Joseph awoke, he did as the angel of the Lord had commanded him and took his wife into his home. He had no relations with her until she bore a son, and he named him Jesus.

Practice of Faith

Joseph is a righteous Jew, firmly grounded in the Torah, when he stakes his entire reputation and future on trusting God. When an angel tells him to take Mary into his home, and later to flee to Egypt, Joseph doesn't question or fret. He immediately acts as he is commanded. In doing so, Joseph protects his family and faithfully cooperates in God's glorious plan of salvation. ◆ With your family or household, read aloud the two infancy stories (Matthew 1:18—2:15 and Luke 1:5—2:20). Ask each listener: As you listen to these two stories, which person are you thinking about most? Did you notice anything this year that you didn't notice before? What special message do these stories hold for you? ◆ Listen to "O Come, O Come Emmanuel": https://www.youtube.com/watch?v=7xtpJ4Q_Q-4. Prayerfully reflect on how you would like Christ to come into your life as it is now. ◆ Read Pope Francis' homily from Christmas 2014: http://w2.vatican.va/content/francesco/en/homilies/2014/documents/papa-francesco_20141224_omelia-natale.html. Reflect on his question: Do I allow God to love me?

Download more questions and activities for families, Christian initiation groups, and other adult groups at http://www.ltp.org/t-productsupplements.aspx.

Scripture Insights

Tonight's readings for the Nativity of the Lord present the beautiful imagery of Jesus as Emmanuel, God-with-us. In the First Reading, from Isaiah, the prophet is excited and impatient to sing of Jerusalem's vindication, saying that she will be given a new name—implying a new destiny—and that she will be cherished by God like a crown in God's hand or like God's bride. Thus the prophet describes Jerusalem's experience of God-with-us in the most encouraging images as the Judean people struggle to put their lives back together after the Babylonian exile.

The Second Reading further develops this idea of God-with-us in human history. Paul is described as giving a speech to his fellow Jews in Antioch of Pisidia (central Turkey) whereby he traces God's relationship with Israel from the time of the patriarchs through David to Israel's savior, Jesus.

Likewise, the Gospel's genealogy (in the longer version of the reading) identifies Jesus as the Christ (Greek, meaning "anointed"), the son of David, and son of Abraham, but the pattern of three groups of fourteen generations puts the focus on Jesus as the Son of David who would appear at the end time and restore Israel to its special place as God's sovereign people. In early rabbinic gematria, a form of Hebrew numerology, fourteen was David's number. The Gospel writer goes on to tell the story of how a fearful and troubled man named Joseph came to understand that he should not turn away his already pregnant fiancée, because her child was conceived of the Holy Spirit and would be named Jesus (in Hebrew, Yeshua, meaning "God saves"). All this was to fulfill the words of the prophet, Matthew says: "And they shall name him Emmanuel."

◆ Carefully read the short form of today's Gospel. What can you conclude about Matthew's understanding of who Jesus is and what he was destined to do?

◆ What does the Responsorial Psalm suggest about our covenant relationship with God?

◆ The image of God's people as a "glorious crown in the hand of the LORD" is unusual. What does it evoke for you?

READING I *Genesis 15:1–6; 21:1–3*

Alternate: Sirach 3:2–6, 12–14

The word of the LORD came to Abram in a vision, saying:

"Fear not, Abram!
I am your shield;
I will make your reward very great."

But Abram said, "O Lord GOD, what good will your gifts be, if I keep on being childless and have as my heir the steward of my house, Eliezer?" Abram continued, "See, you have given me no offspring, and so one of my servants will be my heir." Then the word of the LORD came to him: "No, that one shall not be your heir; your own issue shall be your heir." The Lord took Abram outside and said, "Look up at the sky and count the stars, if you can. Just so," he added, "shall your descendants be." Abram put his faith in the LORD, who credited it to him as an act of righteousness.

The LORD took note of Sarah as he had said he would; he did for her as he had promised. Sarah became pregnant and bore Abraham a son in his old age, at the set time that God had stated. Abraham gave the name Isaac to this son of his whom Sarah bore him.

RESPONSORIAL PSALM
Psalm 105:1–2, 3–4, 6–7, 8–9 (7a, 8a)

Alternate: Psalm 128:1–2, 3, 4–5 (see 1)

R. The Lord remembers his covenant forever.

Give thanks to the LORD, invoke his name;
    make known among the nations his deeds.
Sing to him, sing his praise,
    proclaim all his wondrous deeds. R.

Glory in his holy name;
    rejoice, O hearts that seek the LORD!
Look to the LORD in his strength;
    constantly seek his face. R.

You descendants of Abraham, his servants,
    sons of Jacob, his chosen ones!
He, the LORD, is our God;

throughout the earth his judgments
        prevail. R.

He remembers forever his covenant
    which he made binding for a
        thousand generations
which he entered into with Abraham
    and by his oath to Isaac. R.

READING II *Hebrews 11:8, 11–12, 17–19*

Alternate: Colossians 3:12–21 or 3:12–17

Brothers and sisters: By faith Abraham obeyed when he was called to go out to a place that he was to receive as an inheritance; he went out, not knowing where he was to go. By faith he received power to generate, even though he was past the normal age—and Sarah herself was sterile—for he thought that the one who had made the promise was trustworthy. So it was that there came forth from one man, himself as good as dead, descendants as numerous as the stars in the sky and as countless as the sands on the seashore.

By faith Abraham, when put to the test, offered up Isaac, and he who had received the promises was ready to offer his only son, of whom it was said, "Through Isaac descendants shall bear your name." He reasoned that God was able to raise even from the dead, and he received Isaac back as a symbol.

GOSPEL *Luke 2:22–40*

Shorter: Luke 2:22, 39–40

When the days were completed for their purification according to the law of Moses, they took him up to Jerusalem to present him to the Lord, just as it is written in the law of the Lord, *Every male that opens the womb shall be consecrated to the Lord,* and to offer the sacrifice of *a pair of turtledoves or two young pigeons,* in accordance with the dictate in the law of the Lord.

Now there was a man in Jerusalem whose name was Simeon. This man was righteous and devout, awaiting the consolation of Israel, and the Holy Spirit was upon him. It had been revealed to him by the Holy Spirit that he should not see death before he had seen the Christ of the Lord. He came in the Spirit into the temple; and when the parents brought in the child Jesus to perform the custom of the law in regard to him, he took him into his arms and blessed God, saying:

"Now, Master, you may let your servant go
in peace, according to your word,
for my eyes have seen your salvation,
which you prepared in sight of all
the peoples,
a light for revelation to the Gentiles,
and glory for your people Israel."

The child's father and mother were amazed at what was said about him; and Simeon blessed them and said to Mary his mother, "Behold, this child is destined for the fall and rise of many in Israel, and to be a sign that will be contradicted—and you yourself a sword will pierce—so that the thoughts of many hearts may be revealed." There was also a prophetess, Anna, the daughter of Phanuel, of the tribe of Asher. She was advanced in years, having lived seven years with her husband after her marriage, and then as a widow until she was eighty-four. She never left the temple, but worshiped night and day with fasting and prayer. And coming forward at that very time, she gave thanks to God and spoke about the child to all who were awaiting the redemption of Jerusalem.

When they had fulfilled all the prescriptions of the law of the Lord, they returned to Galilee, to their own town of Nazareth. The child grew and became strong, filled with wisdom; and the favor of God was upon him.

Practice of Charity

◆ Learn how Catholic Charities USA helps homeless families: https://catholiccharitiesusa.org/efforts/sheltering-those-in-need. ◆ Build up your domestic church: http://www.usccb.org/beliefs-and-teachings/vocations/parents/tools-for-building-a-domestic-church.cfm. ◆ Find out what the Church is celebrating each day with the *Year of Grace* liturgical calendar: www.ltp.org (search "Year of Grace 2018").

Scripture Insights

Family is a wonderful thing. But many of us also know the pain and suffering of family life. Today's Scripture readings invite us to reflect on biblical families, in particular the Holy Family, so that we can see what holds them together through times of trouble—faith in God who is always faithful.

In the First Reading, we hear Abram complaining about how God promised him a horde of descendants, but, as an old man, he still does not have a single son. In spite of Abram's rudeness, God simply repeats his promise of many descendants (Genesis 12:1–9). Abram responds in faith, and God gives him a son, Isaac. The Abraham stories (Genesis 12–22) remind us how hard it is for humans to trust in God's faithfulness.

The Second Reading reinforces this theme of faith and faithfulness by recalling the stories of Abraham in a repeated pattern reminiscent of a litany, each section beginning with the words "by faith." The author of this letter finds Abraham's faith exemplary since he even when he could not see God's promise fully realized, he still believed.

In the Gospel, we hear about Mary and Joseph traveling with the infant Jesus to the Temple in Jerusalem. Luke portrays them as people of deep faith since Jewish Law did not require them to come to Jerusalem to perform this sacrifice. Because of their poverty, instead of the year-old lamb prescribed in the Law, they brought a poor woman's offering—two pigeons. Yet their trust in God's faithfulness was genuine.

◆ Carefully read today's Gospel. What do the prophecies of Simeon and Anna tell us about the destiny of Jesus and what is in store for this little family?

◆ Reflect on the dialog between Abram and God as it is described in the First Reading. What does it reveal about the relationship between Abram and God? Have you ever felt like praying to God in this way?

◆ Write a litany of faith patterned after the one in today's Second Reading, but use people who have been models for you in your own faith journey.

January 7, 2018 THE EPIPHANY OF THE LORD

READING I *Isaiah 60:1–6*

Rise up in splendor, Jerusalem!
    Your light has come,
    the glory of the Lord shines upon you.
See, darkness covers the earth,
    and thick clouds cover the peoples;
but upon you the LORD shines,
    and over you appears his glory.
Nations shall walk by your light,
    and kings by your shining radiance.
Raise your eyes and look about;
    they all gather and come to you:
your sons come from afar,
    and your daughters in the arms of
        their nurses.

Then you shall be radiant at what you see,
    your heart shall throb and overflow,
for the riches of the sea shall be
        emptied out before you,
    the wealth of nations shall be brought to you.
Caravans of camels shall fill you,
    dromedaries from Midian and Ephah;
all from Sheba shall come
    bearing gold and frankincense,
    and proclaiming the praises of the LORD.

RESPONSORIAL PSALM
Psalm 72:1–2, 7–8, 10–11, 12–13 (see 11)

R. Lord, every nation on earth will adore you.

O God, with your judgment endow the king,
    and with your justice, the king's son;
he shall govern your people with justice
    and your afflicted ones with judgment. R.

Justice shall flower in his days,
    and profound peace, till the moon be no more.
May he rule from sea to sea,
    and from the River to the ends of the earth. R.

The kings of Tarshish and the Isles shall offer gifts;
    the kings of Arabia and Seba shall
        bring tribute.
All kings shall pay him homage,
    all nations shall serve him. R.

For he shall rescue the poor when he cries out,
    and the afflicted when he has
        no one to help him.
He shall have pity for the lowly and the poor;
    the lives of the poor he shall save. R.

READING II *Ephesians 3:2–3a, 5–6*

Brothers and sisters: You have heard of the stewardship of God's grace that was given to me for your benefit, namely, that the mystery was made known to me by revelation. It was not made known to people in other generations as it has now been revealed to his holy apostles and prophets by the Spirit: that the Gentiles are coheirs, members of the same body, and copartners in the promise in Christ Jesus through the gospel.

GOSPEL *Matthew 2:1–12*

When Jesus was born in Bethlehem of Judea, in the days of King Herod, behold, magi from the east arrived in Jerusalem, saying, "Where is the newborn king of the Jews? We saw his star at its rising and have come to do him homage." When King Herod heard this, he was greatly troubled, and all Jerusalem with him. Assembling all the chief priests and the scribes of the people, he inquired of them where the Christ was to be born. They said to him, "In Bethlehem of Judea, for thus it has been written through the prophet:

And you, Bethlehem, land of Judah,
    are by no means least among the rulers
        of Judah;
since from you shall come a ruler,
    who is to shepherd my people Israel."

Then Herod called the magi secretly and ascertained from them the time of the star's appearance. He sent them to Bethlehem and said, "Go and search diligently for the child. When you have found him, bring me word, that I too may go and do him homage." After their audience with the king they set out. And behold, the star that they had seen at its rising preceded them, until it came and stopped over the place where the child was. They were overjoyed at seeing the star, and on entering the house they saw the child with Mary his mother. They prostrated themselves and did him homage. Then they opened their treasures and offered him gifts of gold, frankincense, and myrrh. And having been warned in a dream not to return to Herod, they departed for their country by another way.

Practice of Hope

For the surrounding culture, Christmas is "over." The decorations are put away, the children are back in school, and we are back to "normal." Meanwhile, in our faith tradition, the Magi have steadfastly made their way to Jesus to worship and honor him with their treasures. They protect the child from Herod's evil intent by avoiding the despot's request for information about his location. In this blessed and holy season, let us not lose focus on the infant Jesus in his parents' arms, and let us protect the hope his birth brings us. ✦ Read Pope Francis' address (Angelus, January 5, 2014) on the joy of the Incarnation: http://w2.vatican.va /content/francesco/en/angelus/2014/documents /papa-francesco_angelus_20140105.html. ✦ Epiphany comes from the ancient Greek *epiphaneia*, which means "manifestation." We celebrate the visit of the Magi as the revelation of the Incarnation. The Magi recognize that God has taken human flesh—has been born as this child. Prayerfully reflect on what God's Incarnation means for you and write your thoughts in your journal. ✦ All vulnerable children need love and protection. Help by sponsoring a child through organizations such as Caritas for Children (caritas. us) or Unbound (unbound.org).

Download more questions and activities for families, Christian initiation groups, and other adult groups at http://www.ltp.org/t-productsupplements.aspx.

Scripture Insights

The Epiphany of the Lord, which invites us to reflect on God's manifestation in the world, gets its name from the Greek word *epiphaneia* meaning "appearing" or "manifestation." For western Christians, the solemnity commemorates the revelation of Christ to the Gentiles as told in the story of the Magi. For Christians in the East, Epiphany celebrates several of the earliest manifestations of Christ's divinity, including his baptism in the Jordan.

The First Reading celebrates the splendor of the New Jerusalem as God's glory shines upon it. A city that was desolate after the exile, the prophet says, will now be filled with peoples from all over the world and the kings of nations will bring gold, frankincense, and sacrificial animals to worship Israel's God.

Continuing the theme of God's manifestation to the world, the Second Reading presents Paul as one who has been called to reveal the mystery of Christ—that Gentiles are coheirs with their Jewish brethren in the one body which is the Church.

The Gospel's story of the visit of the Magi also focuses on God's manifestation in the world. Although the identity of the Magi and even their number is unknown, most experts believe that they were scholars of the esoteric sciences, such as dream interpretation or astrology, not kings as they are later depicted in story and art. However, the gifts that they brought—gold, frankincense, and myrrh—were the gifts of kings (see Isaiah 60:1–6). The story teaches that we may fail to recognize God's presence in our midst, and may need insight from the strangers God sends to help us.

✦ Carefully read today's Gospel, paying attention to every detail that Mary, as a character in the story, might have observed. Notice that she never speaks. What do you think she might have wanted to say as the story unfolded?

✦ What does the Second Reading say about how we should be Church in light of the revelation of the mystery of Christ?

✦ When in your life have you experienced the manifestation of God? What do you think keeps us from recognizing God's presence more often?

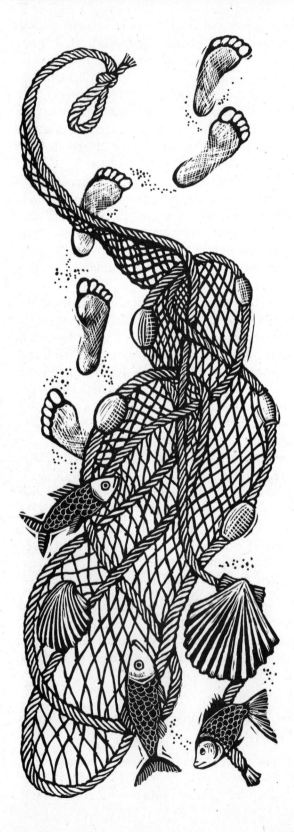

Prayer before Reading the Word

God of mystery,
whose voice whispers our name;
God in our midst,
whose Lamb walks among us unknown;
in every generation you reveal yourself
to those who long to know your dwelling place.

Speak now, Lord, for your servants are listening.
Draw us to you, that with you we may
always remain.

We ask this through our Lord Jesus Christ,
your Son, who lives and reigns with you
in the unity of the Holy Spirit,
one God, for ever and ever. Amen.

Prayer after Reading the Word

In your Son, O God, you have given us
your Word in all its fullness
and the greatest of all your gifts.
Rouse our hearts to grasp the urgent need
of conversion,
and stir up our souls with longing to embrace
your Gospel.

May our lives proclaim to those far away
from you
and to those filled with doubt
that the one Savior of us all is your Son,
our Lord Jesus Christ,
who lives and reigns with you
in the unity of the Holy Spirit,
one God, for ever and ever. Amen.

Weekday Readings

January 9: *1 Samuel 1:9–20; Mark 1:21–28*
January 10: *1 Samuel 3: 1–10, 19–20; Mark 1:29–39*
January 11: *1 Samuel 4:1–11; Mark 1:40–45*
January 12: *1 Samuel 8: 4–7, 10–22a; Mark 2:1–12*
January 13: *1 Samuel 9:1–4, 17–19; 10:1a; Mark 2:13–17*

January 15: *1 Samuel 15:16–23; Mark 2:18–22*
January 16: *1 Samuel 16:1–13; Mark 2:23–28*
January 17: *1 Samuel 17: 32–33, 37, 40–51; Mark 3:1–6*
January 18: *1 Samuel 18:6–9; 19:1–7; Mark 3:7–12*
January 19: *1 Samuel 24:3–21; Mark 3:13–19*
January 20: *2 Samuel 1:1–4, 11–12, 19, 23–27; Mark 3:20–21*

January 22: *2 Samuel 5:1–7, 10; Mark 3:22–30*
January 23: *2 Samuel 6:12b–15, 17–19; Mark 3:31–35*
January 24: *2 Samuel 7:4–17; Mark 4:1– 20*
January 25: Feast of the Conversion of Saint Paul
Acts 22:3–16 or Acts 9:1–22; Mark 16:15–18
January 26: *2 Timothy 1:1–8 or Titus 1:1–5; Mark 4:26–34*
January 27: *2 Samuel 12:1–7a, 10–17; Mark 4:35–41*

January 29: *2 Samuel 15:13–14, 30; 16:5–13; Mark 5:1–20*
January 30: *2 Samuel 18:9–10, 14b, 24–25a,*
30—19:3;Mark 5:21–43
January 31: *2 Samuel 24:2, 9–17; Mark 6:1–6*
February 1: *1 Kings 2:1–4, 10–12; Mark 6:7–13*
February 2: Feast of the Presentation of the Lord
Malachi 3:1–4; Hebrews 2:14–18; Luke 2:22–40
or 2:22–32
February 3: *1 Kings 3:4–13; Mark 6:30–34*

February 5: *1 Kings 8:1–7, 9–13; Mark 6:53–56*
February 6: *1 Kings 8:22–23, 27–30; Mark 7:1–13*
February 7: *1 Kings 10:1–10; Mark 7:14–23*
February 8: *1 Kings 11:4–13; Mark 7:24–30*
February 9: *1 Kings 11:29–32; 12:19; Mark 7:31–37*
February 10: *1 Kings 12:26–32; 13:33–34; Mark 8:1–10*

February 12: *James 1:1–11; Mark 8:11–13*
February 13: *James 1:12–18; Mark 8:14–21*

READING I *1 Samuel 3:3b–10, 19*

Samuel was sleeping in the temple of the LORD where the ark of God was. The LORD called to Samuel, who answered, "Here I am." Samuel ran to Eli and said, "Here I am. You called me." "I did not call you," Eli said. "Go back to sleep." So he went back to sleep. Again the LORD called Samuel, who rose and went to Eli. "Here I am," he said. "You called me." But Eli answered, "I did not call you, my son. Go back to sleep."

At that time Samuel was not familiar with the LORD, because the LORD had not revealed anything to him as yet. The LORD called Samuel again, for the third time. Getting up and going to Eli, he said, "Here I am. You called me." Then Eli understood that the LORD was calling the youth. So he said to Samuel, "Go to sleep, and if you are called, reply, 'Speak, LORD, for your servant is listening.'" When Samuel went to sleep in his place, the LORD came and revealed his presence, calling out as before, "Samuel, Samuel!" Samuel answered, "Speak, for your servant is listening."

Samuel grew up, and the LORD was with him, not permitting any word of his to be without effect.

RESPONSORIAL PSALM
Psalm 40:2, 4, 7–8, 8–9, 10 (8a, 9a)

R. Here am I, Lord; I come to do your will.

I have waited, waited for the LORD,
   and he stooped toward me and heard my cry.
And he put a new song into my mouth,
   a hymn to our God. R.

Sacrifice or offering you wished not,
   but ears open to obedience you gave me.
Holocausts or sin-offerings you sought not;
   then said I, "Behold I come." R.

"In the written scroll it is prescribed for me,
to do your will, O my God, is my delight,
   and your law is within my heart!" R.

I announced your justice in the vast assembly;
   I did not restrain my lips, as you,
      O LORD, know. R.

READING II
1 Corinthians 6:13c–15a, 17–20

Brothers and sisters: The body is not for immorality, but for the Lord, and the Lord is for the body; God raised the Lord and will also raise us by his power.

Do you not know that your bodies are members of Christ? But whoever is joined to the Lord becomes one Spirit with him. Avoid immorality. Every other sin a person commits is outside the body, but the immoral person sins against his own body. Do you not know that your body is a temple of the Holy Spirit within you, whom you have from God, and that you are not your own? For you have been purchased at a price. Therefore glorify God in your body.

GOSPEL *John 1:35–42*

John was standing with two of his disciples, and as he watched Jesus walk by, he said, "Behold, the Lamb of God." The two disciples heard what he said and followed Jesus. Jesus turned and saw them following him and said to them, "What are you looking for?" They said to him, "Rabbi"— which translated means Teacher—, "where are you staying?" He said to them, "Come, and you will see." So they went and saw where Jesus was staying, and they stayed with him that day. It was about four in the afternoon. Andrew, the brother of Simon Peter, was one of the two who heard John and followed Jesus. He first found his own brother Simon and told him, "We have found the Messiah"—which is translated Christ. Then he brought him to Jesus. Jesus looked at him and said, "You are Simon the son of John; you will be called Cephas"—which is translated Peter.

Practice of Charity

After the lights and carols of Christmas, Ordinary Time—which actually means counted time (we number the weeks of Ordinary Time)—can seem so, well, ordinary. But it is in the ordinary days of our ordinary lives that God asks us to build his Kingdom. The Lectionary readings during these weeks take us through the life of Christ. Striving to live Jesus' example of love, reconciliation, and healing can transform our most ordinary moments into extraordinary moments of charity. ◆ St. Thérèse of Lisieux wrote: "What matters in life is not great deeds, but great love." Thérèse's gift was recognizing God in the little, every day moments. To learn more about Thérèse and her "little way," visit http://www.littleflower.org /therese/ or read her autobiography, *Story of a Soul.* ◆ Take time this week to look for God in the ordinary moments of your life. Write in your journal about where you find him and give thanks! ◆ What ordinary moments in your life repeatedly invite frustration? The drive to work? The mess left in the kitchen? Brainstorm ways to invite God into these moments. Notice what happens when you do!

Download more questions and activities for families, Christian initiation groups, and other adult groups at http://www.ltp.org/t-productsupplements.aspx.

Scripture Insights

Christmas Time ended with the Feast of the Baptism of the Lord on Monday, January 8, and now we enter "Ordinary Time," a time to reflect on the life of Jesus and commit ourselves to following him. Appropriately, then, the theme of today's Scripture readings is God's invitation and our response.

The First Reading tells the story of young Samuel who was serving in the Israelite sanctuary in Shiloh under the priest, Eli. During the night Samuel was sleeping in the temple when he heard someone call, "Samuel!" He ran to Eli saying, "Here I am," but Eli had not called him. Three times Samuel heard the voice, until Eli realized that God was calling his servant. He instructed Samuel to respond, "Speak, Lord, for your servant is listening." From that time, we are told, God was with Samuel, making all of his words effective.

Today's Gospel invites us to reflect on another calling—that of Jesus' disciples. In this call story it is John the Baptist who helps two of his own disciples recognize the Lord. When they go to Jesus, he initiates the encounter by asking, "What are you looking for?"—a key question for any seeker. Their response—"Where are you staying?" —has profound implications. The Greek word *menein* means "to remain" or "to stay with," and in John's Gospel it also describes the divine dwelling within a person, like the relationship that Jesus has with the Father (see John 14:9–11; 15:4). The seeking and finding theme is also important here. Like those who seek Lady Wisdom in the Old Testament books of Wisdom and Proverbs, those who seek Jesus will find him and become one with him as he is one with the Father.

◆ Why was Samuel so slow in recognizing the voice that was calling him? How was he helped to understand?

◆ How might Paul's words, "Whoever is joined to the Lord becomes one spirit with him" (Second Reading), relate to today's theme of invitation and response?

◆ Reflect on your own call to discipleship with Jesus. In what ways do you feel you are abiding with Christ?

READING I *Jonah 3:1–5, 10*

The word of the LORD came to Jonah, saying: "Set out for the great city of Nineveh, and announce to it the message that I will tell you." So Jonah made ready and went to Nineveh, according to the LORD's bidding. Now Nineveh was an enormously large city; it took three days to go through it. Jonah began his journey through the city, and had gone but a single day's walk announcing, "Forty days more and Nineveh shall be destroyed," when the people of Nineveh believed God; they proclaimed a fast and all of them, great and small, put on sackcloth.

When God saw by their actions how they turned from their evil way, he repented of the evil that he had threatened to do to them; he did not carry it out.

RESPONSORIAL PSALM
Psalm 25:4–5, 6–7, 8–9 (4a)

R. Teach me your ways, O Lord.

Your ways, O LORD, make known to me;
    teach me your paths,
guide me in your truth and teach me,
    for you are God my savior. R.

Remember that your compassion, O LORD,
    and your love are from of old.
In your kindness remember me,
    because of your goodness, O LORD. R.

Good and upright is the LORD;
    thus he shows sinners the way.
He guides the humble to justice
    and teaches the humble his way. R.

READING II *1 Corinthians 7:29–31*

I tell you, brothers and sisters, the time is running out. From now on, let those having wives act as not having them, those weeping as not weeping, those rejoicing as not rejoicing, those buying as not owning, those using the world as not using it fully. For the world in its present form is passing away.

GOSPEL *Mark 1:14–20*

After John had been arrested, Jesus came to Galilee proclaiming the gospel of God: "This is the time of fulfillment. The kingdom of God is at hand. Repent, and believe in the gospel."

As he passed by the Sea of Galilee, he saw Simon and his brother Andrew casting their nets into the sea; they were fishermen. Jesus said to them, "Come after me, and I will make you fishers of men." Then they abandoned their nets and followed him. He walked along a little farther and saw James, the son of Zebedee, and his brother John. They too were in a boat mending their nets. Then he called them. So they left their father Zebedee in the boat along with the hired men and followed him.

Practice of Hope

On this Third Sunday in Ordinary Time, Jesus proclaims, "This is the time of fulfillment. The kingdom of God is at hand." That kingdom—so long promised by the prophets—is unfolding. And what does this mean? How are we to be part of this unfolding? "Repent, and believe in the gospel." Apparently living in the new kingdom requires us to hope and to change the way we live. ◆ Are you purposefully growing your knowledge of the Kingdom of God and all that it requires? Make a point of participating in a parish adult education activity or small group study. ◆ Reflect on your prayer life. Is it time to begin praying again? Is it time to explore new ways of praying or revisit old, treasured ones? Ask the Holy Spirit to guide you. ◆ This Thursday the Church will celebrate the Feast of the Conversion of St. Paul the Apostle. As Jesus called Simon, Andrew, James, John, and Paul, he also calls us. What a reason for hope! Read Paul's conversion story in Acts 22:3–16. Then think or write about your own conversion journey. Where are you today in that journey?

Download more questions and activities for families, Christian initiation groups, and other adult groups at http://www.ltp.org/t-productsupplements.aspx.

Scripture Insights

Today's readings invite us to reflect on the quality of our response to Jesus' invitation to walk in the spirit of Christ in our daily lives. Will our response be half-hearted, or are we willing to allow ourselves to be radically changed by our calling?

The First Reading tells a parable about Jonah, who was called to announce a message of repentance to the people of Nineveh in ancient Assyria. The city was so big that Jonah walked for three days to get across it. Immediately on hearing Jonah's words every person in Nineveh believed God and repented. But some verses of Jonah's story are missing from this reading. In them we see that Jonah was a self-righteous prophet. When God first called him to go to Nineveh, he ran the other way! And when he finally warned the Ninevites and God forgave them, Jonah became furious because he wanted God to destroy Nineveh, not treat them with compassion and mercy. Guess who most needed to experience conversion of heart!

Today's Gospel story also focuses on conversion of heart. Jesus appears on the scene at the beginning of his public ministry proclaiming God's Gospel—that God's reign is already on the doorstep—and shouting, "Repent and believe in the gospel." The energy and immediacy of the story is palpable. Thus, when Jesus calls his disciples, they respond immediately, leaving their old lives behind and following Jesus.

In today's Second Reading, Paul describes the radical conversion of heart required of those who would follow Christ. Everything they would normally be expected to do should be done in entirely new ways in the light of the coming reign of God.

◆ Carefully reread the First Reading and the Gospel. These two stories are very similar but also complete opposites. What are their similarities and differences?

◆ As you reflect on today's Second Reading, ask yourself what conversion of heart God wants of you today.

◆ Pray the words of today's Responsorial Psalm, and ask for the grace of conversion of heart so that you can respond wholeheartedly to the call of discipleship.

READING I *Deuteronomy 18:15–20*

Moses spoke to all the people, saying: "A prophet like me will the LORD, your God, raise up for you from among your own kin; to him you shall listen. This is exactly what you requested of the LORD, your God, at Horeb on the day of the assembly, when you said, 'Let us not again hear the voice of the LORD, our God, nor see this great fire any more, lest we die.' And the LORD said to me, 'This was well said. I will raise up for them a prophet like you from among their kin, and will put my words into his mouth; he shall tell them all that I command him. Whoever will not listen to my words which he speaks in my name, I myself will make him answer for it. But if a prophet presumes to speak in my name an oracle that I have not commanded him to speak, or speaks in the name of other gods, he shall die.'"

RESPONSORIAL PSALM
Psalm 95:1–2, 6–7, 7–9 (8)

R. If today you hear his voice, harden not
      your hearts.

Come, let us sing joyfully to the LORD;
    let us acclaim the rock of our salvation.
Let us come into his presence with thanksgiving;
    let us joyfully sing psalms to him. R.

Come, let us bow down in worship;
    let us kneel before the LORD who made us.
For he is our God,
    and we are the people he shepherds, the flock
      he guides. R.

Oh, that today you would hear his voice:
    "Harden not your hearts as at Meribah,
    as in the day of Massah in the desert,
where your fathers tempted me;
    they tested me though they had seen
      my works." R.

READING II *1 Corinthians 7:32–35*

Brothers and sisters: I should like you to be free of anxieties. An unmarried man is anxious about the things of the Lord, how he may please the Lord. But a married man is anxious about the things of the world, how he may please his wife, and he is divided. An unmarried woman or a virgin is anxious about the things of the Lord, so that she may be holy in both body and spirit. A married woman, on the other hand, is anxious about the things of the world, how she may please her husband. I am telling you this for your own benefit, not to impose a restraint upon you, but for the sake of propriety and adherence to the Lord without distraction.

GOSPEL *Mark 1:21–28*

Then they came to Capernaum, and on the sabbath Jesus entered the synagogue and taught. The people were astonished at his teaching, for he taught them as one having authority and not as the scribes. In their synagogue was a man with an unclean spirit; he cried out, "What have you to do with us, Jesus of Nazareth? Have you come to destroy us? I know who you are—the Holy One of God!" Jesus rebuked him and said, "Quiet! Come out of him!" The unclean spirit convulsed him and with a loud cry came out of him. All were amazed and asked one another, "What is this? A new teaching with authority. He commands even the unclean spirits and they obey him." His fame spread everywhere throughout the whole region of Galilee.

Practice of Faith

"Quiet!" This is the word Jesus speaks to the unclean spirit before commanding it to depart. It is the same word Jesus later uses to command the storm to "be still." In the face of our own demons, both internal and external, perhaps the command "Quiet!" is the one we first need to obey in faith. Only when we become quiet can God's words of direction, mercy, and healing enter our lives. ◆ Gather your family before bedtime and pray together silently for five minutes. Ask your children how it felt to visit with God in this way. ◆ When do you usually plug into the noise of TV or radio? During the car ride home? While prepping the evening meal? Purposely unplug and get quiet while still engaging the task at hand. Offer this time in prayer. What do you notice? ◆ Sacred music can help calm our restlessness. Take a few minutes to listen to music from a Renaissance Mass by Thomas Tallis, sung by the Collegium Regale at https://www.youtube.com/watch?v=kEwQ51ziCU8, or Gregorian chant by the monks of Santo Domingo de Silos in Spain at https://www.youtube.com/watch?v=zmxCfpsX9Xo.

Download more questions and activities for families, Christian initiation groups, and other adult groups at http://www.ltp.org/t-productsupplements.aspx.

Scripture Insights

Today's readings speak to us about why God chose to come to us in human form in the person of Jesus. The First Reading is part of a very long speech presented as if given by Moses before the Israelites prepared to enter the Promised Land after their Exodus from slavery and their long journey. In the verses we hear today, the author is describing the role of the prophets in the land of Israel. They will be the mediators between God and the people, mediators whom God will raise up from among the people at the appropriate time, and they will speak God's Word to the people. Thus the prophet is given to humans as an accommodation, since the people cannot endure regular, direct encounters with God like the ones they experienced in the Exodus. Christians later reinterpreted this idea of a "prophet like Moses" as fulfilled in Jesus, the prophet par excellence.

In today's Gospel, we hear of Jesus' first miracle as told in Mark's Gospel—the story of Jesus driving an unclean spirit out of a man. Ancients believed that certain diseases were caused by unclean spirits inhabiting the person. Mark shapes the meaning of this story by giving it a rather lengthy introduction and conclusion. "What is this? A new teaching with authority?" (Mark 1:27). The story prompts us to ask about the source of Jesus' authority both in speech and in action. Notice the irony—that the unclean spirit is the one who reveals Jesus' true identity! Why is that?

◆ Reflect on the Gospel story by separating Mark's introduction and conclusion from the miracle story itself. What more do we learn from that beginning and ending? How does Mark's use of this technique shape the meaning of the story?

◆ Imagine what it might have been like for the Israelites to encounter God face-to-face on Mount Sinai. In what ways is it easier or harder to experience God through the prophet's voice?

◆ Pray today's Responsorial Psalm and let it speak to you about where you encounter God's voice and what keeps you from truly hearing it in your life.

READING I *Job 7:1–4, 6–7*

Job spoke, saying:
  Is not man's life on earth a drudgery?
    Are not his days those of hirelings?
  He is a slave who longs for the shade,
    a hireling who waits for his wages.
  So I have been assigned months of misery,
    and troubled nights have been allotted to me.
  If in bed I say, "When shall I arise?"
    then the night drags on;
    I am filled with restlessness until the dawn.
  My days are swifter than a weaver's shuttle;
    they come to an end without hope.
  Remember that my life is like the wind;
    I shall not see happiness again.

RESPONSORIAL PSALM
Psalm 147:1–2, 3–4, 5–6 (see 3a)

R. Praise the Lord, who heals the brokenhearted.
  or: Alleluia.

Praise the LORD, for he is good;
    sing praise to our God, for he is gracious;
    it is fitting to praise him.
The LORD rebuilds Jerusalem;
    the dispersed of Israel he gathers. R.

He heals the brokenhearted
    and binds up their wounds.
He tells the number of the stars;
    he calls each by name. R.

Great is our Lord and mighty in power;
    to his wisdom there is no limit.
The LORD sustains the lowly;
    the wicked he casts to the ground. R.

READING II
1 Corinthians 9:16–19, 22–23

Brothers and sisters: If I preach the gospel, this is no reason for me to boast, for an obligation has been imposed on me, and woe to me if I do not preach it! If I do so willingly, I have a recompense, but if unwillingly, then I have been entrusted with a stewardship. What then is my recompense? That, when I preach, I offer the gospel free of charge so as not to make full use of my right in the gospel.

Although I am free in regard to all, I have made myself a slave to all so as to win over as many as possible. To the weak I became weak, to win over the weak. I have become all things to all, to save at least some. All this I do for the sake of the gospel, so that I too may have a share in it.

GOSPEL *Mark 1:29–39*

On leaving the synagogue Jesus entered the house of Simon and Andrew with James and John. Simon's mother-in-law lay sick with a fever. They immediately told him about her. He approached, grasped her hand, and helped her up. Then the fever left her and she waited on them.

When it was evening, after sunset, they brought to him all who were ill or possessed by demons. The whole town was gathered at the door. He cured many who were sick with various diseases, and he drove out many demons, not permitting them to speak because they knew him.

Rising very early before dawn, he left and went off to a deserted place, where he prayed. Simon and those who were with him pursued him and on finding him said, "Everyone is looking for you." He told them, "Let us go on to the nearby villages that I may preach there also. For this purpose have I come." So he went into their synagogues, preaching and driving out demons throughout the whole of Galilee.

Practice of Hope

Job's hopelessness in today's First Reading may stir memories of our own moments of darkness, or may remind us of so many others who suffer—from illness, poverty, or threat of violence. Jesus, who acted in the world as the Lord who heals the brokenhearted, showed us how he expects his disciples to care for people in need. ◆ More than twenty-one million refugees across the world must wonder, as Job did, if they will ever see happiness again. (Find the most current statistics from the United Nations High Commission on Refugees at http://www.unhcr.org/en-us/figures-at-a-glance.html.) Learn more about the plight of displaced people and the Church's response from the United States Conference of Catholic Bishops' Migration & Refugee Services: http://www.usccb.org/about/migration-and-refugee-services/. ◆ Become a regular donor to organizations that help refugees and learn how you might assist in resettling a family in your community. ◆ With migrants and refugees in mind, pray today's Responsorial Psalm each day this week.

Download more questions and activities for families, Christian initiation groups, and other adult groups at http://www.ltp.org/t-productsupplements.aspx.

Scripture Insights

Today's readings remind us of our constant need for healing and of the salvation that can be found in Jesus. The Greek word for salvation is *soteria*, meaning "rescue," "deliverance," or "wellbeing." In the First Reading, Job, once a wealthy and highly respected man, now finds himself undone through no fault of his own. His oxen and asses were stolen, lightning killed his sheep, and a great wind blew down his house while his kids were partying inside, and everyone was killed. Now he has come down with the worst case of boils that anyone could imagine! And so he laments his very existence and the apparent meaninglessness of life.

The Gospel provides a counterpoint to Job's lament as we see Jesus first raising Peter's mother-in-law from her sick bed, healing the crowds of people who came to the door later that evening, rising early the next day to go off to pray, and then telling his disciples that they must be off to the nearby villages to preach. What is Jesus preaching? In words and actions, he is preaching the Good News that God's reign is at hand. God's salvation is upon us!

In today's Second Reading, Paul reminds us of what ought to motivate the preaching of the Good News. It is an obligation given by God, not so that he can boast of his own powers, but as a means of salvation for himself and as many as he can reach in this world. How will he do that? By becoming the vehicle for others to encounter the saving power of God. Will you also take up the challenge?

◆ In the Gospel look for details that suggest what the reign of God will be like when it fully arrives.

◆ As you reflect on the First Reading, think about times in your life when you might have felt like Job. What gave you hope and helped you to step out of that dark place?

◆ Identify some concrete ways that you could preach the Good News of God's coming kingdom—either in words or actions. What barriers stand in your way?

READING I *Leviticus 13:1–2, 44–46*

The LORD said to Moses and Aaron, "If someone has on his skin a scab or pustule or blotch which appears to be the sore of leprosy, he shall be brought to Aaron, the priest, or to one of the priests among his descendants. If the man is leprous and unclean, the priest shall declare him unclean by reason of the sore on his head.

"The one who bears the sore of leprosy shall keep his garments rent and his head bare, and shall muffle his beard; he shall cry out, 'Unclean, unclean!' As long as the sore is on him he shall declare himself unclean, since he is in fact unclean. He shall dwell apart, making his abode outside the camp."

RESPONSORIAL PSALM
Psalm 32:1–2, 5, 11 (7)

R. I turn to you, Lord, in time of trouble,
and you fill me with the joy of salvation.

Blessed is he whose fault is taken away,
whose sin is covered.
Blessed the man to whom the LORD imputes
not guilt,
in whose spirit there is no guile. R.

Then I acknowledged my sin to you,
my guilt I covered not.
I said, "I confess my faults to the LORD,"
and you took away the guilt of my sin. R.

Be glad in the LORD and rejoice, you just;
exult, all you upright of heart. R.

READING II *1 Corinthians 10:31—11:1*

Brothers and sisters, whether you eat or drink, or whatever you do, do everything for the glory of God. Avoid giving offense, whether to the Jews or Greeks or the church of God, just as I try to please everyone in every way, not seeking my own benefit but that of the many, that they may be saved. Be imitators of me, as I am of Christ.

GOSPEL *Mark 1:40–45*

A leper came to Jesus and kneeling down begged him and said, "If you wish, you can make me clean." Moved with pity, he stretched out his hand, touched him, and said to him, "I do will it. Be made clean." The leprosy left him immediately, and he was made clean. Then, warning him sternly, he dismissed him at once.

He said to him, "See that you tell no one anything, but go, show yourself to the priest and offer for your cleansing what Moses prescribed; that will be proof for them."

The man went away and began to publicize the whole matter. He spread the report abroad so that it was impossible for Jesus to enter a town openly. He remained outside in deserted places, and people kept coming to him from everywhere.

Practice of Hope

The sufferers of leprosy in today's First Reading and Gospel were not necessarily sinners, but the illness that caused them to be labeled "unclean" can serve as a metaphor for the sins that burden us. This week on Ash Wednesday we begin the Lenten season—our time to pay attention to our ongoing conversion. There is great and surprising hope in remembering "you are dust and to dust you shall return," or "turn away from sin and believe in the Gospel," for it reminds us that God is in charge. When we approach God with due humility and repentance, we effectively invite God to live in us anew. ◆ This year, "give up" something to help you grow in faith or charity. Brew your own coffee and donate the money saved. Purposely replace your anger toward fellow drivers with blessing. Give up a half hour of TV and replace it with reading Scripture. ◆ Set up a place in your home for family or household prayer during Lent. Place on a table a purple cloth, an image of Christ, a homemade cross, an alms jar decorated by the children, a Bible, candles, or a container of Holy water. Pray together and bless one another as you move through Lent. ◆ Participate in Catholic Relief Services' Rice Bowl. To learn more about Rice Bowl, and how it relates to Lent, visit http://www.crsricebowl.org/about.

Download more questions and activities for families, Christian initiation groups, and other adult groups at http://www.ltp.org/t-productsupplements.aspx.

Scripture Insights

All of today's readings involve Jewish purity regulations. Cultural anthropologists suggest that purity regulations are a kind of symbol system in which whatever constitutes an orderly cosmos (everything in its place) should be considered "clean." Whatever interferes with this orderly cosmos should be considered "unclean."

The First Reading describes how early Judaism treated one issue involving ritual purity—namely, skin infections. In an orderly cosmos, the skin is supposed to be intact. Therefore, someone with a rupture of the skin, especially an oozing sore, was declared "unclean." Although it is often translated as such, the Hebrew word *tzaraat* does not refer to leprosy or Hansen's disease. The ancient rabbis believed that *tzaraat* was a skin disease that doctors could not heal because it was caused by sin.

This is what makes today's Gospel reading so extraordinary. A man who was known to have *tzaraat* defied the Law and approached Jesus. In response, Jesus did the unthinkable! He had compassion for the man, touched him, and healed him. The point of the story is that the coming Kingdom of God is not about excluding sinners but welcoming them and treating them with compassion so that they can be healed.

In the Second Reading, Paul expands on Jewish purity regulations in another way. He tells the Corinthian community that, whatever individuals decide to do about kosher regulations and the like, they should seek to do what is best for others to the glory of God and the salvation of all.

◆ Carefully read today's Gospel. Why do you imagine that the man went off to tell everyone what Jesus had done for him?

◆ Reflecting on the Psalm, what regrets keep you from feeling included in God's kingdom? Ask for healing.

◆ Think about a time when you were able to set aside cultural or religious expectations in order to do what was most beneficial for another. How did your action glorify God?

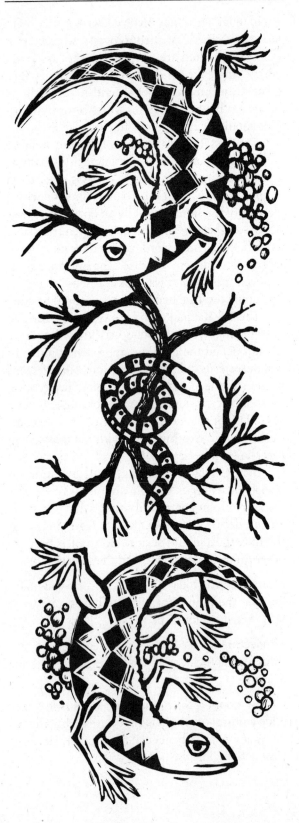

Prayer before Reading the Word

Holy is your name, O Lord our God.
Incline our hearts to keep your Commandments,
and school us in the sublime wisdom of the Cross.
Let us listen to your Son
and bear witness in the world
to that love from which nothing can separate us.

We ask this through Christ,
your power and your wisdom,
the Lord who lives and reigns with you
in the unity of the Holy Spirit,
one God, for ever and ever. Amen.

Prayer after Reading the Word

Deep within our hearts, O God,
you have written your law,
and high upon the Cross
you have lifted up our salvation,
the Savior made perfect in suffering.

Grant us the abundant riches of your grace,
that, with our spirits renewed,
we may be able to respond
to your boundless and eternal love.

We ask this through our Lord Jesus Christ,
your Son, who lives and reigns with you
in the unity of the Holy Spirit,
one God, for ever and ever. Amen.

Weekday Readings

February 14: Ash Wednesday Joel 2:12–18;
   2 Corinthians 5:20—6:2; Matthew 6:1–6, 16–18
February 15: *Deuteronomy 30:15–20; Luke 9:22–25*
February 16: *Isaiah 58:1–9a; Matthew 9:14–15*
February 17: *Isaiah 58:9b–14; Luke 5:27–32*

February 19: *Leviticus 19:1–2, 11–18; Matthew 25:31–46*
February 20: *Isaiah 55:10–11; Matthew 6:7–15*
February 21: *Jonah 3:1–10; Luke 11:29–32*
February 22: Feast of the Chair of Saint Peter
   1 Peter 5:1–4; Matthew 16:13–19
February 23: *Ezekiel 18:21–28; Matthew 5:20–26*
February 24: *Deuteronomy 26:16–19; Matthew 5:43–48*

February 26: *Daniel 9:4b–10; Luke 6:36–38*
February 27: *Isaiah 1:10, 16–20; Matthew 23:1–12*
February 28: *Jeremiah 18:18–20; Matthew 20:17–28*
March 1: *Jeremiah 17:5–10; Luke 16:19–31*
March 2: *Genesis 37:3–4, 12–13a, 17b–28a;*
   Matthew 21:33–43, 45–46
March 3: *Micah 7:14–15, 18–20; Luke 15:1–3, 11–32*

March 5: *2 Kings 5:1–15b; Luke 4:24–30*
March 6: *Daniel 3:25, 34–43; Matthew 18:21–35*
March 7: *Deuteronomy 4:1, 5–9; Matthew 5:17–19*
March 8: *Jeremiah 7:23–28; Luke 11:14–23*
March 9: *Hosea 14:2–10; Mark 12:28–34*
March 10: *Hosea 6:1–6; Luke 18:9–14*

March 12: *Isaiah 65:17–21; John 4:43–54*
March 13: *Ezekiel 47:1–9, 12; John 5:1–16*
March 14: *Isaiah 49:8–15; John 5:17–30*
March 15: *Exodus 32:7–14; John 5:31–47*
March 16: *Wisdom 2:1a, 12–22; John 7:1–2, 10, 25–30*
March 17: *Jeremiah 11:18–20; John 7:40–53*

March 19: Solemnity of St. Joseph, Spouse of the Blessed
   Virgin Mary 2 Samuel 7:4–5a, 12–14a, 16;
   Romans 4:13, 16–18, 22; Matthew 1:16, 18–21, 24a
   or Luke 2:41–51a
March 20: *Numbers 21:4–9; John 8:21–30*
March 21: *Daniel 3:14–20, 91–92, 95; John 8:31–42*
March 22: *Genesis 17:3–9; John 8:51–59*
March 23: *Jeremiah 20:10–13; John 10:31–42*
March 24: *Ezekiel 37:21–28; John 11:45–56*

March 26: *Isaiah 42:1–7; John 12:1–11*
March 27: *Isaiah 49:1–6; John 13:21–33, 36–38*
March 28: *Isaiah 50:4–9a; Matthew 26:14–25*

READING I *Genesis 9:8–15*

God said to Noah and to his sons with him: "See, I am now establishing my covenant with you and your descendants after you and with every living creature that was with you: all the birds, and the various tame and wild animals that were with you and came out of the ark. I will establish my covenant with you, that never again shall all bodily creatures be destroyed by the waters of a flood; there shall not be another flood to devastate the earth." God added: "This is the sign that I am giving for all ages to come, of the covenant between me and you and every living creature with you: I set my bow in the clouds to serve as a sign of the covenant between me and the earth. When I bring clouds over the earth, and the bow appears in the clouds, I will recall the covenant I have made between me and you and all living beings, so that the waters shall never again become a flood to destroy all mortal beings."

RESPONSORIAL PSALM
Psalm 25:4–5, 6–7, 8–9 (see 10)

R. Your ways, O Lord, are love and truth to
    those who keep your covenant.

Your ways, O LORD, make known to me;
    teach me your paths.
Guide me in your truth and teach me,
    for you are God my savior. R.

Remember that your compassion, O LORD,
    and your love are from of old.
In your kindness remember me,
    because of your goodness, O LORD. R.

Good and upright is the LORD,
    thus he shows sinners the way.
He guides the humble to justice,
    and he teaches the humble his way. R.

READING II *1 Peter 3:18–22*

Beloved: Christ suffered for sins once, the righteous for the sake of the unrighteous, that he might lead you to God. Put to death in the flesh, he was brought to life in the Spirit. In it he also went to preach to the spirits in prison, who had once been disobedient while God patiently waited in the days of Noah during the building of the ark, in which a few persons, eight in all, were saved through water. This prefigured baptism, which saves you now. It is not a removal of dirt from the body but an appeal to God for a clear conscience, through the resurrection of Jesus Christ, who has gone into heaven and is at the right hand of God, with angels, authorities, and powers subject to him.

GOSPEL *Mark 1:12–15*

The Spirit drove Jesus out into the desert, and he remained in the desert for forty days, tempted by Satan. He was among wild beasts, and the angels ministered to him.

After John had been arrested, Jesus came to Galilee proclaiming the gospel of God: "This is the time of fulfillment. The kingdom of God is at hand. Repent, and believe in the gospel."

Practice of Faith

Today parishes across the country will send their catechumens (those preparing for Baptism) to their local bishop for the Rite of Election. Through the formation process, which includes much prayer, the catechumens have been growing their faith for many months. They now enter the Period of Purification and Enlightenment, a time of intense spiritual preparation and deepening relationship with Christ, as they prepare to receive the Sacraments of Initiation at the Easter Vigil. ◆ James Dunning writes, "Lent without candidates for baptism is like a Mass without bread and wine. These persons are the sacraments of the dying and rising taking place in all of us" (*New Wine: New Wineskins: Exploring the RCIA*, Sadlier, 1981). Learn the names of the catechumens in your parish and pray for them throughout Lent. ◆ Reflect on what is dying and rising in you this Lenten season. How might it be reflected in those persons preparing for the sacraments of initiation? ◆ To inspire your own Lenten Journey, read Bishop Ricken's "Journey to the Foot of the Cross: 10 Things to Remember for Lent": http://www.usccb.org/prayer-and-worship/liturgical-year/lent/journey-to-the-foot-of-the-cross-10-things-to-remember-for-lent.cfm.

Download more questions and activities for families, Christian initiation groups, and other adult groups at http://www.ltp.org/t-productsupplements.aspx.

Scripture Insights

For the next several weeks the Church celebrates Lent. Lasting a symbolic forty days (it doesn't count out to precisely forty days), Lent reminds us of times of testing described in the Bible, such as the forty years the Jews wandered in the wilderness after the Exodus and many other stories we will hear about during Lent. It is a time of preparation for the great celebration of Easter.

Today's First Reading recalls an important "forty" story—in which God grieved all the evil that had come into the world and decided to renew creation through a flood. For forty days it rained! When Noah and his family were finally able to return to dry land, God established a new, everlasting covenant with humanity that was signified by a rainbow in the clouds.

The Second Reading draws upon the Noah story to explain how Christ suffered for our sins but was brought to life in the Spirit. Biblical scholars do not know the identity of the "spirits in prison," but the phrase may refer to the spirits of the unrighteous who died in the flood. More importantly, the author suggests that the flood story was a prefiguring of Christian Baptism, in which we join ourselves to Christ's Death so that we can come to new life with him.

The Gospel continues the theme of testing and preparation by recalling the story of Jesus' sojourn in the wilderness, where he was tested by Satan for forty days, and then appeared in public proclaiming the nearness of the reign of God and preaching the need for repentance.

◆ Carefully reread the Second Reading. What do you think the author meant when he described the flood story as a prefiguring of Christian Baptism? How is Christian Baptism different from the flood story that prefigures it?

◆ Consider the Gospel reading and Jesus' proclamation of the coming reign of God. What kind of reaction does its message evoke in you? Why?

◆ Prayerfully reflect on today's Responsorial Psalm. What words or images speak most vividly to you? Use those words or images to write your own personal prayer to God.

February 25, 2018 SECOND SUNDAY OF LENT

READING I
Genesis 22:1–2, 9a, 10–13, 15–18

God put Abraham to the test. He called to him, "Abraham!" "Here I am!" he replied. Then God said: "Take your son Isaac, your only one, whom you love, and go to the land of Moriah. There you shall offer him up as a holocaust on a height that I will point out to you."

When they came to the place of which God had told him, Abraham built an altar there and arranged the wood on it. Then he reached out and took the knife to slaughter his son. But the LORD's messenger called to him from heaven, "Abraham, Abraham!" "Here I am!" he answered. "Do not lay your hand on the boy," said the messenger. "Do not do the least thing to him. I know now how devoted you are to God, since you did not withhold from me your own beloved son." As Abraham looked about, he spied a ram caught by its horns in the thicket. So he went and took the ram and offered it up as a holocaust in place of his son.

Again the LORD's messenger called to Abraham from heaven and said: "I swear by myself, declares the Lord, that because you acted as you did in not withholding from me your beloved son, I will bless you abundantly and make your descendants as countless as the stars of the sky and the sands of the seashore; your descendants shall take possession of the gates of their enemies, and in your descendants all the nations of the earth shall find blessing—all this because you obeyed my command."

RESPONSORIAL PSALM
Psalm 116:10, 15, 16–17, 18–19 (9)

R. I will walk before the Lord,
      in the land of the living.

I believed, even when I said,
  "I am greatly afflicted."
Precious in the eyes of the LORD
  is the death of his faithful ones. R.

O LORD, I am your servant;
  I am your servant, the son of your handmaid;
  you have loosed my bonds.
To you will I offer sacrifice of thanksgiving,
  and I will call upon the name of the LORD. R.

My vows to the LORD I will pay
  in the presence of all his people,
in the courts of the house of the LORD,
  in your midst, O Jerusalem. R.

READING II Romans 8:31b–34

Brothers and sisters: If God is for us, who can be against us? He who did not spare his own Son but handed him over for us all, how will he not also give us everything else along with him?

Who will bring a charge against God's chosen ones? It is God who acquits us, who will condemn? Christ Jesus it is who died—or, rather, was raised—who also is at the right hand of God, who indeed intercedes for us.

GOSPEL Mark 9:2–10

Jesus took Peter, James, and John and led them up a high mountain apart by themselves. And he was transfigured before them, and his clothes became dazzling white, such as no fuller on earth could bleach them. Then Elijah appeared to them along with Moses, and they were conversing with Jesus. Then Peter said to Jesus in reply, "Rabbi, it is good that we are here! Let us make three tents: one for you, one for Moses, and one for Elijah." He hardly knew what to say, they were so terrified. Then a cloud came, casting a shadow over them; from the cloud came a voice, "This is my beloved Son. Listen to him." Suddenly, looking around, they no longer saw anyone but Jesus alone with them.

As they were coming down from the mountain, he charged them not to relate what they had seen to anyone, except when the Son of Man had risen from the dead. So they kept the matter to themselves, questioning what rising from the dead meant.

Practice of Hope

In response to his experience of God's glory at the Transfiguration, Peter wants to build tents to house Jesus, Elijah, and Moses. We, too, can be awestruck when God reveals to us his great and magnificent love, but God never allows us to stay on the mountaintop. Rather, he asks us to descend with him and, in hope, get to work building his kingdom. ◆ Have you had a "mountaintop" experience of God? Write down what occurred and how you felt. What do you think God was trying to communicate to you through this experience? ◆ During Lent, invite your family to brainstorm a way to tangibly make life better for someone in your neighborhood or parish community. ◆ Ignatian Volunteer Corp (IVC) provides the opportunity for mature men and women to work for justice and serve the needs of the poor in their community while being supported in deepening their faith. To find out about IVC and its locations, visit http://www.ivcusa.org/.

Download more questions and activities for families, Christian initiation groups, and other adult groups at http://www.ltp.org/t-productsupplements.aspx.

Scripture Insights

On first view, today's First Reading and Gospel appear to have little in common: Abraham nearly sacrifices his son and Jesus is transfigured before two of his disciples. When we dig deeper, however, we discover in both readings a profound message about God's mercy and faithfulness in times of trouble.

The First Reading comes from a story that our Jewish friends call the *Akedah*, the binding of Isaac. It is referred to in the prayers of *Rosh Hashanah*, the first day of the Jewish calendar year. On this day Jews all over the world pray that God will overlook human sinfulness and remember the compassion that he had for Abraham in sparing his son, because Abraham was willing to fully obey God. Ultimately, the story reminds us of our need to depend fully and without question on the tender mercies of God.

In addition to some superficial similarities between the sacrifice of Isaac and the Transfiguration (both are set on a mountain, and in both a voice from the heavens speaks) they both teach about God's restorative love and mercy. To recognize this in the Transfiguration story we need to remember that in Mark's Gospel the Transfiguration episode comes directly after Jesus tells his disciples that he must be killed before he returns in the Father's glory. The transfigured Jesus on the mountain prefigures this return, evidence of God's faithfulness to Jesus and to anyone who is fully obedient to God's will.

The Second Reading reinforces the teaching of the other two readings: Paul speaks with wonderment about the greatness of God's love for us—so great that he would sacrifice his own son for our salvation.

◆ Rereading the First Reading and the Gospel, find as many similarities and divergences as you can between the two stories.

◆ Reflect on the Second Reading as a commentary on the rewards of suffering as a disciple of Jesus. What message do you draw from it?

◆ What phrases or images in today's Responsorial Psalm might help you cultivate greater trust in God's love for you?

READING I *Exodus 20:1–17*

Shorter: Exodus 20:1–3, 7–8, 12–17

In those days, God delivered all these commandments: "I, the LORD, am your God, who brought you out of the land of Egypt, that place of slavery. You shall not have other gods besides me. You shall not carve idols for yourselves in the shape of anything in the sky above or on the earth below or in the waters beneath the earth; you shall not bow down before them or worship them. For I, the LORD, your God, am a jealous God, inflicting punishment for their fathers' wickedness on the children of those who hate me, down to the third and fourth generation; but bestowing mercy down to the thousandth generation on the children of those who love me and keep my commandments.

"You shall not take the name of the LORD, your God, in vain. For the LORD will not leave unpunished the one who takes his name in vain.

"Remember to keep holy the sabbath day. Six days you may labor and do all your work, but the seventh day is the sabbath of the LORD, your God. No work may be done then either by you, or your son or daughter, or your male or female slave, or your beast, or by the alien who lives with you. In six days the LORD made the heavens and the earth, the sea and all that is in them; but on the seventh day he rested. That is why the LORD has blessed the sabbath day and made it holy.

"Honor your father and your mother, that you may have a long life in the land which the LORD, your God, is giving you. You shall not kill. You shall not commit adultery. You shall not steal. You shall not bear false witness against your neighbor. You shall not covet your neighbor's house. You shall not covet your neighbor's wife, nor his male or female slave, nor his ox or ass, nor anything else that belongs to him."

RESPONSORIAL PSALM
Psalm 19:8, 9, 10, 11 (John 6:68c)

R. Lord, you have the words of everlasting life.

The law of the LORD is perfect,
    refreshing the soul;
the decree of the LORD is trustworthy,
    giving wisdom to the simple. R.

The precepts of the LORD are right,
    rejoicing the heart;
the command of the LORD is clear,
    enlightening the eye. R.

The fear of the LORD is pure,
    enduring forever;
the ordinances of the LORD are true,
    all of them just. R.

They are more precious than gold,
    than a heap of purest gold;
sweeter also than syrup
    or honey from the comb. R.

READING II *1 Corinthians 1:22–25*

Brothers and sisters: Jews demand signs and Greeks look for wisdom, but we proclaim Christ crucified, a stumbling block to Jews and foolishness to Gentiles, but to those who are called, Jews and Greeks alike, Christ the power of God and the wisdom of God. For the foolishness of God is wiser than human wisdom, and the weakness of God is stronger than human strength.

GOSPEL *John 2:13–25*

Since the Passover of the Jews was near, Jesus went up to Jerusalem. He found in the temple area those who sold oxen, sheep, and doves, as well as the money changers seated there. He made a whip out of cords and drove them all out of the temple area, with the sheep and oxen, and spilled the coins of the money changers and overturned their tables, and to those who sold doves he said, "Take these out of here, and stop making my Father's house a marketplace." His disciples recalled the words of Scripture, *Zeal for your house will consume me.* At this the Jews answered and said to him, "What sign can you show us for doing this?" Jesus answered and said to them, "Destroy this temple and in three days I will raise it up." The Jews said, "This temple has been under construction for forty-six years, and you will raise it up in three days?" But he was speaking about the temple of his body. Therefore, when he was raised from the dead, his disciples remembered that he had said this, and they came to believe the Scripture and the word Jesus had spoken.

While he was in Jerusalem for the feast of Passover, many began to believe in his name when they saw the signs he was doing. But Jesus would not trust himself to them because he knew them all, and did not need anyone to testify about human nature. He himself understood it well.

Practice of Hope

We know God's Law is "more desirable than gold," yet it is easy for us to get off track. Before we know it, we find ourselves serving idols of our own or society's making, be it success, prestige, or security. Secular and commercial values creep into time and places meant to be holy. Thankfully, God continually invites us to repentance, to turn away from sin and toward himself, where his love and mercy await. ◆ What idols have lately crept into your life? How can you return time and worship to God? ◆ Make a point of participating in the Sacrament of Reconciliation during Lent. "The Sacrament of Penance is an experience of the gift of God's boundless mercy," says the United States Conference of Catholic Bishops. Refresh your understanding of this sacrament at http://www.usccb.org/prayer-and-worship/sacraments-and-sacramentals/penance. ◆ Consider working with a qualified spiritual director to deepen your faith life. Directors can be found through your diocese or local retreat centers. Spiritual Directors International at www.sdiworld.org is a reputable online resource.

Download more questions and activities for families, Christian initiation groups, and other adult groups at http://www.ltp.org/t-productsupplements.aspx.

Scripture Insights

The Ten Commandments are at the heart of the covenant Moses made with God for the Israelites. Today Jews and Christians understand them to be central to their relationship with God and the foundation of the moral life. That covenant relationship with God carries obligations—the point of today's readings.

The First Reading takes place on a sacred mountain in the Sinai wilderness. Having brought the Israelites out of slavery in Egypt, now, on the mountain, God speaks to Moses, making a covenant with the people, declaring that he is their God and they are his people. Then God outlines what they must do in order to keep the covenant with him. Today we know these obligations as the Ten Commandments.

The Gospel story also takes place on a sacred mountain, a traditional place of encounter with God (Jerusalem, God's holy mountain). Just before Passover Jesus enters the Jerusalem Temple, driving out the money changers and those who sell animals for sacrifice. Many readers assume these people were doing something terrible; actually, they were doing only what was necessary for the operation of the Temple. Jesus' action drew attention to another way his understanding of his obligation to his Father would upend religious life. Notice that the author takes a verse from Psalm 69—"Zeal for your house has consumed me"—and changes the verb tense so that it now reads, "Zeal for your house will consume me." Indeed, it will. What was once a part of a lament psalm now has become a prophecy about Jesus' Death, and Jesus' words about raising up "this temple" extend that prophecy.

◆ In the Gospel, the religious authorities ask Jesus for a sign; later we hear that people came to him because of the signs, but Jesus would not trust himself to them. Why isn't faith prompted by signs enough?

◆ In the Ten Commandments, observe how often the phrase "the Lord, your God" appears. What does that tell you about the nature of God's relationship with humanity?

◆ In the Second Reading, where do you see yourself fitting? How do you see Christ crucified?

READING I *Exodus 17:3–7*

In those days, in their thirst for water, the people grumbled against Moses, saying, "Why did you ever make us leave Egypt? Was it just to have us die here of thirst with our children and our livestock?" So Moses cried out to the LORD, "What shall I do with this people? A little more and they will stone me!" The LORD answered Moses, "Go over there in front of the people, along with some of the elders of Israel, holding in your hand, as you go, the staff with which you struck the river. I will be standing there in front of you on the rock in Horeb. Strike the rock, and the water will flow from it for the people to drink." This Moses did, in the presence of the elders of Israel. The place was called Massah and Meribah, because the Israelites quarreled there and tested the LORD, saying, "Is the LORD in our midst or not?"

RESPONSORIAL PSALM
Psalm 95:1–2, 6–7, 8–9 (8)

R. If today you hear his voice, harden not
      your hearts.

Come, let us sing joyfully to the LORD;
  let us acclaim the Rock of our salvation.
Let us come into his presence with thanksgiving;
  let us joyfully sing psalms to him. R.

Come, let us bow down in worship;
  let us kneel before the LORD who made us.
For he is our God,
  and we are the people he shepherds, the flock
      he guides. R.

Oh, that today you would hear his voice:
  "Harden not your hearts as at Meribah,
  as in the day of Massah in the desert.
Where your fathers tempted me;
  they tested me though they had seen
      my works." R.

READING II *Romans 5:1–2, 5–8*

Brothers and sisters: Since we have been justified by faith, we have peace with God through our Lord Jesus Christ, through whom we have gained access by faith to this grace in which we stand, and we boast in hope of the glory of God.

And hope does not disappoint, because the love of God has been poured out into our hearts through the Holy Spirit who has been given to us. For Christ, while we were still helpless, died at the appointed time for the ungodly. Indeed, only with difficulty does one die for a just person, though perhaps for a good person one might even find courage to die. But God proves his love for us in that while we were still sinners Christ died for us.

GOSPEL
John 4:5–15, 19b–26, 39a, 40–42
Longer: John 4:5–42

Jesus came to a town of Samaria called Sychar, near the plot of land that Jacob had given to his son Joseph. Jacob's well was there. Jesus, tired from his journey, sat down there at the well. It was about noon.

A woman of Samaria came to draw water. Jesus said to her, "Give me a drink." His disciples had gone into the town to buy food. The Samaritan woman said to him, "How can you, a Jew, ask me, a Samaritan woman, for a drink?"—For Jews use nothing in common with Samaritans.— Jesus answered and said to her, "If you knew the gift of God and who is saying to you, 'Give me a drink,' you would have asked him and he would have given you living water." The woman said to him, "Sir, you do not even have a bucket and the cistern is deep; where then can you get this living water? Are you greater than our father Jacob, who gave us this cistern and drank from it himself with his children and his flocks?" Jesus answered and said to her, "Everyone who drinks this water will be thirsty again; but whoever drinks the water I shall give will never thirst; the water I shall give will become in him a spring of water welling up to eternal life." The woman said to him, "Sir, give me this water, so that I may not be thirsty or have to keep coming here to draw water.

"I can see that you are a prophet. Our ancestors worshiped on this mountain; but you people say that the place to worship is in Jerusalem." Jesus said to her, "Believe me, woman, the hour is coming when you will worship the Father neither on this mountain nor in Jerusalem. You people worship what you do not understand; we worship what we understand, because salvation is from the Jews. But the hour is coming, and is now here, when true worshipers will worship the Father in Spirit and truth; and indeed the Father seeks such people to worship him. God is Spirit, and those who worship him must worship in Spirit and truth." The woman said to him, "I know that the Messiah is coming, the one called the Christ; when he comes, he will tell us everything." Jesus said to her, "I am he, the one who is speaking with you."

Many of the Samaritans of that town began to believe in him. When the Samaritans came to him, they invited him to stay with them; and he stayed there two days. Many more began to believe in him because of his word, and they said to the woman, "We no longer believe because of your word; for we have heard for ourselves, and we know that this is truly the savior of the world."

Practice of Hope

Today the elect, supported by their sponsors, celebrate the first scrutiny, which helps them discern what needs healing in their hearts. Together we pray with our elect that, like the Samaritan woman at the well, we might all experience the healing power of Christ who is our living water. ◆ In prayer, ask God to reveal what needs healing in your life, and use this to guide your prayer time between now and Easter. ◆ Conversion is a lifelong process. At Mass, listen carefully to the prayers offered during the scrutinies and open your heart to their healing power. ◆ In our culture, poor and homeless women are often disregarded. At Rosehaven, a shelter in Portland, Oregon, these women are considered guests. Learn more at http://rosehaven.org/.

Download more questions and activities for families, Christian initiation groups, and other adult groups at http://www.ltp.org/t-productsupplements.aspx.

Scripture Insights

This is the first of three Sundays in Lent in which those preparing for Baptism celebrate the scrutinies —opportunities to reflect on human sinfulness and desire for healing. The focus of this week's scrutiny is Jesus, the living water.

In the First Reading, we hear the story of the Israelites grumbling against Moses as they wander thirstily in the wilderness. Moses concludes that their grousing about his leadership was a test of for God. Would he care for them? ("Is the Lord in our midst or not?") Standing up to the test, God gives them water from a rock! But it will always be known as the place of the Israelites' strife (the Hebrew word, *Meribah*) and rebellion (*Massah*).

In the Second Reading, Paul describes the peace that comes to those who are justified—literally "acquitted" by God as in a court of law—by their trust in Jesus Christ. This trust brings us hope, Paul says, because of God's love which floods our hearts through the activity of the Holy Spirit. Clearly, Paul's words are an antithesis to those grumbling in the wilderness.

Today's Gospel is the beautiful story of the Samaritan woman at the well. In it, we see a woman whose first encounter with Jesus takes a hostile, partisan tone as he tells her that he can give her "living" water (spring water). John's Gospel is well known for its symbolism and double meanings. The Samaritan woman did not realize that Jesus was talking about "water" that gives everlasting life. Gradually she goes from curiosity about Jesus to recognition of his true identity and becomes an agent of his message to the world.

◆ Why do you think the people quarreled with Moses? What lesson do you draw from God's response?

◆ As you reflect on the Second Reading, consider how you have experienced the peace that comes to those who are justified by faith.

◆ In your Bible read the longer version of the Gospel story. When have you had a feisty conversation with the Lord—similar to the Samaritan woman's or that of the Israelites in the desert?

READING I
2 Chronicles 36:14–16, 19–23

In those days, all the princes of Judah, the priests, and the people added infidelity to infidelity, practicing all the abominations of the nations and polluting the LORD's temple which he had consecrated in Jerusalem.

Early and often did the LORD, the God of their fathers, send his messengers to them, for he had compassion on his people and his dwelling place. But they mocked the messengers of God, despised his warnings, and scoffed at his prophets, until the anger of the LORD against his people was so inflamed that there was no remedy. Their enemies burnt the house of God, tore down the walls of Jerusalem, set all its palaces afire, and destroyed all its precious objects. Those who escaped the sword were carried captive to Babylon, where they became servants of the king of the Chaldeans and his sons until the kingdom of the Persians came to power. All this was to fulfill the word of the LORD spoken by Jeremiah: "Until the land has retrieved its lost sabbaths, during all the time it lies waste it shall have rest while seventy years are fulfilled."

In the first year of Cyrus, king of Persia, in order to fulfill the word of the LORD spoken by Jeremiah, the LORD inspired King Cyrus of Persia to issue this proclamation throughout his kingdom, both by word of mouth and in writing: "Thus says Cyrus, king of Persia: All the kingdoms of the earth the LORD, the God of heaven, has given to me, and he has also charged me to build him a house in Jerusalem, which is in Judah. Whoever, therefore, among you belongs to any part of his people, let him go up, and may his God be with him!"

RESPONSORIAL PSALM
Psalm 137:1–2, 3, 4–5, 6 (6ab)

R. Let my tongue be silenced, if I ever forget you!

By the streams of Babylon
    we sat and wept
    when we remembered Zion.
On the aspens of that land
    we hung up our harps. R.

For there our captors asked of us
    the lyrics of our songs,
and our despoilers urged us to be joyous:
    "Sing for us the songs of Zion!" R.

How could we sing a song of the LORD
    in a foreign land?
If I forget you, Jerusalem,
    may my right hand be forgotten! R.

May my tongue cleave to my palate
    if I remember you not,
if I place not Jerusalem
    ahead of my joy. R.

READING II *Ephesians 2:4–10*

Brothers and sisters: God, who is rich in mercy, because of the great love he had for us, even when we were dead in our transgressions, brought us to life with Christ—by grace you have been saved—, raised us up with him, and seated us with him in the heavens in Christ Jesus, that in the ages to come he might show the immeasurable riches of his grace in his kindness to us in Christ Jesus. For by grace you have been saved through faith, and this is not from you; it is the gift of God; it is not from works, so no one may boast. For we are his handiwork, created in Christ Jesus for the good works that God has prepared in advance, that we should live in them.

GOSPEL *John 3:14–21*

Jesus said to Nicodemus: "Just as Moses lifted up the serpent in the desert, so must the Son of Man be lifted up, so that everyone who believes in him may have eternal life."

For God so loved the world that he gave his only Son, so that everyone who believes in him might not perish but might have eternal life. For God did not send his Son into the world to condemn the world, but that the world might be saved through him. Whoever believes in him will not be condemned, but whoever does not believe has already been condemned, because he has not believed in the name of the only Son of God. And this is the verdict, that the light came into the world, but people preferred darkness to light, because their works were evil. For everyone who does wicked things hates the light and does not come toward the light, so that his works might not be exposed. But whoever lives the truth comes to the light, so that his works may be clearly seen as done in God.

Practice of Hope

St. Paul tells us we are God's "handiwork," plain and simple. Nothing we do can earn God's love or win God's favor. Rather, God's love and mercy are woven into our very being through Jesus Christ. What an astonishing truth this is, and the reason for our hope! ◆ Think of the last time you created something you were proud of. How did you feel while creating it, and then when you were finished? Imagine how God feels toward you! ◆ Read Psalm 139 and choose a couple verses that strike you. Take time to meditate on them. What is God saying to you through these verses? ◆ Read *The Runaway Bunny* by Margaret Wise Brown to your children or grandchildren. Talk to them about how we can never escape God's love, just as the runaway bunny cannot escape his mother's love.

Download more questions and activities for families, Christian initiation groups, and other adult groups at http://www.ltp.org/t-productsupplements.aspx.

Scripture Insights

This is Laetare Sunday. *Laetare* means "rejoice" and comes from the introit, or entrance verse, for this Sunday, taken from Isaiah 66:10: "Rejoice, O Jerusalem!" The beginning of today's First Reading, however, gives little cause for rejoicing. It describes how the leaders and people of Judah (under the evil influence of King Zedekiah) "added infidelity to infidelity" against God and so suffered defeat at the hands of the Babylonians. The Temple was destroyed and many people were carried off to exile in Babylon. But, of course, God is always faithful to his covenant people and eventually will arrange for them to return to Jerusalem by dictate of Cyrus, the king of Persia.

The Second Reading and the Gospel continue this theme of human infidelity and divine faithfulness. The author of the Letter to the Ephesians praises God, who brought us out of the death of sin through his loving mercy and raised us up in glory with Christ not through our own merit but as a gift from God. In other words, we are saved by grace (the Greek word is *charis* meaning "favor" or "kindness").

The Gospel recalls a scene from Numbers 21:4–9, which describes God's punishment of the Israelites for their infidelity during the Exodus. He sent "fiery" serpents into the desert to attack the people. But when they repented, God instructed Moses to make a bronze serpent and mount it on a pole so that anyone who looked upon the serpent would be healed and live. In this symbolic Gospel of John, Jesus is the one on the pole. He is to be "lifted up" in crucifixion, because God loved the world so much that he was willing to give up his only Son. Truly this is cause for rejoicing.

◆ What does the Second Reading have to say about the gift that Baptism offers us?

◆ Carefully reread today's Gospel. What does it mean to you to walk in the light?

◆ Slowly pray today's Responsorial Psalm, mindful of times when you have felt exiled from God. How was your suffering eventually turned to joy?

READING I *1 Samuel 16:1b, 6–7, 10–13a*

The LORD said to Samuel: "Fill your horn with oil, and be on your way. I am sending you to Jesse of Bethlehem, for I have chosen my king from among his sons."

As Jesse and his sons came to the sacrifice, Samuel looked at Eliab and thought, "Surely the LORD's anointed is here before him." But the LORD said to Samuel: "Do not judge from his appearance or from his lofty stature, because I have rejected him. Not as man sees does God see, because man sees the appearance but the LORD looks into the heart." In the same way Jesse presented seven sons before Samuel, but Samuel said to Jesse, "The LORD has not chosen any one of these." Then Samuel asked Jesse, "Are these all the sons you have?" Jesse replied, "There is still the youngest, who is tending the sheep." Samuel said to Jesse, "Send for him; we will not begin the sacrificial banquet until he arrives here." Jesse sent and had the young man brought to them. He was ruddy, a youth handsome to behold and making a splendid appearance. The LORD said, "There—anoint him, for this is the one!" Then Samuel, with the horn of oil in hand, anointed David in the presence of his brothers; and from that day on, the spirit of the LORD rushed upon David.

RESPONSORIAL PSALM
Psalm 23:1–3a, 3b–4, 5, 6 (1)

R. The Lord is my shepherd;
      there is nothing I shall want.

The LORD is my shepherd; I shall not want.
  In verdant pastures he gives me repose;
beside restful waters he leads me;
  he refreshes my soul. R.

He guides me in right paths
  for his name's sake.
Even though I walk in the dark valley
  I fear no evil; for you are at my side
with your rod and your staff
  that give me courage. R.

You spread the table before me
  in the sight of my foes;
you anoint my head with oil;
  my cup overflows. R.

Only goodness and kindness follow me
  all the days of my life;
and I shall dwell in the house of the LORD
  for years to come. R.

READING II *Ephesians 5:8–14*

Brothers and sisters: You were once darkness, but now you are light in the Lord. Live as children of light, for light produces every kind of goodness and righteousness and truth. Try to learn what is pleasing to the Lord. Take no part in the fruitless works of darkness; rather expose them, for it is shameful even to mention the things done by them in secret; but everything exposed by the light becomes visible, for everything that becomes visible is light. Therefore, it says:
  "Awake, O sleeper,
  and arise from the dead,
  and Christ will give you light."

GOSPEL *John 9:1, 6–9, 13–17, 34–38*

Longer: John 9:1–41

As Jesus passed by he saw a man blind from birth. He spat on the ground and made clay with the saliva, and smeared the clay on his eyes, and said to him, "Go wash in the Pool of Siloam"—which means Sent—. So he went and washed, and came back able to see.

His neighbors and those who had seen him earlier as a beggar said, "Isn't this the one who used to sit and beg?" Some said, "It is," but others said, "No, he just looks like him." He said, "I am."

They brought the one who was once blind to the Pharisees. Now Jesus had made clay and opened his eyes on a sabbath. So then the Pharisees also asked him how he was able to see. He said to them, "He put clay on my eyes, and I washed, and now I can see." So some of the Pharisees said, "This man is not from God, because he does not keep the sabbath." But others said, "How can a sinful man do such signs?" And there was a division among them. So they said to the blind man again, "What do you have to say about him, since he opened your eyes?" He said, "He is a prophet."

They answered and said to him, "You were born totally in sin, and are you trying to teach us?" Then they threw him out.

When Jesus heard that they had thrown him out, he found him and said, "Do you believe in the Son of Man?" He answered and said, "Who is he, sir, that I may believe in him?" Jesus said to him, "You have seen him, and the one speaking with you is he." He said, "I do believe, Lord," and he worshiped him.

Practice of Faith

Today the Elect are presented with our Creed. In the early centuries of our Church, Ecumenical Councils developed the Creed to clarify what we believe about God and to defend those beliefs against misunderstanding or heresy. The Creed helps us to see God more clearly, and "as it recalls the wonderful deeds of God for the salvation of the human race, [it] suffuses the vision of the elect with the sure light of faith" (RCIA 147). ◆ Read more about the Nicene Creed and its origins at http://www.catholicnewsherald.com/our-faith/200-news/roknewspager-yearfaith/2718-the-nicene-creed-and-its-origins?showall=&start=1. ◆ So often at Mass we reel off the Creed mechanically. Take time this week to pray with the Creed. What do you notice? Do any questions arise for you about what we believe? ◆ As a Lenten meditation, listen to the Agnus Dei, also recited each week at Mass, here performed by the Choir of New College, Oxford: https://www.youtube.com/watch?v=aRwhkBAeheM.

Download more questions and activities for families, Christian initiation groups, and other adult groups at http://www.ltp.org/t-productsupplements.aspx.

Scripture Insights

Today those preparing for Baptism celebrate the second scrutiny—an opportunity to reflect on sin, evil, and the desire for healing. The focus of this week's scrutiny is Jesus, the light of the world.

In the First Reading God sends Samuel to Jesse, the father of David, whom God called to be the anointed of God. Amazingly but rightfully, Samuel allows himself to see as God sees and to anoint the youngest of Jesse's eight sons as the one upon whom the Holy Spirit will rush.

In the Second Reading, Paul invites us to live as children of light, producing goodness, righteousness, and truth. Light, he says, makes us visible and transparent. And what is the light of which he speaks? Jesus Christ who awakens us to life!

Today's Gospel tells the story of a blind man who is healed by Jesus and who then reveals Jesus' identity and calls others to conversion. After Jesus smeared clay on the eyes of the man born blind, the man "went and washed, and came back able to see" (John 9:7)—notice the three action verbs! The man is healed but then faces his own call to conversion. As he is confronted by neighbors and by the Pharisees about the identity of this man who healed him, he calls him a prophet, a man from God, and finally the Messiah. At this moment his eyes are truly opened and he fully embraces the light of the world, who fills him with everlasting light.

◆ Carefully reread the First Reading. What did God teach Samuel during the search for a king? What message do you take from this story?

◆ As you reflect on the Second Reading, remember a time when you "were once darkness" and a time when you felt strongly that you were "light in the Lord." What made the difference?

◆ Ancients thought that people could see not because of the light that entered the eye, but because of the light that went out from within them. What is the light that God put within you and that enlightens the world?

READING I *Jeremiah 31:31–34*

The days are coming, says the LORD, when I will make a new covenant with the house of Israel and the house of Judah. It will not be like the covenant I made with their fathers the day I took them by the hand to lead them forth from the land of Egypt; for they broke my covenant, and I had to show myself their master, says the LORD. But this is the covenant that I will make with the house of Israel after those days, says the LORD. I will place my law within them and write it upon their hearts; I will be their God, and they shall be my people. No longer will they have need to teach their friends and relatives how to know the LORD. All, from least to greatest, shall know me, says the LORD, for I will forgive their evildoing and remember their sin no more.

RESPONSORIAL PSALM
Psalm 51:3–4, 12–13, 14–15 (12a)

R. Create a clean heart in me, O God.

Have mercy on me, O God, in your goodness;
    in the greatness of your compassion wipe out
        my offense.
Thoroughly wash me from my guilt
    and of my sin cleanse me. R.

A clean heart create for me, O God,
    and a steadfast spirit renew within me.
Cast me not out from your presence,
    and your Holy Spirit take not from me. R.

Give me back the joy of your salvation,
    and a willing spirit sustain in me.
I will teach transgressors your ways,
    and sinners shall return to you. R.

READING II *Hebrews 5:7–9*

In the days when Christ Jesus was in the flesh, he offered prayers and supplications with loud cries and tears to the one who was able to save him from death, and he was heard because of his reverence. Son though he was, he learned obedience from what he suffered; and when he was made perfect, he became the source of eternal salvation for all who obey him.

GOSPEL *John 12:20–33*

Some Greeks who had come to worship at the Passover Feast came to Philip, who was from Bethsaida in Galilee, and asked him, "Sir, we would like to see Jesus." Philip went and told Andrew; then Andrew and Philip went and told Jesus. Jesus answered them, "The hour has come for the Son of Man to be glorified. Amen, amen, I say to you, unless a grain of wheat falls to the ground and dies, it remains just a grain of wheat; but if it dies, it produces much fruit. Whoever loves his life loses it, and whoever hates his life in this world will preserve it for eternal life. Whoever serves me must follow me, and where I am, there also will my servant be. The Father will honor whoever serves me.

"I am troubled now. Yet what should I say? 'Father, save me from this hour'? But it was for this purpose that I came to this hour. Father, glorify your name." Then a voice came from heaven, "I have glorified it and will glorify it again." The crowd there heard it and said it was thunder; but others said, "An angel has spoken to him." Jesus answered and said, "This voice did not come for my sake but for yours. Now is the time of judgment on this world; now the ruler of this world will be driven out. And when I am lifted up from the earth, I will draw everyone to myself." He said this indicating the kind of death he would die.

Practice of Charity

Jesus tells us that he, like a grain of wheat, must fall to the ground and die in order to bear fruit for God's Kingdom. Lenten observances of prayer, fasting, and almsgiving (charity) similarly help us die to ourselves and our selfishness and draw us closer to him. ◆ In prayer, ask God to show you when and where during your life you have been charitable to others. What stands out? Is God calling you to be charitable in a specific way today? ◆ Is there a relationship in your life in need of healing? What steps can you take, in charity and with God's grace, to mend what is broken? Consider seeking counsel or support as you work toward reconciliation. ◆ "Ubi caritas" is a chant used during the Mass of the Lord's Supper on Holy Thursday. It translates: "Where charity is true, God is there." Listen and pray with its words during these last weeks of Lent: https://www.youtube.com/watch?v=R6w5F1-ceIU&index=187&list=PL323D9781654AF975.

Download more questions and activities for families, Christian initiation groups, and other adult groups at http://www.ltp.org/t-productsupplements.aspx.

Scripture Insights

Today's readings offer sober prompts for reflection. In the First Reading, from Jeremiah 31, God promises to renew the old, broken covenant by putting his law within the people, and the psalmist, in Psalm 51, cries out for the grace of internal renewal on a personal level. These passages are easily understood. But the Second Reading and Gospel demand pondering.

Both readings focus on Jesus' agony in anticipation of the Passion. In Hebrews, the author recounts that because of Jesus' reverence, God, the only one who could save him from death, heard his "prayers and supplications . . . loud cries and tears." Jesus was certainly not spared from death, but he was indeed saved from death in the sense of being raised from the dead. The Gospel conveys another insight about Jesus' reflections (placed by John among the Last Supper discourses rather than in the garden at Gethsemane): "I am troubled now. Yet what should I say? 'Father, save me from this hour'? But it was for this purpose that I came to this hour." Jesus was not backing off from trust in the Father. After acknowledging his inner state, Jesus was able to move through the natural human fear to see the place his coming Death would have in the victorious plan of the Father—that his Crucifixion would result in a "lifting up," bringing about an ingathering of "everyone."

Finally, how can the author of Hebrews say that Jesus "learned obedience from what he suffered" and "was made perfect"? He was, after all, the eternal Son of God! These are assertions about the consequences of his humanity. Incarnate as Jesus, the Son really did learn experientially what it is for a human being to suffer. And in this experience of solidarity with humanity, he was perfected precisely as a mediator between the divine and the human.

◆ How has your understanding of Jesus' suffering deepened over time?

◆ How does Jesus' obedience to his Father lead you to think about your own feelings about obedience?

◆ How do these descriptions of Jesus' reflections on the coming ordeal give us a model?

March 18, 2018 FIFTH SUNDAY OF LENT, YEAR A

READING I *Ezekiel 37:12–14*

Thus says the Lord GOD: O my people, I will open your graves and have you rise from them, and bring you back to the land of Israel. Then you shall know that I am the LORD, when I open your graves and have you rise from them, O my people! I will put my spirit in you that you may live, and I will settle you upon your land; thus you shall know that I am the LORD. I have promised, and I will do it, says the LORD.

RESPONSORIAL PSALM
Psalm 130:1–2, 3–4, 5–6, 7–8 (7)

R. With the Lord there is mercy and fullness
of redemption.

Out of the depths I cry to you, O LORD;
　　LORD, hear my voice!
Let your ears be attentive
　　to my voice in supplication. R.

If you, O LORD, mark iniquities,
　　LORD, who can stand?
But with you is forgiveness,
　　that you may be revered. R.

I trust in the LORD;
　　my soul trusts in his word.
More than sentinels wait for the dawn,
　　let Israel wait for the LORD. R.

For with the LORD is kindness
　　and with him is plenteous redemption;
and he will redeem Israel
　　from all their iniquities. R.

READING II *Romans 8:8–11*

Brothers and sisters: Those who are in the flesh cannot please God. But you are not in the flesh; on the contrary, you are in the spirit, if only the Spirit of God dwells in you. Whoever does not have the Spirit of Christ does not belong to him. But if Christ is in you, although the body is dead because of sin, the spirit is alive because of righteousness. If the Spirit of the One who raised Jesus from the dead dwells in you, the One who raised Christ from the dead will give life to your mortal bodies also, through his Spirit dwelling in you.

GOSPEL *John 11:3–7, 17, 20–27, 33b–45*

Longer: John 11:1–45

The sisters of Lazarus sent word to Jesus, saying, "Master, the one you love is ill." When Jesus heard this he said, "This illness is not to end in death, but is for the glory of God, that the Son of God may be glorified through it." Now Jesus loved Martha and her sister and Lazarus. So when he heard that he was ill, he remained for two days in the place where he was. Then after this he said to his disciples, "Let us go back to Judea."

When Jesus arrived, he found that Lazarus had already been in the tomb for four days. When Martha heard that Jesus was coming, she went to meet him; but Mary sat at home. Martha said to Jesus, "Lord, if you had been here, my brother would not have died. But even now I know that whatever you ask of God, God will give you." Jesus said to her, "Your brother will rise." Martha said, "I know he will rise, in the resurrection on the last day." Jesus told her, "I am the resurrection and the life; whoever believes in me, even if he dies, will live, and everyone who lives and believes in me will never die. Do you believe this?" She said to him, "Yes, Lord. I have come to believe that you are the Christ, the Son of God, the one who is coming into the world."

He became perturbed and deeply troubled, and said, "Where have you laid him?" They said to him, "Sir, come and see." And Jesus wept. So the Jews said, "See how he loved him." But some of them said, "Could not the one who opened the eyes of the blind man have done something so that this man would not have died?"

So Jesus, perturbed again, came to the tomb. It was a cave, and a stone lay across it. Jesus said, "Take away the stone." Martha, the dead man's sister, said to him, "Lord, by now there will be a stench; he has been dead for four days." Jesus said to her, "Did I not tell you that if you believe you will see the glory of God?" So they took away the stone. And Jesus raised his eyes and said, "Father,

I thank you for hearing me. I know that you always hear me; but because of the crowd here I have said this, that they may believe that you sent me." And when he had said this, he cried out in a loud voice, "Lazarus, come out!" The dead man came out, tied hand and foot with burial bands, and his face was wrapped in a cloth. So Jesus said to them, "Untie him and let him go."

Now many of the Jews who had come to Mary and seen what he had done began to believe in him.

Practice of Hope

"I trust in the LORD, / my soul trusts in his word / More than sentinels wait for the dawn, / let Israel wait for the LORD." The psalmist's words this Sunday are especially relevant for our elect, who near the end of their hopeful waiting, soon to be adopted into the Body of Christ through Baptism, Eucharist, and Confirmation. This week they will receive The Lord's Prayer, and after receiving the sacraments at the Easter Vigil, will recite it with us as disciples of Christ in our Catholic family.
◆ Reflect on the first two words of The Lord's Prayer. What does it mean for you to be part of a Catholic family that calls God "Our Father"?
◆ Help new members of your parish feel welcome: introduce yourself at coffee, write a note of welcome, or invite them to a parish activity.
◆ Churches United for the Homeless, in Moorehead, Minnesota, has created a large, ecumenical family of care. Partnering with parishes, churches, and community organizations, CUH runs a community center, emergency and transitional shelters, and offers food, medical care, social services, and spiritual support. Find them at http://www.churches-united.org/.

Download more questions and activities for families, Christian initiation groups, and other adult groups at http://www.ltp.org/t-productsupplements.aspx.

Scripture Insights

This Sunday the prayers of the third scrutiny for the elect will focus on Jesus, the Resurrection and the life. The First Reading is the conclusion of a vision in which Ezekiel is transported to a plain filled with dry bones and told to prophesy to the bones so that they might be brought back to life. When he does, the bones clang together and take on flesh. But Judah remains lifeless until God breathes his spirit into them and brings them again to their own land. The vision reassures the people of restoration after their exile in Babylon. In the Second Reading, Paul explains what it means to have the Spirit of God dwelling in us. But be aware that when he writes about flesh and spirit, he does not mean a dichotomy between body versus soul. Instead, he refers to the "old self," before knowing Christ, and the "new self," baptized in Christ's name.

Today's Gospel relates that Mary and Martha send word when their brother, Lazarus, is ill. The disciples are confused because Jesus tells them that this incident will not end in death, yet he delays before leaving for Bethany. When he finally arrives, Martha and Mary are distraught over the loss of their brother and over Jesus' failure to arrive in time to heal him. They are shocked when he orders the tomb opened. After four days, Lazarus' body would be rotting already! But Jesus calls him, and he comes out of the tomb—still bound in his burial cloths—but fully alive. What are they to think when only God can raise the dead!

◆ Carefully read and analyze today's Gospel. What prompted Jesus to delay going to see Lazarus? To what extent did Martha believe that Jesus was the Resurrection and the life?

◆ Both the First and Second Readings associate new life with the indwelling of the Spirit of God. How do you experience the Spirit within you?

◆ As you pray over today's Responsorial Psalm, write an additional stanza that expresses, in your own words, your need for forgiveness and your desire to know God's kindness.

March 25, 2018

Gospel at procession with palms: Mark 11:1–10 or John 12:12–16

READING I *Isaiah 50:4–7*

The Lord GOD has given me
 a well-trained tongue,
that I might know how to speak to the weary
 a word that will rouse them.
Morning after morning
 he opens my ear that I may hear;
and I have not rebelled,
 have not turned back.
I gave my back to those who beat me,
 my cheeks to those who plucked my beard;
my face I did not shield
 from buffets and spitting.

The Lord GOD is my help,
 therefore I am not disgraced;
I have set my face like flint,
 knowing that I shall not be put to shame.

RESPONSORIAL PSALM *Psalm 22:8–9, 17–18, 19–20, 23–24 (2a)*

R. My God, my God, why have you
 abandoned me?

All who see me scoff at me;
 they mock me with parted lips,
 they wag their heads:
"He relied on the LORD; let him deliver him,
 let him rescue him, if he loves him." R.

Indeed, many dogs surround me,
 a pack of evildoers closes in upon me;
they have pierced my hands and my feet;
 I can count all my bones. R.

They divide my garments among them,
 and for my vesture they cast lots.
But you, O LORD, be not far from me;
 O my help, hasten to aid me. R.

I will proclaim your name to my brethren;
 in the midst of the assembly I will praise you:
"You who fear the LORD, praise him;
 all you descendants of Jacob,
 give glory to him;
 revere him, all you descendants of Israel!" R.

READING II *Philippians 2:6–11*

Christ Jesus, though he was in the form of God,
  did not regard equality with God
  something to be grasped.
Rather, he emptied himself,
  taking the form of a slave,
  coming in human likeness;
  and found human in appearance,
  he humbled himself,
  becoming obedient to the point of death,
  even death on a cross.
Because of this, God greatly exalted him
  and bestowed on him the name
  which is above every name,
  that at the name of Jesus
  every knee should bend,
  of those in heaven and on earth and under
      the earth,
  and every tongue confess that
  Jesus Christ is Lord,
  to the glory of God the Father.

GOSPEL *Mark 14:1 — 15:47*

Shorter: Mark 15:1–39

The Passover and the Feast of Unleavened Bread were to take place in two days' time. So the chief priests and the scribes were seeking a way to arrest him by treachery and put him to death. They said, "Not during the festival, for fear that there may be a riot among the people."

When he was in Bethany reclining at table in the house of Simon the leper, a woman came with an alabaster jar of perfumed oil, costly genuine spikenard. She broke the alabaster jar and poured it on his head. There were some who were indignant. "Why has there been this waste of perfumed oil? It could have been sold for more than three hundred days' wages and the money given to the poor." They were infuriated with her. Jesus said, "Let her alone. Why do you make trouble for her? She has done a good thing for me. The poor you will always have with you, and whenever you wish you can do good to them, but you will not always have me. She has done what she could. She has anticipated anointing my body for burial. Amen, I say to you, wherever the gospel is proclaimed to the whole world, what she has done will be told in memory of her."

Then Judas Iscariot, one of the Twelve, went off to the chief priests to hand him over to them. When they heard him they were pleased and promised to pay him money. Then he looked for an opportunity to hand him over.

On the first day of the Feast of Unleavened Bread, when they sacrificed the Passover lamb, his disciples said to him, "Where do you want us to go and prepare for you to eat the Passover?" He sent two of his disciples and said to them, "Go into the city and a man will meet you, carrying a jar of water. Follow him. Wherever he enters, say to the master of the house, 'The Teacher says, "Where is my guest room where I may eat the Passover with my disciples?"' Then he will show you a large upper room furnished and ready. Make the preparations for us there." The disciples then went off, entered the city, and found it just as he had told them; and they prepared the Passover.

When it was evening, he came with the Twelve. And as they reclined at table and were eating, Jesus said, "Amen, I say to you, one of you will betray me, one who is eating with me." They began to be distressed and to say to him, one by one, "Surely it is not I?" He said to them, "One of the Twelve, the one who dips with me into the dish. For the Son of Man indeed goes, as it is written of him, but woe to that man by whom the Son of Man is betrayed. It would be better for that man if he had never been born."

While they were eating, he took bread, said the blessing, broke it, and gave it to them, and said, "Take it; this is my body." Then he took a cup, gave thanks, and gave it to them, and they all drank from it. He said to them, "This is my blood of the covenant, which will be shed for many. Amen, I say to you, I shall not drink again the fruit of the vine until the day when I drink it new in the kingdom of God." Then, after singing a hymn, they went out to the Mount of Olives.

Then Jesus said to them, "All of you will have your faith shaken, for it is written:

I will strike the shepherd,
and the sheep will be dispersed.

But after I have been raised up, I shall go before you to Galilee." Peter said to him, "Even though all should have their faith shaken, mine will not be." Then Jesus said to him, "Amen, I say to you, this very night before the cock crows twice you will deny me three times." But he vehemently replied, "Even though I should have to die with you, I will not deny you." And they all spoke similarly.

Then they came to a place named Gethsemane, and he said to his disciples, "Sit here while I pray." He took with him Peter, James, and John, and began to be troubled and distressed. Then he said to them, "My soul is sorrowful even to death. Remain here and keep watch." He advanced a little and fell to the ground and prayed that if it were possible the hour might pass by him; he said, "Abba, Father, all things are possible to you. Take this cup away from me, but not what I will but what you will." When he returned he found them asleep. He said to Peter, "Simon, are you asleep? Could you not keep watch for one hour? Watch and pray that you may not undergo the test. The spirit is willing but the flesh is weak." Withdrawing again, he prayed, saying the same thing. Then he returned once more and found them asleep, for they could not keep their eyes open and did not know what to answer him. He returned a third time and said to them, "Are you still sleeping and taking your rest? It is enough. The hour has come. Behold, the Son of Man is to be handed over to sinners. Get up, let us go. See, my betrayer is at hand."

Then, while he was still speaking, Judas, one of the Twelve, arrived, accompanied by a crowd with swords and clubs who had come from the chief priests, the scribes, and the elders. His betrayer had arranged a signal with them, saying, "The man I shall kiss is the one; arrest him and lead him away securely." He came and immediately went over to him and said, "Rabbi." And he kissed him. At this they laid hands on him and arrested him. One of the bystanders drew his sword, struck the high priest's servant, and cut off his ear. Jesus said to them in reply, "Have you come out as against a robber, with swords and clubs, to seize me? Day after day I was with you teaching in the temple area, yet you did not arrest me; but that the Scriptures may be fulfilled." And they all left him and fled. Now a young man followed him wearing nothing but a linen cloth about his body. They seized him, but he left the cloth behind and ran off naked.

They led Jesus away to the high priest, and all the chief priests and the elders and the scribes came together. Peter followed him at a distance into the high priest's courtyard and was seated with the guards, warming himself at the fire. The chief priests and the entire Sanhedrin kept trying to obtain testimony against Jesus in order to put him to death, but they found none. Many gave false witness against him, but their testimony did not agree. Some took the stand and testified falsely against him, alleging, "We heard him say, 'I will destroy this temple made with hands and within three days I will build another not made with hands.'" Even so their testimony did not agree. The high priest rose before the assembly and questioned Jesus, saying, "Have you no answer? What are these men testifying against you?" But he was silent and answered nothing. Again the high priest asked him and said to him, "Are you the Christ, the son of the Blessed One?" Then Jesus answered, "I am;

and 'you will see the Son of Man
    seated at the right hand of the Power
    and coming with the clouds of heaven.'"

At that the high priest tore his garments and said, "What further need have we of witnesses? You have heard the blasphemy. What do you think?" They all condemned him as deserving to die. Some began to spit on him. They blindfolded him and struck him and said to him, "Prophesy!" And the guards greeted him with blows.

While Peter was below in the courtyard, one of the high priest's maids came along. Seeing Peter warming himself, she looked intently at him and said, "You too were with the Nazarene, Jesus." But he denied it saying, "I neither know nor understand what you are talking about." So he went out into the outer court. Then the cock crowed. The maid saw him and began again to say to the bystanders, "This man is one of them." Once again he denied it. A little later the bystanders said to Peter once more, "Surely you are one of them; for you too are a Galilean." He began to curse and to swear, "I do not know this man about whom you are talking." And immediately a cock crowed a second time. Then Peter remembered the word that Jesus had said to him, "Before the cock crows twice you will deny me three times." He broke down and wept.

As soon as morning came, the chief priests with the elders and the scribes, that is, the whole Sanhedrin held a council. They bound Jesus, led him away, and handed him over to Pilate. Pilate questioned him, "Are you the king of the Jews?" He said to him in reply, "You say so." The chief priests accused him of many things. Again Pilate questioned him, "Have you no answer? See how many things they accuse you of." Jesus gave him no further answer, so that Pilate was amazed.

Now on the occasion of the feast he used to release to them one prisoner whom they requested. A man called Barabbas was then in prison along with the rebels who had committed murder in a rebellion. The crowd came forward and began to ask him to do for them as he was accustomed. Pilate answered, "Do you want me to release to you the king of the Jews?" For he knew that it was out of envy that the chief priests had handed him over. But the chief priests stirred up the crowd to have him release Barabbas for them instead. Pilate again said to them in reply, "Then what do you want me to do with the man you call the king of the Jews?" They shouted again, "Crucify him." Pilate said to them, "Why? What evil has he done?" They only shouted the louder, "Crucify him." So Pilate, wishing to satisfy the crowd, released Barabbas to them and, after he had Jesus scourged, handed him over to be crucified.

The soldiers led him away inside the palace, that is, the praetorium, and assembled the whole cohort. They clothed him in purple and, weaving a crown of thorns, placed it on him. They began to salute him with, "Hail, King of the Jews!" and kept striking his head with a reed and spitting upon him. They knelt before him in homage. And when they had mocked him, they stripped him of the purple cloak, dressed him in his own clothes, and led him out to crucify him.

They pressed into service a passer-by, Simon, a Cyrenian, who was coming in from the country, the father of Alexander and Rufus, to carry his cross.

They brought him to the place of Golgotha—which is translated Place of the Skull—. They gave him wine drugged with myrrh, but he did not take it. Then they crucified him and divided his garments by casting lots for them to see what each should take. It was nine o'clock in the morning when they crucified him. The inscription of the charge against him read, "The King of the Jews." With him they crucified two revolutionaries, one on his right and one on his left. Those passing by reviled him, shaking their heads and saying, "Aha! You who would destroy the temple and rebuild it in three days, save yourself by coming down from the cross." Likewise the chief priests, with the scribes, mocked him among themselves and said, "He saved others; he cannot save himself. Let the

Christ, the King of Israel, come down now from the cross that we may see and believe." Those who were crucified with him also kept abusing him.

At noon darkness came over the whole land until three in the afternoon. And at three o'clock Jesus cried out in a loud voice, "*Eloi, Eloi, lema sabachthani?*" which is translated, "My God, my God, why have you forsaken me?" Some of the bystanders who heard it said, "Look, he is calling Elijah." One of them ran, soaked a sponge with wine, put it on a reed and gave it to him to drink saying, "Wait, let us see if Elijah comes to take him down." Jesus gave a loud cry and breathed his last.

[Here all kneel and pray for a short time.]

The veil of the sanctuary was torn in two from top to bottom. When the centurion who stood facing him saw how he breathed his last he said, "Truly this man was the Son of God!" There were also women looking on from a distance. Among them were Mary Magdalene, Mary the mother of the younger James and of Joses, and Salome. These women had followed him when he was in Galilee and ministered to him. There were also many other women who had come up with him to Jerusalem.

When it was already evening, since it was the day of preparation, the day before the sabbath, Joseph of Arimathea, a distinguished member of the council, who was himself awaiting the king-dom of God, came and courageously went to Pilate and asked for the body of Jesus. Pilate was amazed that he was already dead. He summoned the centurion and asked him if Jesus had already died. And when he learned of it from the centurion, he gave the body to Joseph. Having bought a linen cloth, he took him down, wrapped him in the linen cloth, and laid him in a tomb that had been hewn out of the rock. Then he rolled a stone against the entrance to the tomb. Mary Magdalene and Mary the mother of Joses watched where he was laid.

Practice of Hope

It is hard to stay awake to the sin and suffering in this world. Even Jesus' disciples failed to keep watch with him in his deep sorrow. But the Gospel urges us to keep trying. It asks us to go with Christ to the heart of sorrow and to stand awake and in solidarity with the poor and suffering, who are Jesus in disguise. Our culture offers us many escapes, many ways to "sleep," but it is by encountering those who suffer, and by bringing God's love to them, that we come to know Christ and his Cross and can look with hope to Resurrection. ◆ Pray the Rosary this week, and with each recitation of the Hail Mary reflect deeply and specifically on the suffering in our world; offer your prayers for the suffering adults and children around the globe. ◆ Do you hold a specific sorrow or suffering in your heart? As you pray this week, imagine being with Christ in the Garden. See that he knows your sorrow. See his willingness to shoulder your burden. Can you offer him your pain? Can you experience God's comfort and presence in this place? ◆ At the Easter Vigil, we will collectively ask all the saints in heaven to pray for us. As you move through Holy Week, pray with the words and images of this Litany of the Saints: https://www.youtube.com/watch?v=kId0NBvNiCk.

Download more questions and activities for families, Christian initiation groups, and other adult groups at http://www.ltp.org/t-productsupplements.aspx.

Scripture Insights

Palm Sunday's opening procession with palms is a commemoration of Jesus' entrance into Jerusalem before his Passion. Palms are a traditional symbol of victory, royalty, and rejoicing. But today's readings are significant for the way they present God's chosen as a servant-king.

The First Reading is one of four poignant passages called "servant songs" in the Book of Isaiah. The servant is unnamed, and some scholars suggest he might have been a disciple of the prophet Isaiah. In the reading the servant credits God with giving him the prophetic words to speak, and he acknowledges the suffering and abuse he has endured. Remarkably, he is not ashamed; he is secure in his role. Later Christians saw the servant songs as fulfilled in Jesus Christ.

The Second Reading is known as the "Christ hymn." Although biblical scholars disagree on how to interpret aspects of the hymn, it clearly follows the pattern of humiliation leading to exaltation. Because Jesus was willing to become like a servant and even give himself over to death, God exalted him and made him Lord over all creation.

Today's Gospel tells the story of Jesus' suffering, Death, and burial—a long narrative with many sub-stories—one of which is particularly meaningful on this Palm Sunday. When the unnamed woman anoints Jesus with a superabundance of perfume, Jesus says that she is doing it for his burial, but anointing of the head would have made most people of his day think of the anointing of a messiah king. *Messiah* means "anointed." Paradoxically, Jesus' messiahship is fully known in his suffering and Death.

◆ Carefully read the Gospel and look for references to Jesus as king. What do they tell us about Mark's understanding of the person and mission of Jesus?

◆ Regarding the Second Reading, Paul tells his readers that that they should have the "same attitude that is also yours in Christ Jesus" (Philippians 2:5). What does this mean for you?

◆ Prayerfully reflect on the Responsorial Psalm. Why is this psalm appropriate for Palm Sunday? Note that Psalm 22 begins, "My God, my God, why have you abandoned me."

Holy Thursday brings to an end the forty days of Lent, which make up the season of anticipation of the great Three Days. Composed of prayer, almsgiving, fasting, and the preparation of the catechumens for Baptism, the season of Lent is now brought to a close, and the Three Days begin as we approach the liturgy of Holy Thursday evening. As those to be initiated into the Church have prepared themselves for their entrance into the fullness of life, so have we been awakening in our hearts, minds, and bodies our own entrances into the life of Christ, experienced in the life of the Church.

Easter Triduum (Latin for "three days") is the center, the core, of the entire year for Christians. These Three Days mark the mystery around which our entire lives are played out. Adults in the community are invited to plan ahead so that the whole time from Thursday night until Easter Sunday is free of social engagements, free of entertainment, and free of meals except for the most basic nourishment. We measure these days—indeed, our very salvation in the life of God—in step with the catechumens themselves; we are revitalized as we support them along the way and participate in their initiation rites.

We are asked to fast on Good Friday and to continue fasting, if possible, all through Holy Saturday as strictly as we can so that we come to the Easter Vigil hungry and full of excitement, parched and longing to feel the sacred water of the font on our skin. We pare down distractions on Good Friday and Holy Saturday so that we may be free for prayer and anticipation, for reflection, preparation, and silence. The Church is getting ready for the great night of the Easter Vigil.

As one who has been initiated into the Church, as one whose life has been wedded to this community gathered at the table, you should anticipate the Triduum with concentration and vigor. With you, the whole Church knows that our presence for the liturgies of the Triduum is not just an invitation. Everyone is needed. We pull out all the stops for these days. As humans, wedded to humanity by the joys and travails of life and grafted onto the body of the Church by the sanctifying waters of Baptism, we lead the new members into new life in this community of faith.

To this end, the Three Days are seen not as three distinct liturgies, but as one movement. These days have been connected liturgically from the early days of the Christian Church. As members of this community, we should be personally committed to preparing for and attending the Triduum and its culmination in the Easter Vigil of Holy Saturday.

The Church proclaims the direction of the Triduum with the opening antiphon of Holy Thursday, which comes from Paul's Letter to the Galatians (6:14). With this verse the Church sets a spiritual environment into which we as committed Christians enter the Triduum:

> *We should glory in the cross of our Lord Jesus Christ, for he is our salvation, our life and resurrection; through him we are saved and made free.*

HOLY THURSDAY

On Thursday evening we enter into this Triduum together. Whether presider, lector, preacher, greeter, altar server, minister of the Eucharist, decorator, or person in the remote corner in the last pew of the church, we begin, as always, by hearkening to the Word of God. These are the Scriptures for the liturgy of Holy Thursday:

Exodus 12:1–8, 11–14
Ancient instructions for the meal of the Passover.

1 Corinthians 11:23–26
Eat the bread and drink the cup until the return of the Lord.

John 13:1–15
Jesus washes the feet of the disciples.

Then the priest, like Jesus, does something strange: he washes feet. Jesus gave us this image of what the Church is supposed to look like, feel like, act like. Our position—whether as observer, washer or washed, servant or served—may be difficult. Yet we learn from the discomfort, from the awkwardness.

Then we celebrate the Eucharist. Because it is connected to the other liturgies of the Triduum on Good Friday and Holy Saturday night, the evening liturgy of Holy Thursday has no ending. Whether we stay to pray awhile or leave, we are now in the quiet, peace, and glory of the Triduum.

GOOD FRIDAY

We gather quietly in community on Friday and again listen to the Word of God:

Isaiah 52:13—53:12
The servant of the Lord was crushed for our sins.

Hebrews 4:14–16; 5:7–9
The Son of God learned obedience through his suffering.

John 18:1—19:42
The Passion of Jesus Christ.

After the sermon, we pray at length for all the world's needs: for the Church; for the pope, the clergy and all the baptized; for those preparing for initiation; for the unity of Christians; for Jews; for non-Christians; for atheists; for all in public office; and for those in special need.

Then there is another once-a-year event: the holy cross is held up in our midst, and we come forward one by one to do reverence with a kiss, bow, or genuflection. This communal reverence of an instrument of torture recalls the painful price, in the past and today, of salvation, the way in which our redemption is wrought, the scourging and humiliation of Jesus Christ that bring direction and life back to a humanity that is lost and dead. During the adoration of the cross, we sing not only of the sorrow, but of the glory of the Cross by which we have been saved.

Again, we bring to mind the words of Paul (Galatians 6:14), on which last night's entrance antiphon is loosely based: "May I never boast except in the cross of our Lord Jesus Christ, through which the world has been crucified to me, and I to the world."

We continue in fasting and prayer and vigil, in rest and quiet, through Saturday. This Saturday for us is God's rest at the end of creation. It is Christ's repose in the tomb. It is Christ's visit with the dead.

EASTER VIGIL

Hungry now, pared down to basics, lightheaded from vigilance and full of excitement, we, the already baptized, gather in darkness and light a new fire. From this blaze we light a great candle that will make this night bright for us and will burn throughout Easter Time.

We hearken again to the Word of God with some of the most powerful narratives and proclamations of our tradition:

Genesis 1:1—2:2
The creation of the world.

Genesis 22:1–18
The sacrifice of Isaac.

Exodus 14:15—15:1
The crossing of the Red Sea.

Isaiah 54:5–14
You will not be afraid.

Isaiah 55:1–11
Come, come to the water.

Baruch 3:9–15, 32—4:4
Walk by the light of wisdom.

Ezekiel 36:16–17a, 18–28
The Lord says: I will sprinkle water.

Romans 6:3–11
United with him in death.

Year A: Matthew 28:1–10, Year B: Mark 16:1–7, Year C: Luke 24:1–12
Jesus has been raised.

After the readings, we call on our saints to stand with us as we go to the font and the priest celebrant blesses the waters. The chosen of all times and all places attend to what is about to take place. The elect renounce evil, profess the faith of the Church, and are baptized and anointed.

All of us renew our Baptism. These are the moments when death and life meet, when we reject evil and make our promises to God. All of this is in the communion of the Church. So together we go to the table and celebrate the Easter Eucharist.

Prayer before Reading the Word

God of Jesus Christ, the holy and righteous one,
by that suffering graciously borne
and that victory gloriously bestowed,
you extend to us all
what you promised through the prophets.

Renew in us the wonders of your power;
open our minds to understand the Scriptures;
open our hearts to true conversion;
make Jesus known to us in the breaking of
        the bread.

We ask this through the Lord Jesus,
our Passover and our Peace,
who lives and reigns with you
in the unity of the Holy Spirit,
one God, for ever and ever. Amen.

Prayer after Reading the Word

What love you have bestowed on us, O God,
that we should be called your children,
born again in Christ by water and the Spirit.

Pour out your Spirit every day,
that, remaining in this world but not
        belonging to it,
we may bear witness to your own abiding love,
made known to us in our Savior, Jesus Christ,
who lives and reigns with you
in the unity of the Holy Spirit,
one God, for ever and ever. Amen.

Weekday Readings

April 2: Solemnity of Monday in the Octave of Easter
Acts 2:14, 22–23; Matthew 28:8–15
April 3: Solemnity of Tuesday in the Octave of Easter
Acts 2:36–41; John 20:11–18
April 4: Solemnity of Wednesday in the Octave of Easter
Acts 3:1–10; Luke 24:13–35
April 5: Solemnity of Thursday in the Octave of Easter
Acts 3:11–26; Luke 24:35–48
April 6: Solemnity of Friday in the Octave of Easter
Acts 4:1–12; John 21:1–14
April 7: Solemnity of Saturday in the Octave of Easter
Acts 4:13–21; Mark 16:9–15

April 9: Solemnity of the Annunciation of the Lord
Isaiah 7:10–14; 8:10; Hebrews 10:4–10; Luke 1:26–38
April 10: *Acts 4:32–37; John 3:7b–15*
April 11: *Acts 5:17–26; John 3:16–21*
April 12: *Acts 5:27–33; John 3:31–36*
April 13: *Acts 5:34–42; John 6:1–15*
April 14: *Acts 6:1–7; John 6:16–21*

April 16: *Acts 6:8–15; John 6:22–29*
April 17: *Acts 7:51—8:1a; John 6:30–35*
April 18: *Acts 8:1b–8; John 6:35–40*
April 19: *Acts 8:26–40; John 6:44–51*
April 20: *Acts 9:1–20; John 6:52–59*
April 21: *Acts 9:31–42; John 6:60–69*

April 23: *Acts 11:1–18; John 10:1–10*
April 24: *Acts 11:19–26; John 10:22–30*
April 25: Feast of Saint Mark
1 Peter 5:5b–14; Mark 16:15–20
April 26: *Acts 13:13–25; John 13:16–20*
April 27: *Acts 13:26–33; John 14:1–6*
April 28: *Acts 13:44–52; John 14:7–14*

April 30: *Acts 14:5–18; John 14:21–26*
May 1: *Acts 14:19–28; John 14:27–31a*
May 2: *Acts 15:1–6; John 15:1–8*
May 3: Feast of Sts. Philip and James
1 Corinthians 15:1–8; John 14:6–14
May 4: *Acts 15:22–31; John 15:12–17*
May 5: *Acts 16:1–10; John 15:18–21*

May 7: *Acts 16:11–15; John 15:26—16:4a*
May 8: *Acts 16:22–34; John 16:5–11*
May 9: *Acts 17:15, 22—18:1; John 16:12–15*
May 10: Solemnity of the Ascension of the Lord
Acts 1:1–11; Ephesians 1:17–23; Mark 16:15–20
(If the Ascension of the Lord is celebrated on the
following Sunday):
May 10: *Acts 18:1–8; John 16:16–20*
May 11: *Acts 18:9–18; John 16:20–23*
May 12: *Acts 18:23–28; John 16:23b–28*

May 14: Feast of St. Matthias
Acts 1:15–17, 20–26; John 15:9–17
May 15: *Acts 20:17–27; John 17:1–11a*
May 16: *Acts 20:28–38 John 17:11b–19*
May 17: *Acts 22:30; 23:6–11; John 17:20–26*
May 18: *Acts 25:13b–21; John 21:15–19*
May 19: *Morning: Acts 28:16–20, 30–31; John 21:20–25*

READING I *Acts 10:34a, 37–43*

Peter proceeded to speak and said: "You know what has happened all over Judea, beginning in Galilee after the baptism that John preached, how God anointed Jesus of Nazareth with the Holy Spirit and power. He went about doing good and healing all those oppressed by the devil, for God was with him. We are witnesses of all that he did both in the country of the Jews and in Jerusalem. They put him to death by hanging him on a tree. This man God raised on the third day and granted that he be visible, not to all the people, but to us, the witnesses chosen by God in advance, who ate and drank with him after he rose from the dead. He commissioned us to preach to the people and testify that he is the one appointed by God as judge of the living and the dead. To him all the prophets bear witness, that everyone who believes in him will receive forgiveness of sins through his name."

RESPONSORIAL PSALM
Psalm 118:1–2, 16–17, 22–23 (24)

R. This is the day the Lord has made;
       let us rejoice and be glad.

or: Alleluia.

Give thanks to the LORD, for he is good,
   for his mercy endures forever.
Let the house of Israel say,
   "His mercy endures forever." R.

"The right hand of the LORD
       has struck with power;
   the right hand of the LORD is exalted.
I shall not die, but live,
   and declare the works of the LORD." R.

The stone which the builders rejected
   has become the cornerstone.
By the LORD has this been done;
   it is wonderful in our eyes. R.

READING II *Colossians 3:1–4*

Alternate: 1 Corinthians 5:6b–8

Brothers and sisters: If then you were raised with Christ, seek what is above, where Christ is seated at the right hand of God. Think of what is above, not of what is on earth. For you have died, and your life is hidden with Christ in God. When Christ your life appears, then you too will appear with him in glory.

GOSPEL *John 20:1–9*

Alternates: Mark 16:1–7; or at an afternoon or evening Mass: Luke 24:13–35

On the first day of the week, Mary of Magdala came to the tomb early in the morning, while it was still dark, and saw the stone removed from the tomb. So she ran and went to Simon Peter and to the other disciple whom Jesus loved, and told them, "They have taken the Lord from the tomb, and we don't know where they put him." So Peter and the other disciple went out and came to the tomb. They both ran, but the other disciple ran faster than Peter and arrived at the tomb first; he bent down and saw the burial cloths there, but did not go in. When Simon Peter arrived after him, he went into the tomb and saw the burial cloths there, and the cloth that had covered his head, not with the burial cloths but rolled up in a separate place. Then the other disciple also went in, the one who had arrived at the tomb first, and he saw and believed. For they did not yet understand the Scripture that he had to rise from the dead.

Practice of Hope

Allelluia! The tomb is empty! After weeks of drawing near to Christ's suffering and Death, we joyously celebrate his Resurrection! How blessed we are to belong to Jesus, who knows our pain, suffering, and sin yet offers us hope through his mercy, forgiveness, and love. ◆ At the Easter Vigil, we proclaim the centuries-old Exsultet. Find the English translation and links to commentary and chant at http://www.usccb.org/prayer-and-worship /liturgical-year/easter/easter-proclamation -exsultet.cfm. ◆ Celebrate the abundance of Easter by having the children of your parish decorate food donation bags for parishioners to fill. Ask your pastor to have returned bags placed near the altar during the Easter season prior to donation. ◆ Sometimes our lives don't align with the liturgy. Are you experiencing pain that separates you from the joy of this holy day? You are not alone. Spend time in prayer, sharing your pain with God. Ask God for what you need. Know that Christ's heart joins with yours and all who are suffering.

Download more questions and activities for families, Christian initiation groups, and other adult groups at http://www.ltp.org/t-productsupplements.aspx.

Scripture Insights

Alleluia! We are witnesses to the power of God who raised Jesus from the dead. This is the theme of the readings on this holy Solemnity of Easter. The First Reading, from Acts of the Apostles, presents the Apostle Peter as proclaiming to the Roman centurion Cornelius and his household the Good News about Jesus Christ. Peter has witnessed those words and deeds and now realizes he is called to preach not only to fellow Jews but to all peoples for the forgiveness of sins. This Good News is a gift for all.

Paul's Letter to the Colossians urgently reinforces primary Gospel teachings about Christ as the source of all salvation. Paul is counteracting false teachings about the powers of angels and the necessity of ascetic practices. In this Second Reading we hear him reassuring the Colossians that they are bonded with Christ in a mystical death and resurrection.

Today's Gospel is part of a longer post-Resurrection narrative, which ends with Mary Magdalene being commissioned to preach to Jesus' disciples saying, "I have seen the Lord!" As the scene opens, we learn that Mary Magdalene came to the garden tomb before dawn. In the first-century Greco-Roman world, a night venture would have been considered strange and dangerous for anyone, but especially for a woman, but it makes her the first witness of the empty tomb. When Peter and the Beloved Disciple respond to her summons, both witness the signs of Jesus' Death—the burial wrappings—but at this moment only one "saw and believed."

◆ Carefully read the First Reading and notice how often the author refers to the act of witness. Why do you think this concept is so important to the author of Acts of the Apostles?

◆ Paul's message is for us as well as the Colossians. Have you ever thought of your life as being "hidden with Christ in God"? What could that mean?

◆ As you pray over the Gospel, enter into dialog with the Beloved Disciple. Ask him what he saw in the empty tomb that caused him to believe and how you might deepen your own faith.

READING I   *Acts 4:32–35*

The community of believers was of one heart and mind, and no one claimed that any of his possessions was his own, but they had everything in common. With great power the apostles bore witness to the resurrection of the Lord Jesus, and great favor was accorded them all. There was no needy person among them, for those who owned property or houses would sell them, bring the proceeds of the sale, and put them at the feet of the apostles, and they were distributed to each according to need.

RESPONSORIAL PSALM
Psalm 118:2–4, 13–15, 22–24 (1)

R. Give thanks to the Lord, for he is good; his
      love is everlasting.
  or: Alleluia.

Let the house of Israel say,
   "His mercy endures forever."
Let the house of Aaron say,
   "His mercy endures forever."
Let those who fear the LORD say,
   "His mercy endures forever." R.

I was hard pressed and was falling,
   but the LORD helped me.
My strength and my courage is the LORD,
   and he has been my savior.
The joyful shout of victory
   in the tents of the just. R.

The stone which the builders rejected
   has become the cornerstone.
By the LORD has this been done;
   it is wonderful in our eyes.
This is the day the LORD has made;
   let us be glad and rejoice in it. R.

READING II   *1 John 5:1–6*

Beloved: Everyone who believes that Jesus is the Christ is begotten by God, and everyone who loves the Father loves also the one begotten by him. In this way we know that we love the children of God when we love God and obey his commandments. For the love of God is this, that we keep his commandments. And his commandments are not burdensome, for whoever is begotten by God conquers the world. And the victory that conquers the world is our faith. Who indeed is the victor over the world but the one who believes that Jesus is the Son of God?

This is the one who came through water and blood, Jesus Christ, not by water alone, but by water and blood. The Spirit is the one that testifies, and the Spirit is truth.

GOSPEL   *John 20:19–31*

On the evening of that first day of the week, when the doors were locked, where the disciples were, for fear of the Jews, Jesus came and stood in their midst and said to them, "Peace be with you." When he had said this, he showed them his hands and his side. The disciples rejoiced when they saw the Lord. Jesus said to them again, "Peace be with you. As the Father has sent me, so I send you." And when he had said this, he breathed on them and said to them, "Receive the Holy Spirit. Whose sins you forgive are forgiven them, and whose sins you retain are retained."

Thomas, called Didymus, one of the Twelve, was not with them when Jesus came. So the other disciples said to him, "We have seen the Lord." But he said to them, "Unless I see the mark of the nails in his hands and put my finger into the nailmarks and put my hand into his side, I will not believe."

Now a week later his disciples were again inside and Thomas was with them. Jesus came, although the doors were locked, and stood in their midst and said, "Peace be with you." Then he said to Thomas, "Put your finger here and see my hands, and bring your hand and put it into my side, and do not be unbelieving, but believe." Thomas answered and said to him, "My Lord and my God!" Jesus said to him, "Have you come to believe because you have seen me? Blessed are those who have not seen and have believed."

Now Jesus did many other signs in the presence of his disciples that are not written in this book. But these are written that you may come to believe that Jesus is the Christ, the Son of God, and that through this belief you may have life in his name.

Practice of Faith

After his Resurrection, Jesus breathes the Holy Spirit upon his disciples. Through the sacraments of the Easter Vigil, newborn Christians receive the Holy Spirit and begin the last stage of their initiation. Mystagogy, the "revelation of the mysteries," is the final period of the initiation process and lasts until Pentecost. ◆ Actually, Easter Time is a time of mystagogy for the entire assembly because the mysteries keep unfolding to us all during our lives. You can do a version of what the newly initiated are doing during the fifty days of Easter: reflect on the rituals of initiation you witnessed, on the symbols and Scriptures of the liturgy. They will offer you insights about the Paschal Mystery (the Passion, Death, and Resurrection of Jesus Christ). ◆ What thoughts arise from your reflections about how to lead your life in the world as Christ's disciple? What is your sense of your mission at this moment? ◆ Offer to befriend some of the new initiates in your parish. Invite them to attend a parish or diocesan activity with you, or share your own faith journey.

Download more questions and activities for families, Christian initiation groups, and other adult groups at http://www.ltp.org/t-productsupplements.aspx.

Scripture Insights

If we choose to live as Easter people, our lives will be radically transformed. This is what happened to Jesus' disciples. They went from being cowards, afraid for their lives, to bold messengers of the Gospel. The earliest Christian communities were also transformed, aspiring to live a way of life radically different from their previous one. The question for us today is whether we will allow ourselves to be profoundly transformed by the Easter message and so become revealers of God.

Today's First Reading describes the radical ideals of the first Christian community living in Jerusalem. They joined as one family, we are told, sharing all things in common so that no one was in need of anything. This sharing was no small thing, as we see, since some people sold houses and donated the proceeds. Further, we learn that the Apostles enjoyed God's favor in their powerful acts of witness.

In the Second Reading, we learn that love of God is intimately connected to the commandment to love our brothers and sisters. For those who believe that Jesus is the Son of God, one cannot stand without the other.

At the beginning of today's Gospel, we see the disciples hiding in the upper room of a house in Jerusalem. Suddenly Jesus appears before them, showing himself alive, offering peace (the Greek word, *eirene*), breathing the Holy Spirit on them, and sending them to do what the Father sent Jesus to do—to be revealers of God in the world.

◆ If you could create a modern Christian community following the same principles that we read about in the First Reading, what might it look like?

◆ Considering the Second Reading, how have you experienced the link between love of God, love of others, and keeping the commandments? When have the commandments felt burdensome? Not burdensome? What makes the difference for you?

◆ In the story of Thomas' encounter with the risen Jesus, imagine that you are Thomas. What would you say to Jesus? What does he say to you?

READING I *Acts 3:13–15, 17–19*

Peter said to the people: "The God of Abraham, the God of Isaac, and the God of Jacob, the God of our fathers, has glorified his servant Jesus, whom you handed over and denied in Pilate's presence when he had decided to release him. You denied the Holy and Righteous One and asked that a murderer be released to you. The author of life you put to death, but God raised him from the dead; of this we are witnesses. Now I know, brothers, that you acted out of ignorance, just as your leaders did; but God has thus brought to fulfillment what he had announced beforehand through the mouth of all the prophets, that his Christ would suffer. Repent, therefore, and be converted, that your sins may be wiped away."

RESPONSORIAL PSALM
Psalm 4:2, 4, 7–8, 9 (7a)

R. Lord, let your face shine on us.
 or: Alleluia.

When I call, answer me, O my just God,
 you who relieve me when I am in distress;
 have pity on me, and hear my prayer! R.

Know that the LORD does wonders for his
   faithful one;
 the LORD will hear me when I call
   upon him. R.

O LORD, let the light of your countenance shine
   upon us!
 You put gladness into my heart. R.

As soon as I lie down, I fall peacefully asleep,
 for you alone, O LORD,
 bring security to my dwelling. R.

READING II *1 John 2:1–5a*

My children, I am writing this to you so that you may not commit sin. But if anyone does sin, we have an Advocate with the Father, Jesus Christ the righteous one. He is expiation for our sins, and not for our sins only but for those of the whole world. The way we may be sure that we know him is to keep his commandments. Those who say, "I know him," but do not keep his commandments are liars, and the truth is not in them. But whoever keeps his word, the love of God is truly perfected in him.

GOSPEL *Luke 24:35–48*

The two disciples recounted what had taken place on the way, and how Jesus was made known to them in the breaking of bread.

While they were still speaking about this, he stood in their midst and said to them, "Peace be with you." But they were startled and terrified and thought that they were seeing a ghost. Then he said to them, "Why are you troubled? And why do questions arise in your hearts? Look at my hands and my feet, that it is I myself. Touch me and see, because a ghost does not have flesh and bones as you can see I have." And as he said this, he showed them his hands and his feet. While they were still incredulous for joy and were amazed, he asked them, "Have you anything here to eat?" They gave him a piece of baked fish; he took it and ate it in front of them.

He said to them, "These are my words that I spoke to you while I was still with you, that everything written about me in the law of Moses and in the prophets and psalms must be fulfilled." Then he opened their minds to understand the Scriptures. And he said to them, "Thus it is written that the Christ would suffer and rise from the dead on the third day and that repentance, for the forgiveness of sins, would be preached in his name to all the nations, beginning from Jerusalem. You are witnesses of these things."

Practice of Hope

As followers of Christ, we are called to constant conversion. The ecumenical Taizé community in Taizé, France, is a pilgrimage site for people throughout the world to come listen for Christ's voice. It especially attracts young people, and thousands arrive each year to experience the community and its daily common prayer. "God is love alone," writes Brother Roger, founder of the community. Taizé brothers live to be signs of Christ to others, bearers of hope and joy! ♦ Learn more about the Taizé community through their website: http://www.taize.fr/en. ♦ For images and music from a Taizé prayer service, visit https://www.youtube.com/watch?v=go1-BoDD7CI. ♦ This week, pray each day with the Taizé's chant, "Lord Hear my Prayer," found at https://www.youtube.com/watch?v=f51n-yb11dY.

Download more questions and activities for families, Christian initiation groups, and other adult groups at http://www.ltp.org/t-productsupplements.aspx

Scripture Insights

In today's readings we hear that Christ is expiation for the sins of all the world and wants all the world to hear that message from his followers. In the Gospel, two disciples have returned from Emmaus to tell their colleagues about meeting the risen Jesus on the road and recognizing him finally in the "breaking of the bread." Suddenly Jesus appears before the whole group, giving them proof that he is alive and not a ghost. He reminds them that the Scriptures about a suffering messiah had to be fulfilled and that they could trust his words because he had told them these things before they happened. Now that they are witnesses of all that has been said about Jesus, they must go out to preach repentance for the forgiveness of sin.

We can see an example of this preaching in the First Reading: Peter's speech to the Jews who had witnessed the healing of a crippled man at the Temple's beautiful gate. When the people come rushing toward them to see what is happening, Peter tells the story of the Jewish people's rejection of Jesus and the prophets and calls for their repentance. A word of caution: this text can sound painfully hostile toward Jews. It's important to remember that the Gospel writer recognized that they were the first and rightful heirs of the covenant and that God would never abandon them. The only way for the Good News to extend to the Gentile (non-Jewish) world was if Israel rejected God's covenant. Hence Peter's message of repentance indicates that the writer believes God will continue to be faithful to the Chosen People.

♦ Examine the context for Jesus' commissioning of the disciples in today's Gospel—their fear and their difficulty believing in him. Why do you think repentance and forgiveness are so important in Luke's story?

♦ As you reflect on the Second Reading, what clues can you find about the type of sin that the author is concerned about? Have you ever found yourself committing this sin?

♦ Slowly pray today's Responsorial Psalm. How might it bring consolation to one of a repentant heart.

READING I *Acts 4:8–12*

Peter, filled with the Holy Spirit, said: "Leaders of the people and elders: If we are being examined today about a good deed done to a cripple, namely, by what means he was saved, then all of you and all the people of Israel should know that it was in the name of Jesus Christ the Nazorean whom you crucified, whom God raised from the dead; in his name this man stands before you healed. He is *the stone rejected by you, the builders, which has become the cornerstone.* There is no salvation through anyone else, nor is there any other name under heaven given to the human race by which we are to be saved."

RESPONSORIAL PSALM *Psalm 118:1, 8–9, 21–23, 26, 28, 29 (22)*

R. The stone rejected by the builders has become
        the cornerstone.
    or: Alleluia.

Give thanks to the LORD, for he is good,
    for his mercy endures forever.
It is better to take refuge in the LORD
    than to trust in man.
It is better to take refuge in the LORD
    than to trust in princes. R.

I will give thanks to you, for you have
        answered me
    and have been my savior.
The stone which the builders rejected
    has become the cornerstone.
By the LORD has this been done;
    it is wonderful in our eyes. R.

Blessed is he who comes in the name of the LORD;
    we bless you from the house of the LORD.
I will give thanks to you,
        for you have answered me
    and have been my savior.
Give thanks to the LORD, for he is good;
    for his kindness endures forever. R.

READING II *1 John 3:1–2*

Beloved: See what love the Father has bestowed on us that we may be called the children of God. Yet so we are. The reason the world does not know us is that it did not know him. Beloved, we are God's children now; what we shall be has not yet been revealed. We do know that when it is revealed we shall be like him, for we shall see him as he is.

GOSPEL *John 10:11–18*

Jesus said: "I am the good shepherd. A good shepherd lays down his life for the sheep. A hired man, who is not a shepherd and whose sheep are not his own, sees a wolf coming and leaves the sheep and runs away, and the wolf catches and scatters them. This is because he works for pay and has no concern for the sheep. I am the good shepherd, and I know mine and mine know me, just as the Father knows me and I know the Father; and I will lay down my life for the sheep. I have other sheep that do not belong to this fold. These also I must lead, and they will hear my voice, and there will be one flock, one shepherd. This is why the Father loves me, because I lay down my life in order to take it up again. No one takes it from me, but I lay it down on my own. I have power to lay it down, and power to take it up again. This command I have received from my Father."

Practice of Charity

The powerful image of Jesus as the Good Shepherd expresses Christ's love and care for us, especially in his act of laying down his life for ours. Yet his sacrifice is part of a relationship in which we too have a role to play. In today's Gospel Jesus emphasizes the importance of a mutual, charitable relationship with him. ◆ What does it mean to have Jesus "know" you? How have you felt his knowing you in the past? Read Psalm 139. How does Christ speak to you in this passage? How does Jesus' knowing you affect your life today? ◆ Pope Francis spoke of the relationship between Jesus, the Shepherd, and his sheep during his April 17, 2016, Regina Coeli address. Read it here: http://en.radio vaticana.va/news/2016/04/17/full_text_of _pope_francis_regina_coeli_address/1223525. ◆ One of the best ways to get to know Jesus is to read the Gospels. Choose your favorite Gospel and reread it, or engage in a parish Bible Study. Notice where and how you come to know Jesus in a new way.

Download more questions and activities for families, Christian initiation groups, and other adult groups at http://www.ltp.org/t-productsupplements.aspx.

Scripture Insights

Today's readings crackle with the Apostles' excitement over the new understandings they were experiencing after the Resurrection and with their work of creating a new way of life, a community of the resurrected Christ—living and life-giving. In the light of Resurrection, Jesus' words in the Gospel, spoken before the Passion, take on new meaning.

The First Reading is part of a lengthy story that began with Peter healing a crippled man near the Jerusalem Temple and then addressing the people who stood around him, amazed at what he had done. As the crowds continued to grow, Peter and John were arrested, and his accusers demanded to know by whose authority they did such a thing. Peter is answering that question in today's First Reading. His sense of urgency and conviction ring out as he testifies that "there is no salvation through anyone else." He is, after all, "filled with the Holy Spirit."

Likewise, in the Second Reading we can hear a deep sense of community identity. Thanks to the loving gift of the Father, which is his Son, we have become "children of God" both now and in the future, when God (or Christ) is fully revealed and we become like him.

In today's Gospel, John uses the image of the Good Shepherd to explain what it means to be a faith community. It is about our shared trust in Christ who put his life on the line to take care of his flock and keep them secure. It is about a flock that can be open and welcoming to others without fear for its safety, because the one who laid down his life for them has taken it up again as the Father commanded.

◆ What does the author of the First Reading mean by "the stone rejected by the builders, which has become the cornerstone?"

◆ How does the Responsorial Psalm help your understanding of the rejected stone becoming the cornerstone?

◆ Take some time to pray over the Second Reading. How does it speak to you about what it means to be God's children and, in the end of time, to become like him?

READING I *Acts 9:26–31*

When Saul arrived in Jerusalem he tried to join the disciples, but they were all afraid of him, not believing that he was a disciple. Then Barnabas took charge of him and brought him to the apostles, and he reported to them how he had seen the Lord, and that he had spoken to him, and how in Damascus he had spoken out boldly in the name of Jesus. He moved about freely with them in Jerusalem, and spoke out boldly in the name of the Lord. He also spoke and debated with the Hellenists, but they tried to kill him. And when the brothers learned of this, they took him down to Caesarea and sent him on his way to Tarsus.

The church throughout all Judea, Galilee, and Samaria was at peace. It was being built up and walked in the fear of the Lord, and with the consolation of the Holy Spirit it grew in numbers.

RESPONSORIAL PSALM
Psalm 22:26–27, 28, 30, 31–32 (26a)

R. I will praise you, Lord, in the assembly of
     your people.
  or: Alleluia.

I will fulfill my vows before those who fear
    the LORD.
  The lowly shall eat their fill;
they who seek the LORD shall praise him:
  "May your hearts live forever!" R.

All the ends of the earth
  shall remember and turn to the LORD;
all the families of the nations
  shall bow down before him. R.

To him alone shall bow down
  all who sleep in the earth;
before him shall bend
  all who go down into the dust. R.

And to him my soul shall live;
  my descendants shall serve him.
Let the coming generation be told of the LORD
  that they may proclaim to a people yet
    to be born
  the justice he has shown. R.

READING II *1 John 3:18–24*

Children, let us love not in word or speech but in deed and truth.

Now this is how we shall know that we belong to the truth and reassure our hearts before him in whatever our hearts condemn, for God is greater than our hearts and knows everything. Beloved, if our hearts do not condemn us, we have confidence in God and receive from him whatever we ask, because we keep his commandments and do what pleases him. And his commandment is this: we should believe in the name of his Son, Jesus Christ, and love one another just as he commanded us. Those who keep his commandments remain in him, and he in them, and the way we know that he remains in us is from the Spirit he gave us.

GOSPEL *John 15:1–8*

Jesus said to his disciples: "I am the true vine, and my Father is the vine grower. He takes away every branch in me that does not bear fruit, and every one that does he prunes so that it bears more fruit. You are already pruned because of the word that I spoke to you. Remain in me, as I remain in you. Just as a branch cannot bear fruit on its own unless it remains on the vine, so neither can you unless you remain in me. I am the vine, you are the branches. Whoever remains in me and I in him will bear much fruit, because without me you can do nothing. Anyone who does not remain in me will be thrown out like a branch and wither; people will gather them and throw them into a fire and they will be burned. If you remain in me and my words remain in you, ask for whatever you want and it will be done for you. By this is my Father glorified, that you bear much fruit and become my disciples."

Practice of Faith

Jesus asks us to "remain in me, as I remain in you," and by this to bear fruit for the Kingdom. How do we do this? There are many practices that help us, such as prayer, Scripture study, and acts of charity. But perhaps the best way is by receiving the gift of the Eucharist, where we and Christ abide together in the most intimate of ways. ◆ Think about your experience of the Eucharist. What has this sacrament meant to you? Sometimes we fall into the habit of approaching the Eucharist in a mechanical manner. Next time you are at Mass, pray to experience Christ in you more deeply as you receive his Body and Blood. ◆ The Eucharist is the "heart and center of our lives as Christians," writes Kathleen Hughes, RSCJ, ". . . familiar in its every contour, it is mystery at its core." To read more about the beautiful mystery of the Eucharist and other sacraments, see Sr. Kathleen's book, *Saying Amen: A Mystagogy of Sacrament* (LTP, 1999). ◆ The United States Conference of Catholic Bishops shares answers to basic questions about the Eucharist on their website: http://www.usccb.org /prayer-and-worship/the-mass/order-of-mass /liturgy-of-the-eucharist/the-real-presence-of -jesus-christ-in-the-sacrament-of-the-eucharist -basic-questions-and-answers.cfm.

Download more questions and activities for families, Christian initiation groups, and other adult groups at http://www.ltp.org/t-productsupplements.aspx.

Scripture Insights

Today's readings continue the previous Sunday's emphasis on the community of the resurrected Christ—living and life giving. The First Reading gives us a thumbnail sketch of the illustrious teacher and missionary Paul, who began as Saul, a zealous Jew and persecutor of the Jesus followers, who experienced conversion, was persecuted by fellow Jews, and for some time was viewed warily by Jesus' disciples. Eventually he became the missionary to the Gentiles.

The reading from the First Letter of John highlights the most important attribute that makes the Church truly alive and authentic—love. But this love is not simply a warm feeling or tender words. Rather, it is love "in deed and truth." If we stay grounded in God's command to believe in his Son and love one another, we remain in him and he remains in us.

In today's Gospel, John gives us another metaphor for understanding what it means to be Church—the vineyard, for wine was considered a necessity of life. First-century vineyards were constructed differently from today's vineyards. They were surrounded by a stone wall to keep animals from trampling the vines, which were allowed to spread along the ground. When the vines were pruned to increase production, the discarded branches were placed on the wall to dry so that they could later be used for fuel. Vineyards also had towers, where the owner and his workers kept watch during harvest time to protect their produce from thieves and marauders. This is the cultural context for understanding the metaphor of the vineyard.

◆ Carefully analyze today's Gospel and unpack its metaphor. Who is the vineyard owner? The vine and its branches? What does it mean to remain part of the vine? To be cut off from the vine? To bear much fruit?

◆ The Second Reading invites us to love "in deed and truth." What does that phrase mean to you?

◆ Today's Responsorial Psalm is the concluding section of Psalm 22, a lament psalm that began with a complaint and a call for help. This section promises to praise God. For what would you like to praise God?

May 6, 2018 SIXTH SUNDAY OF EASTER

READING I
Acts 10:25–26, 34–35, 44–48

When Peter entered, Cornelius met him and, falling at his feet, paid him homage. Peter, however, raised him up, saying, "Get up. I myself am also a human being."

Then Peter proceeded to speak and said, "In truth, I see that God shows no partiality. Rather, in every nation whoever fears him and acts uprightly is acceptable to him."

While Peter was still speaking these things, the Holy Spirit fell upon all who were listening to the word. The circumcised believers who had accompanied Peter were astounded that the gift of the Holy Spirit should have been poured out on the Gentiles also, for they could hear them speaking in tongues and glorifying God. Then Peter responded, "Can anyone withhold the water for baptizing these people, who have received the Holy Spirit even as we have?" He ordered them to be baptized in the name of Jesus Christ.

RESPONSORIAL PSALM
Psalm 98:1, 2–3, 3–4 (see 2b)

R. The Lord has revealed to the nations his
          saving power.
     or: Alleluia.

Sing to the LORD a new song,
     for he has done wondrous deeds;
His right hand has won victory for him,
     his holy arm. R.

The LORD has made his salvation known:
     in the sight of the nations he has revealed
               his justice.
He has remembered his kindness and
               his faithfulness
     toward the house of Israel. R.

All the ends of the earth have seen
     the salvation by our God.
Sing joyfully to the LORD, all you lands;
     break into song; sing praise. R.

READING II 1 John 4:7–10

Beloved, let us love one another, because love is of God; everyone who loves is begotten by God and knows God. Whoever is without love does not know God, for God is love. In this way the love of God was revealed to us: God sent his only Son into the world so that we might have life through him. In this is love: not that we have loved God, but that he loved us and sent his Son as expiation for our sins.

GOSPEL John 15:9–17

Jesus said to his disciples: "As the Father loves me, so I also love you. Remain in my love. If you keep my commandments, you will remain in my love, just as I have kept my Father's commandments and remain in his love.

"I have told you this so that my joy may be in you and your joy might be complete. This is my commandment: love one another as I love you. No one has greater love than this, to lay down one's life for one's friends. You are my friends if you do what I command you. I no longer call you slaves, because a slave does not know what his master is doing. I have called you friends, because I have told you everything I have heard from my Father. It was not you who chose me, but I who chose you and appointed you to go and bear fruit that will remain, so that whatever you ask the Father in my name he may give you. This I command you: love one another."

Practice of Charity

In turbulent times, it can be challenging to truly love those who are different from us, who look different, come from a different country or culture, or hold different political or religious views. Our media culture fuels this divisiveness, turning the "other" into the enemy. Yet Jesus commands us: "love one another." Often we love only when it is easy; Jesus asks us to love when it's hard, just as he did. ◆ If we are commanded by Christ to love one another, then contempt or hatred for another is a sin. Is there an individual or group that you find difficult to love? In prayer, ask for God's heart of love and forgiveness. Pray this way each day until you can hold them in God's love. ◆ Make an effort to get to know the "other" in your world. Attend Mass at a parish where the demographic is different from your own. Find a way to meet, work, or volunteer together with persons of a different race, culture, or economic status. ◆ At Catholic Worker Houses throughout the country, people of all races and backgrounds share meals, conversation, and work, in an effort to promote understanding and peace. Consider visiting a Worker House in your area. To learn about Catholic Worker read http://www.uscatholic.org/culture/social-justice/2011/09/house-work-catholic-worker-houses-today. For a directory of Houses visit http://www.catholicworker.org/communities/directory.html.

Download more questions and activities for families, Christian initiation groups, and other adult groups at http://www.ltp.org/t-productsupplements.aspx.

Scripture Insights

On this Sixth Sunday of Easter, we continue our focus on the community of the resurrected Christ, the Easter community that is living and life-giving. In the First Reading, Luke tells the story of Peter's encounter with Cornelius, a Roman centurion and a "God-fearer" (a Gentile proselyte to Judaism). Biblical scholars think that these were the first Gentile followers of Jesus. Peter's speech highlights one of the four marks of the Church, namely, its universality or catholicity. As Peter expresses his new insight, that "God shows no partiality," the Holy Spirit descends on Cornelius and his relatives even *before* they were baptized.

In the Second Reading, we hear again about the love relationship between God and the Christian community. Genuine and self-giving love is an attribute of God, which was revealed in the person of Jesus. But like any good relationship, this divine love comes with an obligation: to love one another.

Using the imagery of slave and friend, today's Gospel continues to explore the theme of divine love and love for one another. During his farewell discourse on the night he is arrested and put to death, Jesus explains to his disciples that they are no longer slaves. Rather, they are his friends. This is possible because he is about to complete the most perfect act of love on their behalf, and because they know him as one who abides with the Father and with them. The lesson is for us as well as the disciples: as a community of faith, we are Jesus' friends if we love one another.

The First Reading is only the dramatic ending of a wonderful story. In your Bible read all of chapter 10 and reflect on how God brings about changes in our thinking. What prompts Peter to say "God shows no partiality" and how does he know that the Holy Spirit had come upon Cornelius and his household?

◆ As you reflect on the Gospel, what does it mean to you to remain in Jesus' love as he remains in the Father's love?

◆ What do you think connects today's Responsorial Psalm with the First Reading?

READING I *Acts 1:1–11*

In the first book, Theophilus, I dealt with all that Jesus did and taught until the day he was taken up, after giving instructions through the Holy Spirit to the apostles whom he had chosen. He presented himself alive to them by many proofs after he had suffered, appearing to them during forty days and speaking about the kingdom of God. While meeting with them, he enjoined them not to depart from Jerusalem, but to wait for "the promise of the Father about which you have heard me speak; for John baptized with water, but in a few days you will be baptized with the Holy Spirit."

When they had gathered together they asked him, "Lord, are you at this time going to restore the kingdom to Israel?" He answered them, "It is not for you to know the times or seasons that the Father has established by his own authority. But you will receive power when the Holy Spirit comes upon you, and you will be my witnesses in Jerusalem, throughout Judea and Samaria, and to the ends of the earth." When he had said this, as they were looking on, he was lifted up, and a cloud took him from their sight. While they were looking intently at the sky as he was going, suddenly two men dressed in white garments stood beside them. They said, "Men of Galilee, why are you standing there looking at the sky? This Jesus who has been taken up from you into heaven will return in the same way as you have seen him going into heaven."

RESPONSORIAL PSALM
Psalm 47:2–3, 6–7, 8–9 (6)

R. God mounts his throne to shouts of joy:
      a blare of trumpets for the Lord.
  or: Alleluia.

All you peoples, clap your hands,
    shout to God with cries of gladness.
For the LORD, the Most High, the awesome,
    is the great king over all the earth. R.

God mounts his throne amid shouts of joy;
    the LORD, amid trumpet blasts.
Sing praise to God, sing praise;
    sing praise to our king, sing praise. R.

For king of all the earth is God;
    sing hymns of praise.
God reigns over the nations,
    God sits upon his holy throne. R.

READING II *Ephesians 4:1–13*

Shorter: Ephesians 4:1–7, 11–13
Alternate: Ephesians 1:17–23

Brothers and sisters, I, a prisoner for the Lord, urge you to live in a manner worthy of the call you have received, with all humility and gentleness, with patience, bearing with one another through love, striving to preserve the unity of the spirit through the bond of peace: one body and one Spirit, as you were also called to the one hope of your call; one Lord, one faith, one baptism; one God and Father of all, who is over all and through all and in all.

But grace was given to each of us according to the measure of Christ's gift. Therefore, it says: *He ascended on high and took prisoners captive; he gave gifts to men.* What does "he ascended" mean except that he also descended into the lower regions of the earth? The one who descended is also the one who ascended far above all the heavens, that he might fill all things.

And he gave some as apostles, others as prophets, others as evangelists, others as pastors and teachers, to equip the holy ones for the work of ministry, for building up the body of Christ, until we all attain to the unity of faith and knowledge of the Son of God, to mature manhood, to the extent of the full stature of Christ.

GOSPEL *Mark 16:15–20*

Jesus said to his disciples: "Go into the whole world and proclaim the gospel to every creature. Whoever believes and is baptized will be saved; whoever does not believe will be condemned. These signs will accompany those who believe: in my name they will drive out demons, they will speak new languages. They will pick up serpents with their hands, and if they drink any deadly thing, it will not harm them. They will lay hands on the sick, and they will recover."

So then the Lord Jesus, after he spoke to them, was taken up into heaven and took his seat at the right hand of God. But they went forth and preached everywhere, while the Lord worked with them and confirmed the word through accompanying signs.

Practice of Charity

As the Apostles watch Jesus ascend into heaven, two angelic figures ask: "Why are you looking at the sky?" Their message seems twofold: "Don't worry, he'll be back," and "Get on with it!" Indeed, the rest of the Acts of the Apostles is about how Jesus works through his people, by the power of the Holy Spirit, to bring about God's purposes. ◆ "We keep the Holy Spirit as a 'luxury prisoner' in our hearts," said Pope Francis at Mass (May 9, 2016), "we do not allow the Spirit to push us forward, to move us." Read a summary of the pope's homily at http://www.catholicnewsagency.com/news/dont-lock-up-the-holy-spirit-in-your-heart-pope-francis-says-11868/. ◆ How might the Holy Spirit be moving you toward action in the world? Bring this question to God in prayer, and discern with other Christian disciples. ◆ The Catherine of Siena Institute is dedicated to the "formation of lay Catholics for the sake of their mission to the world." Through their Called and Gifted workshops and other resources, they help Christians identify their spiritual gifts and calling. Learn more at https://siena.org/Called-Gifted/called-a-gifted.

Download more questions and activities for families, Christian initiation groups, and other adult groups at http://www.ltp.org/t-productsupplements.aspx.

Scripture Insights

The Solemnity of the Ascension of the Lord is celebrated forty days after Easter, commemorating the forty days Jesus appeared to his disciples, reassuring them of his Resurrection and continuing to teach them. His ascent to the Father is the final action of the Paschal Mystery and allows the Holy Spirit to come into the world.

Today's First Reading is one of only two narrative accounts of the Ascension (aside from single verse in Mark, part of today's Gospel). The other appears at the end of the Gospel according to Luke (24:44–53). Both were written by the same author and addressed to someone named Theophilus. In Luke's mind, Jesus' Ascension into heaven is further proof that he truly was raised from the dead. He also understands it to be the birthday of the Church—hence the teaching about the coming Kingdom of God.

In the Second Reading, the letter writer describes how the Church should live its calling as one Body and one Spirit, committed to one Lord, one faith, and one Baptism. And just as a body has many parts, the Body of Christ has many different kinds of ministers who contribute to the building up of the body.

Although today's Gospel is most likely a somewhat later addition to the Gospel of Mark, it provides a fitting closure to the Gospel by recalling the appearances of the risen Christ and recounting his understanding of the disciples' post-Resurrection mission: "Go into the whole world and proclaim the gospel!"

◆ Carefully analyze the First Reading. What clues can you find to explain why Luke introduced his Acts of the Apostles as he did? What did he intend for Theophilus to glean from it?

◆ As you reflect on the Second Reading, consider the phrase, "bearing with one another through love." How have you managed to do that, or failed to it?

◆ For Christians living in today's world, it would be unwise for us to handle poisonous snakes to prove that we are believers. How then will our calling to "go into the whole world and proclaim the gospel" be proven authentic?

READING I *Acts 1:15−17, 20a, 20c−26*

Peter stood up in the midst of the brothers—there was a group of about one hundred and twenty persons in the one place—. He said, "My brothers, the Scripture had to be fulfilled which the Holy Spirit spoke beforehand through the mouth of David, concerning Judas, who was the guide for those who arrested Jesus. He was numbered among us and was allotted a share in this ministry.

"For it is written in the Book of Psalms: *May another take his office.*

"Therefore, it is necessary that one of the men who accompanied us the whole time the Lord Jesus came and went among us, beginning from the baptism of John until the day on which he was taken up from us, become with us a witness to his resurrection." So they proposed two, Judas called Barsabbas, who was also known as Justus, and Matthias. Then they prayed, "You, Lord, who know the hearts of all, show which one of these two you have chosen to take the place in this apostolic ministry from which Judas turned away to go to his own place." Then they gave lots to them, and the lot fell upon Matthias, and he was counted with the eleven apostles.

RESPONSORIAL PSALM
Psalm 103:1−2, 11−12, 19−20 (19a)

R. The Lord has set his throne in heaven.
  or: Alleluia.

Bless the LORD, O my soul;
  and all my being, bless his holy name.
Bless the LORD, O my soul,
  and forget not all his benefits. R.

For as the heavens are high above the earth,
  so surpassing is his kindness toward those
      who fear him.
As far as the east is from the west,
  so far has he put our transgressions
      from us. R.

The LORD has established his throne in heaven,
  and his kingdom rules over all.
Bless the LORD, all you his angels,
  you mighty in strength,
      who do his bidding. R.

READING II *1 John 4:11−16*

Beloved, if God so loved us, we also must love one another. No one has ever seen God. Yet, if we love one another, God remains in us, and his love is brought to perfection in us.

This is how we know that we remain in him and he in us, that he has given us of his Spirit. Moreover, we have seen and testify that the Father sent his Son as savior of the world. Whoever acknowledges that Jesus is the Son of God, God remains in him and he in God. We have come to know and to believe in the love God has for us.

God is love, and whoever remains in love remains in God and God in him.

GOSPEL *John 17:11b−19*

Lifting up his eyes to heaven, Jesus prayed, saying: "Holy Father, keep them in your name that you have given me, so that they may be one just as we are one. When I was with them I protected them in your name that you gave me, and I guarded them, and none of them was lost except the son of destruction, in order that the Scripture might be fulfilled. But now I am coming to you. I speak this in the world so that they may share my joy completely. I gave them your word, and the world hated them, because they do not belong to the world any more than I belong to the world. I do not ask that you take them out of the world but that you keep them from the evil one. They do not belong to the world any more than I belong to the world. Consecrate them in the truth. Your word is truth. As you sent me into the world, so I sent them into the world. And I consecrate myself for them, so that they also may be consecrated in truth."

Practice of Hope

In the days after Jesus' Death and Resurrection, the Apostles moved to make their community whole. They knew that to effectively witness to Jesus' rising, unity was required. ◆ Help create wholeness in your parish, bit by bit. After Mass today, reach out to someone on the margins and invite him or her to sit with you for coffee and a doughnut. ◆ Learn about an effort underway in the Holy Land to bring unity in a most fragile relationship, between Christians and Muslims. The Jordanian Interfaith Coexistence Research Center—http://www.coexistencejordan.org—seeks to repair misunderstandings. ◆ Christians and Muslims address one God. Ramadan, a Muslim holy period, begins this year after sunset on May 15. Say a prayer to God for the wellbeing of our Muslim brothers and sisters.

Download more questions and activities for families, Christian initiation groups, and other adult groups at http://www.ltp.org/t-productsupplements.aspx.

Scripture Insights

One week before Pentecost, today's readings focus on the early Christians and how they managed to continue Jesus' mission after his Death and Resurrection. In the First Reading, we learn how after Jesus' Ascension into heaven Matthias was selected to replace the Apostle Judas, the one who betrayed Jesus. (In case you have ever wondered why Jesus, guided by the Holy Spirit, managed to choose such a flawed follower, Luke makes it clear that God planned it that way.)

The Second Reading reminds us that Jesus did not leave his beloved disciples alone after his mission was completed. The love that they had for one another was the sign that God remained in them and that God's love was perfected in them. And how did they know that? Through the Holy Spirit.

The Resurrection was a great dividing line in human history and also in the development of human consciousness. Teachings of Jesus that were enigmatic and alarming before the Resurrection took on new depth as the disciples slowly came to understand the larger picture. In today's Gospel, Jesus is presented as praying to the Father in the moments before he departed for the garden where he was betrayed by Judas. He asks the Father to keep his disciples in his name so they can be one as he and the Father are one, and, as he sends them out into the world, he asks that they be protected from the evil one. Imagine his disciples' reaction as they overheard his prayer.

◆ The First Reading shows the Apostles asking God to guide the group's choice of the new Apostle. What other ways might group decisions be made under God's guidance?

◆ As you pray over the Gospel, enter into dialog with Jesus over the content of his prayer. What questions would you like to ask of him? What hopes and anxieties does his prayer bring to mind for you?

◆ Reflect on the Second Reading and allow it to challenge you about the decisions you make today. What will you do to show that God remains in you and that his love is perfected in you?

May 20, 2018 PENTECOST SUNDAY

READING I *Acts 2:1–11*

When the time for Pentecost was fulfilled, they were all in one place together. And suddenly there came from the sky a noise like a strong driving wind, and it filled the entire house in which they were. Then there appeared to them tongues as of fire, which parted and came to rest on each one of them. And they were all filled with the Holy Spirit and began to speak in different tongues, as the Spirit enabled them to proclaim.

Now there were devout Jews from every nation under heaven staying in Jerusalem. At this sound, they gathered in a large crowd, but they were confused because each one heard them speaking in his own language. They were astounded, and in amazement they asked, "Are not all these people who are speaking Galileans? Then how does each of us hear them in his native language? We are Parthians, Medes, and Elamites, inhabitants of Mesopotamia, Judea and Cappadocia, Pontus and Asia, Phrygia and Pamphylia, Egypt and the districts of Libya near Cyrene, as well as travelers from Rome, both Jews and converts to Judaism, Cretans and Arabs, yet we hear them speaking in our own tongues of the mighty acts of God."

RESPONSORIAL PSALM *Psalm 104:1, 24, 29–30, 31, 34 (see 30)*

R. Lord, send out your Spirit, and renew the
      face of the earth.
  or: Alleluia.

Bless the LORD, O my soul!
  O LORD, my God, you are great indeed!
How manifold are your works, O LORD!
  The earth is full of your creatures. R.

If you take away their breath, they perish
  and return to their dust.
When you send forth your spirit, they are created,
  and you renew the face of the earth. R.

May the glory of the LORD endure forever;
  may the LORD be glad in his works!
Pleasing to him be my theme;
  I will be glad in the LORD. R.

READING II *Galatians 5:16–25*

Alternate: 1 Corinthians 12:3b–7, 12–13

Brothers and sisters, live by the Spirit and you will certainly not gratify the desire of the flesh. For the flesh has desires against the Spirit, and the Spirit against the flesh; these are opposed to each other, so that you may not do what you want. But if you are guided by the Spirit, you are not under the law. Now the works of the flesh are obvious: immorality, impurity, lust, idolatry, sorcery, hatreds, rivalry, jealousy, outbursts of fury, acts of selfishness, dissensions, factions, occasions of envy, drinking bouts, orgies, and the like. I warn you, as I warned you before, that those who do such things will not inherit the kingdom of God. In contrast, the fruit of the Spirit is love, joy, peace, patience, kindness, generosity, faithfulness, gentleness, self-control. Against such there is no law. Now those who belong to Christ Jesus have crucified their flesh with its passions and desires. If we live in the Spirit, let us also follow the Spirit.

GOSPEL *John 15:26–27; 16:12–15*

Alternate: John 20:19–23

Jesus said to his disciples: "When the Advocate comes whom I will send you from the Father, the Spirit of truth that proceeds from the Father, he will testify to me. And you also testify, because you have been with me from the beginning.

"I have much more to tell you, but you cannot bear it now. But when he comes, the Spirit of truth, he will guide you to all truth. He will not speak on his own, but he will speak what he hears, and will declare to you the things that are coming. He will glorify me, because he will take from what is mine and declare it to you. Everything that the Father has is mine; for this reason I told you that he will take from what is mine and declare it to you."

Practice of Hope

"Bienvenidos! Welcome!" That's a greeting from the Sisters of St. Mary of Oregon, mostly Anglo women in middle age and later. They use their former school building in Beaverton, Oregon, as a place to teach English to immigrants. The sisters say they have benefitted from the multicultural encounter. ◆ Attend Mass in another language. Enjoy Catholicism's paradox—many lands, but one faith, centered on "the mighty acts of God." ◆ Later this year, the Catholic Church in the United States holds "Encuentro," a gathering to assess ministry among Hispanic Catholics. Here is one part of the prayer for Encuentro: "May the fire of your Word rekindle their hearts and prepare them to become missionary disciples ready to share the joy of the Gospel to present and future generations of every race, culture, and language." For more on Encuentro, go to http://www.usccb.org/issues-and-action/cultural-diversity/hispanic-latino/resources/encuentro-in-united-states-hispanic-ministry.cfm. ◆ Learn to pray the Our Father in another language.

Download more questions and activities for families, Christian initiation groups, and other adult groups at http://www.ltp.org/t-productsupplements.aspx.

Scripture Insights

Pentecost celebrates the coming of the Holy Spirit. The Hebrew word for Spirit is *ruah*, meaning "breath or wind." Speak the word *ruah* aloud and you will hear its meaning! In the opening verse of the Bible the writer uses this image of wind to capture God's creating power: "When God created the heavens and the earth . . . a mighty wind was sweeping over the waters" (Genesis 1:1).

When God created the human being, the writer used the image of God "blowing into his nostrils the breath of life" (Genesis 2:7). In a symbolic way, God shows us that life itself is a gift that comes from God. Not only did God bring us into existence, but God also wanted humanity to remain close to God. Humans had more independent schemes—captured in the story of the Tower of Babel (Genesis 11:1–9). The different languages of humanity became a sign that without God we were unable to communicate perfectly with one another, and strife emerged.

The First Reading, from Acts of the Apostles, describes a noise like a *strong driving wind* that points to the presence of the Spirit, *ruah*. That Spirit works through the preaching of the Apostles, enabling everyone to understand the message despite the different languages. Through the Spirit, the human family is recreated into a new people of God that can communicate and understand each other. The Tower of Babel is reversed!

Today's Gospel is a passage prior to Jesus' Death and Resurrection when Jesus promises to send the Spirit on the disciples to continue God's communication with them into the future. "The Spirit of truth" will testify to Jesus and will guide us into a deeper understanding of Jesus' teaching. What role do you find the Spirit playing in today's Responsorial Psalm?

◆ With the caveat that for Paul, "flesh" and "spirit" cannot be equated with body and soul, but rather with the old self (before Baptism) and the new life in Christ, what insights do you find in the Second Reading that could be helpful to your spiritual life at this time?

◆ How are you empowered by the Spirit today?

Prayer before Reading the Word

Let nothing, O God, be dearer to us than
        your Son;
no worldly possessions, no human honors.
Let us prefer nothing whatever to Christ,
who alone makes known to the world the
        mystery of your love.
Stir up within us a longing for your Word,
that we may be able to satisfy that hunger
        for truth
that you have placed within every human heart.
Nourish us on the bread of Christ's teaching.
We ask this through our Lord Jesus Christ,
the Living Bread, who has come down from
        heaven for the life of the world,
who lives and reigns with you
in the unity of the Holy Spirit,
one God, for ever and ever. Amen.

Prayer after Reading the Word

O God of salvation,
you adopt us through Baptism,
you call us to proclaim the Good News of
        Jesus Christ,
your healing power and forgiving love.
Give us an unfailing trust
that the wealth of your Word is sufficient,
the food and drink you provide is ample.
Then send us out with praise on our lips.
We ask this through our Lord Jesus Christ,
your Son, who lives and reigns with you
in the unity of the Holy Spirit,
one God, for ever and ever. Amen.

Weekday Readings

May 21: *James 3:13–18; Mark 9:14–29*
May 22: *James 4:1–10; Mark 9:30–37*
May 23: *James 4:13–17; Mark 9:38–40*
May 24: *James 5:1–6; Mark 9:41–50*
May 25: *James 5:9–12; Mark 10:1–12*
May 26: *James 5:13–20; Mark 10:13–16*

May 28: *1 Peter 1:3–9; Mark 10:17–27*
May 29: *1 Peter 1:10–16; Mark 10:28–31*
May 30: *1 Peter 1:18– 25; Mark 10:32–45*
May 31: Feast of the Visitation of the Blessed Virgin Mary
Zephaniah 3:14–18a or Romans 12:9–16;
Luke 1:39–56
June 1: *1 Peter 4:7–13; Mark 11:11–26*
June 2: *Jude 17, 20b–25; Mark 11:27–33*

June 4: *2 Peter 1:2–7; Mark 12:1–12*
June 5: *2 Peter 3:12–15a, 17–18; Mark 12:13–17*
June 6: *2 Timothy 1:1–3, 6–12; Mark 12:18–27*
June 7: *2 Timothy 2:8–15; Mark 12:28–34*
June 8: Solemnity of the Most Sacred Heart of Jesus
Hosea 11:1, 3–4, 8c–9; Ephesians 3:8–12, 14–19;
John 19:31–37
June 9: *2 Timothy 4:1–8; Luke 2:41–51*

June 11: *Acts 11:21b–26; 13:1–3; Matthew 5:1–12*
June 12: *1 Kings 17:7–16; Matthew 5:13–16*
June 13: *1 Kings 18:20–39; Matthew 5:17–19*
June 14: *1 Kings 18:41–46; Matthew 5:20–26*
June 15: *1 Kings 19:9a, 11–16; Matthew 5:27–32*
June 16: *1 Kings 19:19–21; Matthew 5:33–37*

June 18: *1 Kings 21:1–16; Matthew 5:38–42*
June 19: *1 Kings 21:17–29; Matthew 5:43–48*
June 20: *2 Kings 2:1, 6–14; Matthew 6:1–6, 16–18*
June 21: *Sirach 48:1–14; Matthew 6:7–15*
June 22: *2 Kings 11:1–4, 9–18, 20; Matthew 6:19–23*
June 23: *2 Chronicles 24:17–25; Matthew 6:24 –34*

June 25: *2 Kings 17:5–8, 13–15a, 18; Matthew 7:1–5*
June 26: *2 Kings 19:9b–11, 14–21, 31–35a, 36;*
Matthew 7:6, 12–14
June 27: *2 Kings 22:8–13; 23:1–3; Matthew 7:15–20*
June 28: *2 Kings 24:8–17; Matthew 7:21–29*
June 29: Solemnity of Sts. Peter and Paul, Apostles
Acts 12:1–11; 2 Timothy 4:6–8, 17–18;
Matthew 16:13–19
June 30: *2 Lamentations 2:2, 10–14, 18–19; Matthew 8:5–17*

July 2: *Amos 2:6–10, 13–16; Matthew 8:18–22*
July 3: Feast of St. Thomas the Apostle
Ephesians 2:19–22; John 20:24–29
July 4: *Amos 5:14–15, 21–24; Matthew 8:28–34*
July 5: *Amos 7:10–17; Matthew 9:1–8*
July 6: *Amos 8:4–6, 9–12; Matthew 9:9–13*
July 7: *Amos 9:11–15; Matthew 9:14–17*

July 9: *Hosea 2:16, 17b–18, 21–22; Matthew 9:18–26*
July 10: *Hosea 8:4–7, 11–13; Matthew 9:32–38*
July 11: *Hosea 10:1–3, 7–8, 12; Matthew 10:1–7*
July 12: *Hosea 11:1–4, 8e–9; Matthew 10:7–15*

July 13: *Hosea 14:2–10; Matthew 10:16–23*
July 14: *Isaiah 6:1–8; Matthew 10:24–33*

July 16: *Isaiah 1:10–17; Matthew 10:34 —11:1*
July 17: *Isaiah 7:1–9; Matthew 11:20–24*
July 18: *Isaiah 10:5–7, 13b–16; Matthew 11:25–27*
July 19: *Isaiah 26:7–9, 12, 16–19; Matthew 11:28–30*
July 20: *Isaiah 38:1–6, 21–22, 7–8; Matthew 12:1–8*
July 21: *Micah 2:1–5; Matthew 12:14–21*

July 23: *Micah 6:1–4; Matthew 12:38–42*
July 24: *Micah 7:14–15, 18–20; Matthew 12:46–50*
July 25: Feast of St. James
2 Corinthians 4:7–15; Matthew 20:20–28
July 26: *Jeremiah 2:1–3, 7–8, 12–13; Matthew 13:10–17*
July 27: *Jeremiah 3:14–17; Matthew 13:18–23*
July 28: *Jeremiah 7:1–11; Matthew 13:24–30*

July 30: *Jeremiah 13:1–11; Matthew 13:31–35*
July 31: *Jeremiah 14:17–22; Matthew 13:36–43*
August 1: *Jeremiah 15:10, 16–21; Matthew 13:44–46*
August 2: *Jeremiah 18:1–6; Matthew 13:47–53*
August 3: *Jeremiah 26:1–9; Matthew 13:54–58*
August 4: *Jeremiah 26:11–16, 24; Matthew 14:1–12*

August 6: Feast of the Transfiguration of the Lord
Daniel 7:9–10, 13–14; 2 Peter 1:16–19; Mark 9:2–10
August 7: *Jeremiah 30:1–2, 12–15, 18–22; Matthew 14:22–36*
or Matthew 15:1–2, 10–14
August 8: *Jeremiah 31:1–7; Matthew 15:21–28*
August 9: *Jeremiah 31:31–34; Matthew 16:13–23*
August 10: Feast of St. Lawrence, Deacon and Martyr
2 Corinthians 9:6–10; John 12:24–26
August 11: *Habakkuk 1:12—2:4; Matthew 17:14–20*

August 13: *Ezekiel 1:2–5, 24–28c; Matthew 17:22–27*
August 14: *Ezekiel 2:8—3:4; Matthew 18:1–5, 10, 12–14*
August 15: Solemnity of the Assumption of the Blessed
Virgin Mary Revelation 11:19a; 12:1–6a, 10ab; 1
Corinthians 15:20–27; Luke 1:39–56
August 16: *Ezekiel 12:1–12; Matthew 18:21—19:1*
August 17: *Ezekiel 16:1–15, 60, 63 or 16:59–63;*
Matthew 19:3–12
August 18: *Ezekiel 18:1–10, 13b, 30–32; Matthew 19:1–15*

August 20: *Ezekiel 24:15–24; Matthew 19:16–22*
August 21: *Ezekiel 28:1–10; Matthew 19:23–30*
August 22: *Ezekiel 34:1–11; Matthew 20:1–16*
August 23: *Ezekiel 36:23–28; Matthew 22:1–14*
August 24: Feast of St. Bartholomew, Apostle
Revelation 21:9b–14; John 1:45–51
August 25: *Ezekiel 43:1–7ab; Matthew 23:1–12*

August 27: *2 Thessalonians 1:1–5, 11–12; Matthew 23:13–22*
August 28: *2 Thessalonians 2:1–3a, 14–17;*
Matthew 23:23–26
August 29: *2 Thessalonians 3:6–10, 16–18; Mark 6:17–29*
August 30: *1 Corinthians 1:1–9; Matthew 24:42–51*
August 31: *1 Corinthians 1:17–25; Matthew 25:1–13*
September 1: *1 Corinthians 1:26–31; Matthew 25:14–30*

READING I
Deuteronomy 4:32–34, 39–40

Moses said to the people: "Ask now of the days of old, before your time, ever since God created man upon the earth; ask from one end of the sky to the other: Did anything so great ever happen before? Was it ever heard of? Did a people ever hear the voice of God speaking from the midst of fire, as you did, and live? Or did any god venture to go and take a nation for himself from the midst of another nation, by testings, by signs and wonders, by war, with strong hand and outstretched arm, and by great terrors, all of which the LORD, your God, did for you in Egypt before your very eyes? This is why you must now know, and fix in your heart, that the LORD is God in the heavens above and on earth below, and that there is no other. You must keep his statutes and commandments that I enjoin on you today, that you and your children after you may prosper, and that you may have long life on the land which the LORD, your God, is giving you forever."

RESPONSORIAL PSALM *Psalm 33:4–5, 6, 9, 18–19, 20, 22 (12b)*

R. Blessed the people the Lord has chosen to be
　　his own.

Upright is the word of the LORD,
　　and all his works are trustworthy.
He loves justice and right;
　　of the kindness of the LORD the earth
　　　　is full. R.

By the word of the LORD the heavens were made;
　　by the breath of his mouth all their host.
For he spoke, and it was made;
　　he commanded, and it stood forth. R.

See, the eyes of the LORD are upon those who
　　　　fear him,
　　upon those who hope for his kindness,
to deliver them from death
　　and preserve them in spite of famine. R.

Our soul waits for the LORD,
　　who is our help and our shield.
May your kindness, O LORD, be upon us
　　who have put our hope in you. R.

READING II *Romans 8:14–17*

Brothers and sisters: Those who are led by the Spirit of God are sons of God. For you did not receive a spirit of slavery to fall back into fear, but you received a Spirit of adoption, through whom we cry, "Abba, Father!" The Spirit himself bears witness with our spirit that we are children of God, and if children, then heirs, heirs of God and joint heirs with Christ, if only we suffer with him so that we may also be glorified with him.

GOSPEL *Matthew 28:16–20*

The eleven disciples went to Galilee, to the mountain to which Jesus had ordered them. When they all saw him, they worshiped, but they doubted. Then Jesus approached and said to them, "All power in heaven and on earth has been given to me. Go, therefore, and make disciples of all nations, baptizing them in the name of the Father, and of the Son, and of the Holy Spirit, teaching them to observe all that I have commanded you. And behold, I am with you always, until the end of the age."

Practice of Faith

For a reason we cannot know, God chooses to run the world through human beings. Our Trinitarian God, modeling community for us, continually frees us but also asks us to serve in the Kingdom, healing human community. ◆ Read paragraph 20 from *Evangelii Gaudium*, in which Pope Francis urges us to go out to the "peripheries": http://w2.vatican.va/content/francesco/en/apost_exhortations/documents/papa-francesco_esortazione-ap_20131124_evangelii-gaudium.html. ◆ Still God's Chosen People, our Jewish brothers and sisters are open to service projects done in conjunction with Christians. Join or suggest a joint Jewish-Catholic project in your city. ◆ Before any act of service, pray for the awareness that it is the Lord who is acting, he who is with us always.

Download more questions and activities for families, Christian initiation groups, and other adult groups at http://www.ltp.org/t-productsupplements.aspx.

Scripture Insights

We celebrate today what lies at the heart of the Christian faith and life: the mystery of God as Father, Son, and Holy Spirit. Jesus taught about God in very concrete ways, giving us glimpses into the mystery of God and into the relationship of love that we are called to share. Today's readings shine like three flashlights illuminating different dimensions of God.

In Deuteronomy, Moses reminds the Israelites that God created all things in heaven and on earth. There is no other God. Having loved and cared for his people from the beginning, God wants to be close to them, and they in turn are called to respond by keeping God's laws and commandments.

In his letter, Paul instructs the people of Rome (and us) that we have received God's Spirit. The Spirit dwells within us, liberating us from slavery to the Law and to fear, by adopting us as God's children. The Holy Spirit unites us to the Body of Christ and to the Father whom we can address as "Abba," an intimate term of love used by children for their father.

In the Gospel, Jesus reveals more fully the mystery of God's love by sending his disciples on a mission to bring all people into this relationship of love with God as Father, Son, and Holy Spirit—through Baptism. Jesus promises that he is with us "always, until the end of the age." We are never alone since we are, as God's children, always united with the Father, Son, and Spirit in a relationship of love. We share in God's own life and mission. This Solemnity of the Holy Trinity celebrates what we have received in the sacrament of Baptism: life in a relationship of love with God and one another.

◆ In the First Reading, what specific events from the history of the people's relationship with God do you think Moses refers to?

◆ What new insight do you find in the four readings about any of the three Persons of the Trinity?

◆ When have you felt a close connection with "Abba, Father!" or Christ, our coheir, or the Spirit who leads us?

June 3, 2018 THE MOST HOLY BODY AND BLOOD OF CHRIST

READING I *Exodus 24:3–8*

When Moses came to the people and related all the words and ordinances of the LORD, they all answered with one voice, "We will do everything that the LORD has told us." Moses then wrote down all the words of the LORD and, rising early the next day, he erected at the foot of the mountain an altar and twelve pillars for the twelve tribes of Israel. Then, having sent certain young men of the Israelites to offer holocausts and sacrifice young bulls as peace offerings to the LORD, Moses took half of the blood and put it in large bowls; the other half he splashed on the altar. Taking the book of the covenant, he read it aloud to the people, who answered, "All that the LORD has said, we will heed and do." Then he took the blood and sprinkled it on the people, saying, "This is the blood of the covenant that the LORD has made with you in accordance with all these words of his."

RESPONSORIAL PSALM
Psalm 116:12–13, 15–16, 17–18 (13)

R. I will take the cup of salvation, and call on
　　　the name of the Lord.
　or: Alleluia.

How shall I make a return to the LORD
　for all the good he has done for me?
The cup of salvation I will take up,
　and I will call upon the name
　　　of the LORD. R.

Precious in the eyes of the LORD
　is the death of his faithful ones.
I am your servant, the son of your handmaid;
　you have loosed my bonds. R.

To you will I offer sacrifice of thanksgiving,
　and I will call upon the name of the LORD.
My vows to the LORD I will pay
　in the presence of all his people. R.

READING II *Hebrews 9:11–15*

Brothers and sisters: When Christ came as high priest of the good things that have come to be, passing through the greater and more perfect tabernacle not made by hands, that is, not belonging to this creation, he entered once for all into the sanctuary, not with the blood of goats and calves but with his own blood, thus obtaining eternal redemption. For if the blood of goats and bulls and the sprinkling of a heifer's ashes can sanctify those who are defiled so that their flesh is cleansed, how much more will the blood of Christ, who through the eternal Spirit offered himself unblemished to God, cleanse our consciences from dead works to worship the living God.

For this reason he is mediator of a new covenant: since a death has taken place for deliverance from transgressions under the first covenant, those who are called may receive the promised eternal inheritance.

GOSPEL *Mark 14:12–16, 22–26*

On the first day of the Feast of Unleavened Bread, when they sacrificed the Passover lamb, Jesus' disciples said to him, "Where do you want us to go and prepare for you to eat the Passover?" He sent two of his disciples and said to them, "Go into the city and a man will meet you, carrying a jar of water. Follow him. Wherever he enters, say to the master of the house, 'The Teacher says, "Where is my guest room where I may eat the Passover with my disciples?"' Then he will show you a large upper room furnished and ready. Make the preparations for us there." The disciples then went off, entered the city, and found it just as he had told them; and they prepared the Passover.

While they were eating, he took bread, said the blessing, broke it, gave it to them, and said, "Take it; this is my body." Then he took a cup, gave thanks, and gave it to them, and they all drank from it. He said to them, "This is my blood of the covenant, which will be shed for many. Amen, I say to you, I shall not drink again the fruit of the vine until the day when I drink it new in the kingdom of God." Then, after singing a hymn, they went out to the Mount of Olives.

Practice of Faith

For the Jews of Jesus' day, the Temple was where divine and human mingled. Pilgrims came from desert lands to worship and take joy in the Temple's cool courtyards. Jesus would later be recognized as a walking Temple, an individual in whom divine and human met, and who offers refuge. Today, God and humans meet in humble service, love, and especially the celebration of the Eucharist. ◆ Read more about the meaning of Eucharist in Pope Francis' *Laudato Si'*, paragraph 236 — http://w2.vatican.va/content/francesco /en/encyclicals/documents/papa-francesco _20150524_enciclica-laudato-si.html. ◆ Take the family to church for adoration of Jesus in the Eucharist. ◆ Meditate on these lines from a homily of St. John Chrysostom: "'How many of you say: I wish I could see Christ's form and figure, his clothing, his shoes!' Indeed! You do see him; you do touch him; you even eat him. And you want to see his clothes?! Really! [Christ] has given you the ability not only to see him, but to eat and touch and take him within yourselves" (Sermon 82 on Matthew translated by Nathan Mitchell).

Download more questions and activities for families, Christian initiation groups, and other adult groups at http://www.ltp.org/t-productsupplements.aspx.

Scripture Insights

Today's readings focus on the themes of blood and covenant. The Exodus passage takes us back to the people wandering through the wilderness. When Moses writes down God's commandments, the people accept them as the guide for their lives. To seal this covenant-bond between God and the Israelites, Moses takes the blood of the sacrifices and sprinkles it upon the altar (symbolizing God) and upon the people. The people believed that life itself was in the blood, and life was sacred because it came from God. (Thus, the people of Israel would not eat meat that contained blood.) So through the sprinkled blood, the life element, God and Israel become bound together in a sacred bond, a covenant.

In the Gospel account, just prior to his Death, Jesus shares his last meal with his disciples. There he blesses bread, gives it to his disciples, and tells them "Take it; this is my body." He then blesses the wine, and tells them to drink of it for "This is the blood of the covenant which will be shed for many." Through the shedding of his blood in his Death, Jesus establishes a new covenant between God and his people. The Letter to the Hebrews explains the significance of Jesus' action by contrasting it with the first covenant that Moses established. The blood used to seal the covenant is not that of goats and calves, but the very blood of Christ himself. "For this reason he is mediator of a new covenant."

These readings tell us what we celebrate around the altar. Like the disciples in the room with Jesus, we drink the blood of the Lord, and through his blood we are united to the Lord in a new covenant-bond.

◆ In the rituals described in the First Reading and the Gospel; what things are similar to your experience of the Mass? What things are different?

◆ How do you experience our celebration of the Eucharist binding us together as the Body of Christ?

◆ How might drinking from the chalice help one to unite with Jesus' Death on the Cross?

READING I *Genesis 3:9–15*

After the man, Adam, had eaten of the tree, the LORD God called to the man and asked him, "Where are you?" He answered, "I heard you in the garden; but I was afraid, because I was naked, so I hid myself." Then he asked, "Who told you that you were naked? You have eaten, then, from the tree of which I had forbidden you to eat!" The man replied, "The woman whom you put here with me—she gave me fruit from the tree, and so I ate it." The LORD God then asked the woman, "Why did you do such a thing?" The woman answered, "The serpent tricked me into it, so I ate it."

Then the LORD God said to the serpent:
"Because you have done this,
    you shall be banned
    from all the animals and from all
        the wild creatures;
on your belly shall you crawl,
    and dirt shall you eat
    all the days of your life.
I will put enmity between you and the woman,
    and between your offspring and hers;
he will strike at your head,
    while you strike at his heel."

RESPONSORIAL PSALM
Psalm 130:1–2, 3–4, 5–6, 7–8 (7bc)

R. With the Lord there is mercy, and fullness of
        redemption.

Out of the depths I cry to you, O LORD;
    LORD, hear my voice!
Let your ears be attentive
    to my voice in supplication. R.

If you, O LORD, mark iniquities,
    LORD, who can stand?
But with you is forgiveness,
    that you may be revered. R.

I trust in the LORD;
    my soul trusts in his word.
More than sentinels wait for the dawn,
    let Israel wait for the LORD. R.

For with the LORD is kindness
    and with him is plenteous redemption;
and he will redeem Israel
    from all their iniquities. R.

READING II *2 Corinthians 4:13—5:1*

Brothers and sisters:
Since we have the same spirit of faith, according to what is written, *I believed, therefore I spoke*, we too believe and therefore we speak, knowing that the one who raised the Lord Jesus will raise us also with Jesus and place us with you in his presence. Everything indeed is for you, so that the grace bestowed in abundance on more and more people may cause the thanksgiving to overflow for the glory of God. Therefore, we are not discouraged; rather, although our outer self is wasting away, our inner self is being renewed day by day. For this momentary light affliction is producing for us an eternal weight of glory beyond all comparison, as we look not to what is seen but to what is unseen; for what is seen is transitory, but what is unseen is eternal. For we know that if our earthly dwelling, a tent, should be destroyed, we have a building from God, a dwelling not made with hands, eternal in heaven.

GOSPEL *Mark 3:20–35*

Jesus came home with his disciples. Again the crowd gathered, making it impossible for them even to eat. When his relatives heard of this they set out to seize him, for they said, "He is out of his mind." The scribes who had come from Jerusalem said, "He is possessed by Beelzebul," and "By the prince of demons he drives out demons."

Summoning them, he began to speak to them in parables, "How can Satan drive out Satan? If a kingdom is divided against itself, that kingdom cannot stand. And if a house is divided against itself, that house will not be able to stand. And if Satan has risen up against himself and is divided, he cannot stand; that is the end of him. But no one can enter a strong man's house to plunder his property unless he first ties up the strong man. Then he can plunder the house. Amen, I say to you, all sins and all blasphemies that people utter will be forgiven them. But whoever blasphemes against the Holy Spirit will never have forgiveness, but is guilty of an everlasting sin." For they had said, "He has an unclean spirit."

His mother and his brothers arrived. Standing outside they sent word to him and called him. A crowd seated around him told him, "Your mother and your brothers and your sisters are outside asking for you." But he said to them in reply, "Who are my mother and my brothers?" And looking around at those seated in the circle he said, "Here are my mother and my brothers. For whoever does the will of God is my brother and sister and mother."

Practice of Faith

Jesus' family didn't understand his mission. Who can blame them? What Jesus was about was more than earthshaking. In small ways, the situation parallels relations between parents and young adults today; some parents don't understand what their children must do. ◆ If you are a parent with a child exploring a religious vocation, try to be patient and supportive of their discernment process. Many parents want grandchildren, or imagine that their children will be unhappy as priests or religious, for example. Read a moving letter from a priest to parents at http://www.archdpdx-vocations.org/parents.html, and whether or not you are a parent, consider joining your nearest Serra Club, a vocations promotion group named after St. Junipero Serra. Look for a club here: http://www.serraus.org/serrausa/serra_findclub.htm or call (888) 777-6681. ◆ Whatever vocation the young person in your life is discerning—lay ministry, social sciences, health care, the arts, crafts, communications, trade fields, and so forth, pray that they can be open to the guidance of the Holy Spirit. ◆ The Church and the world need willing hands and hearts of all ages. Pray for all the vocations of helping and serving.

Download more questions and activities for families, Christian initiation groups, and other adult groups at http://www.ltp.org/t-productsupplements.aspx.

Scripture Insights

Today's readings remind us of two foundational aspects of our Christian faith: (1) the sinfulness in our world comes ultimately from pursuing our own will and not God's will, and (2) God liberates us from our sinful condition through the Redeemer.

The First Reading gives an explanation for the presence of sin and evil in our world. God did not intend them when he created the world as "good." But we humans have constantly used the gift of free will to choose our own will instead of carrying out God's will. Because we are so vulnerable to sin, God has promised us the gift of a redeemer who will liberate us from the powers of evil: "I will put enmity between you and the woman and between your offspring and hers; he will strike at your head, while you strike at his heel."

In the Gospel, we see that Jesus is this redeemer, but his own people refuse to accept his message. Instead, they say he is "out of his mind" and attribute everything to the powers of evil. They reject the workings of the Holy Spirit in their lives. Mark's Gospel makes the significant point that Jesus brought about a new kinship, founded not on flesh and blood, but on rebirth by the Spirit. The Spirit enables Jesus' followers to carry out God's will. As the story of Adam and Eve and also the history of humanity have shown, without God's help, human beings are incapable of using their free will to carry out God's will. Instead they follow their own selfish desires. Only those who do the will of God are "Jesus' brother and sister and mother." The Spirit gives us rebirth into this new family of God and enables us to carry out God's will.

◆ How do Adam and Eve refuse to take responsibility for what they have done?

◆ Apart from being his brothers and sisters, we are also, Jesus tells us, his mothers. What could Jesus mean by that?

◆ How do you try to carry out God's will in your life?

READING I *Ezekiel 17:22–24*

Thus says the Lord GOD:
I, too, will take from the crest of the cedar,
    from its topmost branches tear off a
        tender shoot,
and plant it on a high and lofty mountain;
    on the mountain heights of Israel I will
        plant it.
It shall put forth branches and bear fruit,
    and become a majestic cedar.
Birds of every kind shall dwell beneath it,
    every winged thing in the shade of
        its boughs.
And all the trees of the field shall know
    that I, the LORD,
bring low the high tree,
    lift high the lowly tree,
wither up the green tree,
    and make the withered tree bloom.
As I, the LORD, have spoken, so will I do.

RESPONSORIAL PSALM
Psalm 92:2–3, 13–14, 15–16 (see 2a)

R Lord, it is good to give thanks to you.

It is good to give thanks to the LORD,
    to sing praise to your name, Most High,
To proclaim your kindness at dawn
    and your faithfulness throughout
        the night. R.

The just one shall flourish like the palm tree,
    like a cedar of Lebanon shall he grow.
They that are planted in the house of the LORD
    shall flourish in the courts of our God. R.

They shall bear fruit even in old age;
    vigorous and sturdy shall they be,
declaring how just is the LORD,
    my rock, in whom there is no wrong. R.

READING II *2 Corinthians 5:6–10*

Brothers and sisters: We are always courageous, although we know that while we are at home in the body we are away from the Lord, for we walk by faith, not by sight. Yet we are courageous, and we would rather leave the body and go home to the Lord. Therefore, we aspire to please him, whether we are at home or away. For we must all appear before the judgment seat of Christ, so that each may receive recompense, according to what he did in the body, whether good or evil.

GOSPEL *Mark 4:26–34*

Jesus said to the crowds: "This is how it is with the kingdom of God; it is as if a man were to scatter seed on the land and would sleep and rise night and day and through it all the seed would sprout and grow, he knows not how. Of its own accord the land yields fruit, first the blade, then the ear, then the full grain in the ear. And when the grain is ripe, he wields the sickle at once, for the harvest has come."

He said, "To what shall we compare the kingdom of God, or what parable can we use for it? It is like a mustard seed that, when it is sown in the ground, is the smallest of all the seeds on the earth. But once it is sown, it springs up and becomes the largest of plants and puts forth large branches, so that the birds of the sky can dwell in its shade." With many such parables he spoke the word to them as they were able to understand it. Without parables he did not speak to them, but to his own disciples he explained everything in private.

Practice of Hope

Scripture often uses trees and plants as symbols for God's action—in the lives of the Israelites and, in Jesus' ministry, to describe how the Kingdom of God works. God invites us to participate in divine action, and that includes care for the plants of the earth as well as the whole globe. ◆ Read paragraphs 1 and 2 of *Laudato Si'*, Pope Francis' encyclical on care of the earth—http://w2.vatican.va/content/francesco/en/encyclicals/documents/papa-francesco_20150524_enciclica-laudato-si.html. ◆ Consider taking the St. Francis pledge at http://www.catholicclimatecovenant.org/pledge or by calling (202) 756-5545. Catholic Climate Covenant will send you resources to put your faith into action. ◆ In your home, set up a prayer corner (a good idea in any case), including a card with the Canticle of the Sun, composed by St. Francis.

Download more questions and activities for families, Christian initiation groups, and other adult groups at http://www.ltp.org/t-productsupplements.aspx.

Scripture Insights

Today's Word reminds us that the Lord is at work in the world, in us, and in spreading God's Kingdom. The prophet Ezekiel addresses the people of Israel encouraging them never to lose hope. As God's people, they are assured that their fortunes will be reversed. The prophet offers a beautiful image: God takes a shoot from a cedar tree and plants it in the ground, where it grows into a majestic tree. In like manner, this loving God, whose power makes mighty trees grow, will restore the people of Israel.

"We walk by faith, and not by sight" is a call Paul addresses to his friends in Corinth: Remember that life is a journey to the Lord. No matter what happens Christ journeys with us. Our faith in Christ offers the confidence that we can face every challenge. Consequently, we are called to act in a way that pleases the Lord.

The Gospel presents two parables that focus on God's work within us and in the spread of God's Kingdom. In the first parable, Jesus compares the growth of God's Kingdom on earth to God's creative power working mysteriously in the world of nature. In the second parable, Jesus compares the growth of the Kingdom to a small mustard seed planted in the ground that becomes the largest of plants.

All these readings challenge us to remember that the work we do is ultimately not ours, but the Lord's. God works in mysterious ways within our lives and within the world in the growth of God's Kingdom. The future that lies ahead is mysterious, but it is rooted in God's love for his people, beginning with the people of Israel and culminating with Jesus and the growth of the Christian Church.

◆ Reread the first sentence of the Second Reading carefully. What do you think Paul means by "We walk by faith and not by sight"?

◆ In your own life where have you seen God's mysterious power at work lately?

◆ How do the images of God's working in nature help you understand God's working in our lives?

READING I *Isaiah 49:1–6*

Hear me, O coastlands,
  listen, O distant peoples.
The LORD called me from birth,
  from my mother's womb he gave me
      my name.
He made of me a sharp-edged sword
  and concealed me in the shadow of his arm.
He made me a polished arrow,
  in his quiver he hid me.
You are my servant, he said to me,
  Israel, through whom I show my glory.

Though I thought I had toiled in vain,
  and for nothing, uselessly, spent
      my strength,
yet my reward is with the LORD,
  my recompense is with my God.
For now the LORD has spoken
  who formed me as his servant from
      the womb,
that Jacob may be brought back to him
  and Israel gathered to him;
and I am made glorious in the sight of the LORD,
  and my God is now my strength!
It is too little, he says, for you to be my servant,
  to raise up the tribes of Jacob,
  and restore the survivors of Israel;
I will make you a light to the nations,
  that my salvation may reach to the ends of
      the earth.

RESPONSORIAL PSALM *Psalm 139:1b–3, 13–14ab, 14c–15 (14)*

R. I praise you, for I am wonderfully made.

O LORD, you have probed me, you know me:
  you know when I sit and when I stand;
  you understand my thoughts from afar.
My journeys and my rest you scrutinize,
  with all my ways you are familiar. R.

Truly you have formed my inmost being;
  you knit me in my mother's womb.
I give you thanks that I am fearfully,
      wonderfully made;
  wonderful are your works. R.

My soul also you knew full well;
  nor was my frame unknown to you
When I was made in secret,
  when I was fashioned in the depths of
      the earth. R.

READING II *Acts 13:22–26*

In those days, Paul said: "God raised up David as king; of him God testified, *I have found David, son of Jesse, a man after my own heart; he will carry out my every wish.* From this man's descendants God, according to his promise, has brought to Israel a savior, Jesus. John heralded his coming by proclaiming a baptism of repentance to all the people of Israel; and as John was completing his course, he would say, 'What do you suppose that I am? I am not he. Behold, one is coming after me; I am not worthy to unfasten the sandals of his feet.'

"My brothers, sons of the family of Abraham, and those others among you who are God-fearing, to us this word of salvation has been sent."

GOSPEL *Luke 1:57–66, 80*

When the time arrived for Elizabeth to have her child she gave birth to a son. Her neighbors and relatives heard that the Lord had shown his great mercy toward her, and they rejoiced with her. When they came on the eighth day to circumcise the child, they were going to call him Zechariah after his father, but his mother said in reply, "No. He will be called John." But they answered her, "There is no one among your relatives who has this name." So they made signs, asking his father what he wished him to be called. He asked for a tablet and wrote, "John is his name," and all were amazed. Immediately his mouth was opened, his tongue freed, and he spoke blessing God. Then fear came upon all their neighbors, and all these matters were discussed throughout the hill country of Judea. All who heard these things took them to heart, saying, "What, then, will this child be?" For surely the hand of the Lord was with him. The child grew and became strong in spirit, and he was in the desert until the day of his manifestation to Israel.

Practice of Faith

John the Baptist, the great herald of Jesus, came in the spirit of Elijah, a prophet and wonder-worker. The place near the Jordan River where John chose to baptize people, including Jesus, is near where Elijah was taken up to heaven "in a whirlwind." In the 1990s, after a peace accord between Jordan and Israel, the baptism site of Jesus and the wilderness of John the Baptist were made available for pilgrims. Archeologists uncovered the cave where John lived. ◆ Learn more about this holy place at www.baptismsite.com. ◆ If you can't make a pilgrimage to Jordan, go to a local river, the baptismal font at your church, or a fountain near your home and prayerfully imagine the scene—Jesus stepping into the water with John. That began Jesus' public ministry. ◆ Pray for the intercession of St. John the Baptist—that he will help you with your own mission as a disciple of Jesus.

Download more questions and activities for families, Christian initiation groups, and other adult groups at http://www.ltp.org/t-productsupplements.aspx.

Scripture Insights

As we celebrate the birthday of John the Baptist, the readings focus on John's role of inspiring people to prepare for the coming of the Messiah. The First Reading is one of four "Servant Songs" in the book of the prophet Isaiah. For Christians, these songs expressly prepare the way for the Messiah by foreshadowing the coming of Jesus, who fulfilled these prophecies. Here the Servant speaks and describes his call from his mother's womb; how God empowered him with gifts as a speaker; how difficult his task was going to be; how his task was to bring together the people of Israel while also being a light of salvation to the nations of the earth. The servant trusts in God while grieving over the sufferings that he has to face.

The Gospel reading from Luke narrates events surrounding John's birth—focusing on his name. For the people of Israel, a person's name expressed an aspect of their identity. The name, John, a common one among the people of Israel, was not found in his family's lineage. It means "the Lord has been gracious" because the elderly parents, Elizabeth and Zechariah, had lost all hope of conceiving a child in their old age. God had certainly favored them. This raised the question: "What, then, will this child be? For surely the hand of the Lord was with him."

The Second Reading, from Acts of the Apostles, answers this question. When Paul speaks in the synagogue of Antioch, he identifies John's role as preparing the way for the Messiah. This shows how well the early Church understood that the Baptist was the forerunner of Christ.

Like John the Baptist, our task is to continue his work of enabling the light of Christ to shine out more fully in our world.

◆ The Isaiah passage uses several poetic images to describe the Servant. How do you interpret them?

◆ Do you see God's grace blessing your life as God blessed John's life?

◆ How can you continue John's work in your own life?

READING I *Wisdom 1:13–15; 2:23–24*

God did not make death,
  nor does he rejoice in the destruction of
    the living.
For he fashioned all things that they might
      have being;
  and the creatures of the world
    are wholesome,
and there is not a destructive drug among them
  nor any domain of the netherworld on earth,
  for justice is undying.
For God formed man to be imperishable;
  the image of his own nature he made him.
But by the envy of the devil, death entered
    the world,
  and they who belong to his company
    experience it.

RESPONSORIAL PSALM
Psalm 30:2, 4, 5–6, 11, 12, 13 (2a)

R. I will praise you, Lord, for you have
      rescued me.

I will extol you, O LORD, for you drew me clear
  and did not let my enemies rejoice over me.
O LORD, you brought me up
      from the netherworld;
  you preserved me from among those going
      down into the pit. R.

Sing praise to the LORD, you his faithful ones,
  and give thanks to his holy name.
For his anger lasts but a moment;
  a lifetime, his good will.
At nightfall, weeping enters in,
  but with the dawn, rejoicing. R.

Hear, O LORD, and have pity on me;
  O LORD, be my helper.
You changed my mourning into dancing;
  O LORD, my God, forever will I give you
      thanks. R.

READING II *2 Corinthians 8:7, 9, 13–15*

Brothers and sisters: As you excel in every respect, in faith, discourse, knowledge, all earnestness, and in the love we have for you, may you excel in this gracious act also.

For you know the gracious act of our Lord Jesus Christ, that though he was rich, for your sake he became poor, so that by his poverty you might become rich. Not that others should have relief while you are burdened, but that as a matter of equality your abundance at the present time should supply their needs, so that their abundance may also supply your needs, that there may be equality. As it is written: / *Whoever had much did not have more, / and whoever had little did not have less.*

GOSPEL *Mark 5:21–43*

Shorter: Mark 5:21–24, 35b–43

When Jesus had crossed again in the boat to the other side, a large crowd gathered around him, and he stayed close to the sea. One of the synagogue officials, named Jairus, came forward. Seeing him he fell at his feet and pleaded earnestly with him, saying, "My daughter is at the point of death. Please, come lay your hands on her that she may get well and live." He went off with him, and a large crowd followed him and pressed upon him.

There was a woman afflicted with hemorrhages for twelve years. She had suffered greatly at the hands of many doctors and had spent all that she had. Yet she was not helped but only grew worse. She had heard about Jesus and came up behind him in the crowd and touched his cloak. She said, "If I but touch his clothes, I shall be cured." Immediately her flow of blood dried up. She felt in her body that she was healed of her affliction. Jesus, aware at once that power had gone out from him, turned around in the crowd and asked, "Who has touched my clothes?" But his disciples said to Jesus, "You see how the crowd is pressing upon you, and yet you ask, 'Who touched me?'" And he looked around to see who had done it. The woman, realizing what had happened to her, approached in fear and trembling. She fell down before Jesus and told him the whole truth.

He said to her, "Daughter, your faith has saved you. Go in peace and be cured of your affliction."

While he was still speaking, people from the synagogue official's house arrived and said, "Your daughter has died; why trouble the teacher any longer?" Disregarding the message that was reported, Jesus said to the synagogue official, "Do not be afraid; just have faith." He did not allow anyone to accompany him inside except Peter, James, and John, the brother of James. When they arrived at the house of the synagogue official, he caught sight of a commotion, people weeping and wailing loudly. So he went in and said to them, "Why this commotion and weeping? The child is not dead but asleep." And they ridiculed him. Then he put them all out. He took along the child's father and mother and those who were with him and entered the room where the child was. He took the child by the hand and said to her, "*Talitha koum*," which means, "Little girl, I say to you, arise!" The girl, a child of twelve, arose immediately and walked around. At that they were utterly astounded. He gave strict orders that no one should know this and said that she should be given something to eat.

Practice of Charity

Learn about the Church's ministry to the dying. ◆ Read the brief section called "A Better Way" near the end of the United States Conference of Catholic Bishops' 2011 statement on assisted suicide; visit http://www.migrate.usccb.org/issues-and-action /human-life-and-dignity/assisted-suicide/to-live -each-day or call 202-541-3000 to request a copy. The bishops echo St. John Paul's call for Christians to surround patients with love, support, and companionship, easing physical, emotional, and spiritual suffering. Facing death, they say, is one of the most important things we can do. ◆ Learn about your local, faith-based hospice. Send a note of support or a donation. ◆ Seek out someone who has companioned the dying as a volunteer and listen to their stories. Discern if this is a ministry to which you are called.

Download more questions and activities for families, Christian initiation groups, and other adult groups at http://www.ltp.org/t-productsupplements.aspx.

Scripture Insights

Today's readings celebrate God who has blessed us with life and they invite us to share these blessings with others. The Book of Wisdom reminds us that in creation we discover God's goodness, and Paul continues the reminder of God's graciousness, "For you know the gracious act of our Lord Jesus Christ, that though he was rich, for your sake he became poor." We discover God's goodness in creation, but also in his Son's Death and Resurrection, whereby we become a new creation through grace. Since we experience God's life of grace daily, Paul challenges us to imitate God's generosity by caring for those in need.

The two miracles recorded in today's Gospel offer examples of Jesus' generosity. Jesus responds to two people in dire need with his gift of life and grace. Mark narrates these miracles in an interesting way—similar to how we make a sandwich! The first miracle (the two slices of bread) shows Jesus responding to the urgent appeal of a synagogue official, Jairus, by restoring his twelve-year-old daughter to life. On the way (this is the sandwich-filling) Jesus responds to a woman who anxiously touches his cloak. Each takes the initiative in reaching out to Jesus in faith, and Jesus responds to their faith: "Daughter, your faith has saved you. Go in peace and be cured of your affliction." In both healings Jesus breaks taboos of his society: he touches a dead person and is touched by a bleeding woman. These actions make Jesus impure in the eyes of his society. Disregarding society's norms in order to bring life and healing, Jesus proves he is the source of life for all in need. Like Jesus, we are challenged to reach out to those in need and bring them God's love and compassion, making them feel alive again.

◆ How do Jairus and the bleeding woman demonstrate their faith? How might today's Responsorial Psalm be their response to Jesus' care for them?

◆ How do you understand Paul's words that "whoever is in Christ is a new creation"?

◆ What aspects of the Gospel reading inspire your faith?

READING I *Ezekiel 2:2–5*

As the LORD spoke to me, the spirit entered into me and set me on my feet, and I heard the one who was speaking say to me: Son of man, I am sending you to the Israelites, rebels who have rebelled against me; they and their ancestors have revolted against me to this very day. Hard of face and obstinate of heart are they to whom I am sending you. But you shall say to them: Thus says the Lord GOD! And whether they heed or resist—for they are a rebellious house—they shall know that a prophet has been among them.

RESPONSORIAL PSALM
Psalm 123:1–2, 2, 3–4 (2cd)

R. Our eyes are fixed on the Lord, pleading for
           his mercy.

To you I lift up my eyes
     who are enthroned in heaven —
as the eyes of servants
     are on the hands of their masters. R.

As the eyes of a maid
     are on the hands of her mistress,
so are our eyes on the LORD, our God,
     till he have pity on us. R.

Have pity on us, O LORD, have pity on us,
     for we are more than sated with contempt;
our souls are more than sated
     with the mockery of the arrogant,
     with the contempt of the proud. R.

READING II *2 Corinthians 12:7–10*

Brothers and sisters: That I, Paul, might not become too elated, because of the abundance of the revelations, a thorn in the flesh was given to me, an angel of Satan, to beat me, to keep me from being too elated. Three times I begged the Lord about this, that it might leave me, but he said to me, "My grace is sufficient for you, for power is made perfect in weakness." I will rather boast most gladly of my weaknesses, in order that the power of Christ may dwell with me. Therefore, I am content with weaknesses, insults, hardships, persecutions, and constraints, for the sake of Christ; for when I am weak, then I am strong.

GOSPEL *Mark 6:1–6*

Jesus departed from there and came to his native place, accompanied by his disciples. When the sabbath came he began to teach in the synagogue, and many who heard him were astonished. They said, "Where did this man get all this? What kind of wisdom has been given him? What mighty deeds are wrought by his hands! Is he not the carpenter, the son of Mary, and the brother of James and Joses and Judas and Simon? And are not his sisters here with us?" And they took offense at him. Jesus said to them, "A prophet is not without honor except in his native place and among his own kin and in his own house." So he was not able to perform any mighty deed there, apart from curing a few sick people by laying his hands on them. He was amazed at their lack of faith.

Practice of Faith

We often miss the holiness right in front of us. We expect God's action to be flashy and otherworldly, whereas Scripture and theology tell us that God acts through regular people and everyday events. ◆ Reflect on what the Jesuit paleontologist Pierre Teilhard de Chardin wrote: "God is not remote from us. He is at the point of my pen, my pick, my paintbrush, my needle—and my heart and my thoughts" (*Hymn of the Universe*, 1961). ◆ Often, we miss the sacredness of the everyday because we are preoccupied with the past or worried about the future—or, these days, because we have our noses in electronic devices. Take a silent walk in your neighborhood park. Try to be utterly open to what is around you. Cultivate awareness of God's presence. ◆ At the end of the day, journal about all the ways God was present to you in the past twenty-four hours.

Download more questions and activities for families, Christian initiation groups, and other adult groups at http://www.ltp.org/t-productsupplements.aspx.

Scripture Insights

Biblical prophets speak God's Word to God's people. They come as God's messengers proclaiming an uncomfortable message that challenges their hearers. Throughout the Scriptures, God's prophets encounter opposition and rejection. Today's readings offer three examples of God's messengers of mercy and grace being rejected because of their challenging message. "Hard of face and obstinate of heart are they to whom I am sending you," says God to the prophet Ezekiel. Even though the people of Israel continued to rebel against God by worshipping other gods, God never gave up calling them back.

Because of internal jealousy and rivalries, Paul had to defend himself to the Corinthian community that he had founded. Paul lays out his qualifications as an Apostle and prophet sent by God to preach God's message of salvation. When Paul's critics focus on his weaknesses, he shows how God's grace overcomes these weaknesses: "When I am weak, then I am strong."

Jesus also experiences opposition from those who know him best. His home town of Nazareth rejects him. Despite his wisdom and miracles, they arrogantly reject him because, as they say, "Is he not the carpenter, the son of Mary?" Jesus quotes a proverb that says, in essence: "A prophet is only despised in his own country, among his own relatives, and in his own house." He is one of us, so how could he attain such wisdom?

St. Augustine saw jealousy and envy as "the diabolical sin!" Envy keeps us from seeing God working in our world and hinders us from responding to God's vision for our world. Indeed, Jesus "was not able to perform any might deed there."

◆ What does Paul mean when he says: "When I am weak, then I am strong"? Have you ever experienced that in your own life?

◆ How have you ever experienced jealousy as "the diabolical sin"?

◆ What circumstances have made you aware of your prophetic calling as a Christian?

READING I *Amos 7:12–15*

Amaziah, priest of Bethel, said to Amos, "Off with you, visionary, flee to the land of Judah! There earn your bread by prophesying, but never again prophesy in Bethel; for it is the king's sanctuary and a royal temple." Amos answered Amaziah, "I was no prophet, nor have I belonged to a company of prophets; I was a shepherd and a dresser of sycamores. The LORD took me from following the flock, and said to me, Go, prophesy to my people Israel."

RESPONSORIAL PSALM
Psalm 85:9–10, 11–12, 13–14 (8)

R. Lord, let us see your kindness, and grant us
        your salvation.

I will hear what God proclaims;
    the LORD—for he proclaims peace.
Near indeed is his salvation to those who fear him,
    glory dwelling in our land. R.

Kindness and truth shall meet;
    justice and peace shall kiss.
Truth shall spring out of the earth,
    and justice shall look down from heaven. R.

The LORD himself will give his benefits;
    our land shall yield its increase.
Justice shall walk before him,
    and prepare the way of his steps. R.

READING II *Ephesians 1:3–14*

Shorter: Ephesians 1:3–10

Blessed be the God and Father of our Lord Jesus Christ, who has blessed us in Christ with every spiritual blessing in the heavens, as he chose us in him, before the foundation of the world, to be holy and without blemish before him. In love he destined us for adoption to himself through Jesus Christ, in accord with the favor of his will, for the praise of the glory of his grace that he granted us in the beloved. In him we have redemption by his blood, the forgiveness of transgressions, in accord with the riches of his grace that he lavished upon us. In all wisdom and insight, he has made known to us the mystery of his will in accord with his favor that he set forth in him as a plan for the fullness of times, to sum up all things in Christ, in heaven and on earth.

In him we were also chosen, destined in accord with the purpose of the One who accomplishes all things according to the intention of his will, so that we might exist for the praise of his glory, we who first hoped in Christ. In him you also, who have heard the word of truth, the gospel of your salvation, and have believed in him, were sealed with the promised Holy Spirit, which is the first installment of our inheritance toward redemption as God's possession, to the praise of his glory.

GOSPEL *Mark 6:7–13*

Jesus summoned the Twelve and began to send them out two by two and gave them authority over unclean spirits. He instructed them to take nothing for the journey but a walking stick—no food, no sack, no money in their belts. They were, however, to wear sandals but not a second tunic. He said to them, "Wherever you enter a house, stay there until you leave. Whatever place does not welcome you or listen to you, leave there and shake the dust off your feet in testimony against them." So they went off and preached repentance. The Twelve drove out many demons, and they anointed with oil many who were sick and cured them.

Practice of Hope

Few of us are called to be prophets or to wander towns driving out demons. But we all are called to be disciples. It's a matter of finding out how. One wise priest said that the path to finding your calling begins with learning about yourself. ◆ "Oh God ever the same, let me know myself, let me know you!" St. Augustine of Hippo, a seminal Doctor of the Church, made this plea 1,600 years ago, but it still cuts to the core of modern life. For a taste of St. Augustine's searing self-knowledge in his classic work *Confessions*, sample it in book 4, chapter 1: http://www.newadvent.org/fathers/110104.htm. ◆ Jesus asked his disciples to travel without comforts. See how you can simplify your life as a way to increase your dependence on God and enhance your discipleship. ◆ Consider a day of fasting along with your prayer so you can learn more about yourself and your path.

Download more questions and activities for families, Christian initiation groups, and other adult groups at http://www.ltp.org/t-productsupplements.aspx.

Scripture Insights

For today and the following six Sundays, we read from Paul's Letter to the Ephesians, whose theme is captured by these words: "In the Church Christ fulfills and reveals his own mystery as the purpose of God's plan: 'to unite all things in Christ'" (Ephesians 1:10; *Catechism of the Catholic Church*, 772). Our reading today presents a beautiful hymn praising God the Father who has chosen us in Christ and blessed us in the Spirit "with every spiritual blessing" from all eternity.

In the First Reading, God calls Amos from his ordinary life as a "shepherd and a dresser of sycamores" to become a prophet carrying God's Word to God's people. Amos' task is to challenge the people to repent and return to their covenant relationship.

In today's Gospel Jesus sends out the Apostles in pairs to share in his ministry of preaching and healing. Called to "preach repentance," they have no visible means of support, but God's grace was with them as they "drove out many demons and they anointed with oil many who were sick and cured them." This is the first of two places in the New Testament where healing occurs in relation to anointing with oil. The Letter of James shows the early Church continuing Jesus' instruction to heal those who are sick: "Are there any among you sick? They should call for the elders of the church and have them pray over them, anointing them with oil in the name of the Lord" (James 5:13). Today the Church continues this instruction in the Sacrament of the Anointing of the Sick

Like the prophet Amos and the Apostles, we have been chosen to be the Son's coworkers in continuing God's plan of bringing healing and grace to a broken world.

◆ To what is Paul referring when he says: "In him we have redemption by his blood, the forgiveness of transgressions"?

◆ What significance do you see in Amos being a shepherd?

◆ Like the Apostles in the Gospel, have you been able to step forward in total reliance upon Christ's grace? If not, how might you build the trust to do so?

READING I *Jeremiah 23:1–6*

Woe to the shepherds who mislead and scatter the flock of my pasture, says the LORD. Therefore, thus says the LORD, the God of Israel, against the shepherds who shepherd my people: You have scattered my sheep and driven them away. You have not cared for them, but I will take care to punish your evil deeds. I myself will gather the remnant of my flock from all the lands to which I have driven them and bring them back to their meadow; there they shall increase and multiply. I will appoint shepherds for them who will shepherd them so that they need no longer fear and tremble; and none shall be missing, says the LORD.

Behold, the days are coming, says the LORD,
   when I will raise up a righteous shoot
      to David;
as king he shall reign and govern wisely,
   he shall do what is just and
      right in the land.
In his days Judah shall be saved,
   Israel shall dwell in security.
This is the name they give him:
   "The LORD our justice."

RESPONSORIAL PSALM
Psalm 23:1–3, 3–4, 5, 6 (1)

R. The Lord is my shepherd;
      there is nothing I shall want.

The LORD is my shepherd; I shall not want.
   In verdant pastures he gives me repose;
beside restful waters he leads me;
   he refreshes my soul. R.

He guides me in right paths
   for his name's sake.
Even though I walk in the dark valley
   I fear no evil; for you are at my side
with your rod and your staff
   that give me courage. R.

You spread the table before me
   in the sight of my foes;
you anoint my head with oil;
   my cup overflows. R.

Only goodness and kindness follow me
   all the days of my life;
and I shall dwell in the house of the LORD
   for years to come. R.

READING II *Ephesians 2:13–18*

Brothers and sisters: In Christ Jesus you who once were far off have become near by the blood of Christ.

For he is our peace, he who made both one and broke down the dividing wall of enmity, through his flesh, abolishing the law with its commandments and legal claims, that he might create in himself one new person in place of the two, thus establishing peace, and might reconcile both with God, in one body, through the cross, putting that enmity to death by it. He came and preached peace to you who were far off and peace to those who were near, for through him we both have access in one Spirit to the Father.

GOSPEL *Mark 6:30–34*

The apostles gathered together with Jesus and reported all they had done and taught. He said to them, "Come away by yourselves to a deserted place and rest a while." People were coming and going in great numbers, and they had no opportunity even to eat. So they went off in the boat by themselves to a deserted place. People saw them leaving and many came to know about it. They hastened there on foot from all the towns and arrived at the place before them.

When he disembarked and saw the vast crowd, his heart was moved with pity for them, for they were like sheep without a shepherd; and he began to teach them many things.

Practice of Hope

One of the great shepherds of the Catholic Church was St. John Vianney, an early nineteenth-century priest in the small French town of Ars. He had flunked Latin and so was almost not ordained. But a priest took pity. The Curé of Ars, as St. John was called, spent hours listening to confessions made by people from all over the region. He became the patron of pastors. ◆ An acting company based in Washington state has made a film called "Vianney Speaks." You can order it at https://store.stluke productions.com/products/vianney-speaks-dvd or by calling 360-687-8029. ◆ There may be other "slow students" out there with great gifts. Consider volunteering at your local school as a mentor or tutor. ◆ August 4 is the memorial of St. John Vianney. Begin a novena for his intercession on July 27. For prayers, go to http://www.cureprayer group.org/novenaforpriests.htm.

Download more questions and activities for families, Christian initiation groups, and other adult groups at http://www.ltp.org/t-productsupplements.aspx.

Scripture Insights

The familiar image of the Good Shepherd pervades our readings today. The prophet Jeremiah reminds the leaders of God's people that they have wandered far from the vision God had for them. Instead of acting as true shepherds caring for God's flock, they have "scattered the flock of my pasture." Consequently, God presents a vision for the future in which the remnant of God's flock will be gathered together "from all the lands to which I have driven them." God promises to bring them together with a true shepherd guiding them to live in peace.

Paul proclaims that Christ Jesus went farther in fulfilling this vision by uniting all humanity in Christ Jesus, who is, as Paul says, "our peace, who made all one and broke down the dividing wall of enmity" among all people.

The Responsorial Psalm, "The Lord is my shepherd," is a beautiful commentary on how God's care shepherds God's people "near restful waters" and guides them "in right paths." These images are continued in the Gospel account where Jesus prepares to teach and feed the crowd who are "like sheep without a shepherd."

When Jesus looks on the crowds as "sheep without a shepherd," the scene acts as a prelude to the miracle of the feeding of the five thousand that we will hear next Sunday. Jesus' feelings for God's people are captured so graphically when Mark says, "His heart was moved with pity for them." The heart conveys the very depths of the love, compassion, and mercy that Jesus has for those he has come to lead back to his Father.

We are the sheep of his flock. The Lord continues to care for us in the Eucharist where he shepherds us, instructs us, nourishes us.

◆ What does Paul mean when he says that Christ Jesus "is our peace"?

◆ What feelings does the image of the "Lord is my Shepherd" evoke in you?

◆ What connection do you see between the words of the Psalm, "In verdant pastures you give me repose," and Jesus' words to the disciples, "Come away by yourselves to a deserted place and rest a while"?

July 29, 2018 SEVENTEENTH SUNDAY IN ORDINARY TIME

READING I *2 Kings 4:42–44*

A man came from Baal-shalishah bringing to Elisha, the man of God, twenty barley loaves made from the firstfruits, and fresh grain in the ear. Elisha said, "Give it to the people to eat." But his servant objected, "How can I set this before a hundred people?" Elisha insisted, "Give it to the people to eat. For thus says the LORD, 'They shall eat and there shall be some left over.'" And when they had eaten, there was some left over, as the LORD had said.

RESPONSORIAL PSALM *Psalm 145:10–11, 15–16, 17–18 (see 16)*

R. The hand of the Lord feeds us;
he answers all our needs.

Let all your works give you thanks, O LORD,
and let your faithful ones bless you.
Let them discourse of the glory of your kingdom
and speak of your might. R.

The eyes of all look hopefully to you,
and you give them their food in due season;
you open your hand
and satisfy the desire of every living thing. R.

The LORD is just in all his ways
and holy in all his works.
The LORD is near to all who call upon him,
to all who call upon him in truth. R.

READING II *Ephesians 4:1–6*

Brothers and sisters: I, a prisoner for the Lord, urge you to live in a manner worthy of the call you have received, with all humility and gentleness, with patience, bearing with one another through love, striving to preserve the unity of the spirit through the bond of peace: one body and one Spirit, as you were also called to the one hope of your call; one Lord, one faith, one baptism; one God and Father of all, who is over all and through all and in all.

GOSPEL *John 6:1–15*

Jesus went across the Sea of Galilee. A large crowd followed him, because they saw the signs he was performing on the sick. Jesus went up on the mountain, and there he sat down with his disciples. The Jewish feast of Passover was near. When Jesus raised his eyes and saw that a large crowd was coming to him, he said to Philip, "Where can we buy enough food for them to eat?" He said this to test him, because he himself knew what he was going to do. Philip answered him, "Two hundred days' wages worth of food would not be enough for each of them to have a little." One of his disciples, Andrew, the brother of Simon Peter, said to him, "There is a boy here who has five barley loaves and two fish; but what good are these for so many?" Jesus said, "Have the people recline." Now there was a great deal of grass in that place. So the men reclined, about five thousand in number. Then Jesus took the loaves, gave thanks, and distributed them to those who were reclining, and also as much of the fish as they wanted. When they had had their fill, he said to his disciples, "Gather the fragments left over, so that nothing will be wasted." So they collected them, and filled twelve wicker baskets with fragments from the five barley loaves that had been more than they could eat. When the people saw the sign he had done, they said, "This is truly the Prophet, the one who is to come into the world." Since Jesus knew that they were going to come and carry him off to make him king, he withdrew again to the mountain alone.

Practice of Hope

"There is a boy here who has five barley loaves and two fish; but what good are these for so many?" Often, we underestimate what we can do to help people. We can feed them literally, but we can also nourish them with kindness, fellowship, or attentive listening. Small acts can yield big results. ◆ Do you have a family member or friend with whom relations are stressed? Invite that person out for coffee or a meal and simply say, "I want to hear what you are feeling about what's been happening." Then be quiet and listen. ◆ Watch the G-rated 1987 film *Babette's Feast*. A Parisian refugee comes to an austere Nordic village and feeds people in a way that transforms them. ◆ Pray for the intercession of Dorothy Day, a founder of the Catholic Worker Movement, who saw to the physical, social, and spiritual needs of people, even with sparse resources.

Download more questions and activities for families, Christian initiation groups, and other adult groups at http://www.ltp.org/t-productsupplements.aspx.

Scripture Insights

Last week's Gospel acted as an introduction to the miracle of the feeding of five thousand. Instead of continuing with the account from Mark's Gospel, the Church has deliberately chosen to read the narrative from John's Gospel. The reason is two-fold: John gives a longer and more detailed description of the miracle. John also offers us an insight into the deeper meaning of this miracle by using specific details to draw attention to symbolism that foreshadows the Eucharist. For the next four weeks we continue to read from John's narrative as we gain a deeper insight into the meaning of the Eucharist.

Jesus, seated on a mountain beside the Sea of Galilee, reminds us of Moses on Mount Sinai. A boy offers Jesus five barley loaves and two fish that Jesus uses to feed the vast crowd. Many of the details of the story remind us of the Eucharist: the miracle occurs just before the second *Passover*. John uses the Greek word *eucharisteo* for "giving thanks" (from which comes the word "Eucharist"). A further interesting point is that the Greek word *klasma* for "fragment" was used in the early Church to refer to the Communion host.

The references to "young boy" (or "servant") and "barley loaves" are details that John deliberately uses to connect to the First Reading today, in which Elisha orders the servant to distribute "the twenty barley loaves." Just as Elisha's miracle reminded the people of God's care for them in the desert by feeding them with manna from heaven, so Jesus' miracle shows the people that God, through his Son, is again feeding his people. By deliberately connecting the description to the Eucharist, John shows that this miracle of nourishing God's people continues today every time the Eucharist is celebrated.

◆ How do the words that John uses to describe Jesus' actions remind you of the Eucharist?

◆ Why might the writer of John's Gospel deliberately take up images found in the reading from 2 Kings? Why would the Lectionary place these on the same Sunday?

◆ How might today's Responsorial Psalm work as a prayer of thanksgiving for the Eucharist?

READING I *Exodus 16:2–4, 12–15*

The whole Israelite community grumbled against Moses and Aaron. The Israelites said to them, "Would that we had died at the LORD's hand in the land of Egypt, as we sat by our fleshpots and ate our fill of bread! But you had to lead us into this desert to make the whole community die of famine!"

Then the LORD said to Moses, "I will now rain down bread from heaven for you. Each day the people are to go out and gather their daily portion; thus will I test them, to see whether they follow my instructions or not.

"I have heard the grumbling of the Israelites. Tell them: In the evening twilight you shall eat flesh, and in the morning you shall have your fill of bread, so that you may know that I, the LORD, am your God."

In the evening quail came up and covered the camp. In the morning a dew lay all about the camp, and when the dew evaporated, there on the surface of the desert were fine flakes like hoarfrost on the ground. On seeing it, the Israelites asked one another, "What is this?" for they did not know what it was. But Moses told them, "This is the bread that the LORD has given you to eat."

RESPONSORIAL PSALM
Psalm 78:3–4, 23–24, 25, 54 (24b)

R. The Lord gave them bread from heaven.

What we have heard and know,
   and what our fathers have declared to us,
we will declare to the generation to come
   the glorious deeds of the LORD
         and his strength
   and the wonders that he wrought. R.

He commanded the skies above
   and opened the doors of heaven;
he rained manna upon them for food
   and gave them heavenly bread. R.

Man ate the bread of angels,
   food he sent them in abundance.
And he brought them to his holy land,
to the mountains his right hand
      had won. R.

READING II *Ephesians 4:17, 20–24*

Brothers and sisters: I declare and testify in the Lord that you must no longer live as the Gentiles do, in the futility of their minds; that is not how you learned Christ, assuming that you have heard of him and were taught in him, as truth is in Jesus, that you should put away the old self of your former way of life, corrupted through deceitful desires, and be renewed in the spirit of your minds, and put on the new self, created in God's way in righteousness and holiness of truth.

GOSPEL *John 6:24–35*

When the crowd saw that neither Jesus nor his disciples were there, they themselves got into boats and came to Capernaum looking for Jesus. And when they found him across the sea they said to him, "Rabbi, when did you get here?" Jesus answered them and said, "Amen, amen, I say to you, you are looking for me not because you saw signs but because you ate the loaves and were filled. Do not work for food that perishes but for the food that endures for eternal life, which the Son of Man will give you. For on him the Father, God, has set his seal." So they said to him, "What can we do to accomplish the works of God?" Jesus answered and said to them, "This is the work of God, that you believe in the one he sent." So they said to him, "What sign can you do, that we may see and believe in you? What can you do? Our ancestors ate manna in the desert, as it is written: *He gave them bread from heaven to eat.*" So Jesus said to them, "Amen, amen, I say to you, it was not Moses who gave the bread from heaven; my Father gives you the true bread from heaven. For the bread of God is that which comes down from heaven and gives life to the world."

So they said to him, "Sir, give us this bread always." Jesus said to them, "I am the bread of life; whoever comes to me will never hunger, and whoever believes in me will never thirst."

Practice of Faith

Whether through manna in the desert, or Jesus, the bread of life, God feeds his people what they need. But there is also an expectation that the People of God will live right. It's good for us to know that what sustains us comes from God. One good response is to develop habits toward food sustainability. You could eat food produced locally so that transportation does not create greenhouse gases that harm God's earth. ◆ Read about small scale farms in paragraph 129 of Pope Francis' encyclical *Laudato Si'*: http://w2.vatican.va/content/francesco/en/encyclicals/documents/papa-francesco_20150524_enciclica-laudato-si.html. The pope says they are good for the planet and create jobs. ◆ Join a community-supported agriculture farm, which will sell you local produce. ◆ It's prime gardening season, with harvest at hand. Stand in your garden or yard, or over your vegetable drawer, and give thanks to God for the fruits of the earth, one of the oldest kinds of prayer known to humans.

Download more questions and activities for families, Christian initiation groups, and other adult groups at http://www.ltp.org/t-productsupplements.aspx.

Scripture Insights

The people of Israel show in the First Reading how difficult it was for them to allow God to lead them on their journey from slavery to the Promised Land. They complain and long for the old days "as we sat by our fleshpots and ate our fill of bread" in Egypt. How easily they forgot what the Lord had done for them! Despite their ingratitude, God never abandoned them. Instead, God gave them manna, "bread from heaven," as the Responsorial Psalm says.

The Gospel continues John's narrative, setting the stage for a discourse in which Jesus explains the symbolism and significance of the miracle of the feeding of the five thousand. He challenges his hearers about their motivations. They followed him because they focused on the material gift he had given them—namely, bread to eat. Instead, Jesus focuses on the deeper spiritual meaning they should seek, "the food that endures for eternal life, which the Son of Man will give you." When they point to the gift of manna their ancestors ate in the desert, Jesus reminds them that it was not Moses who gave them manna, but the Father who "gives you the true bread form heaven." When Jesus says "I am the bread of life," he shows how the manna in the desert foreshadowed his own coming. "I am" is a way Jesus identifies himself with God, claiming his divinity. He speaks in the manner of God in the Old Testament where "I am" is God's name (Exodus 3:14). As "the bread of life," Jesus is the one who gives bread that is eternal life. Real hunger can only be satisfied through a personal relationship with Jesus.

◆ What does the image of "the fleshpots of Egypt" convey to you?

◆ Reflect on how the Old Testament miracle of the manna in the desert foreshadows the feeding of five thousand. How would you explain that to someone outside the faith?

◆ How do you see the Sacrament of the Eucharist nourishing you on your journey of life? And how does it offer you a foretaste of the eternal life that is to come?

READING I *1 Kings 19:4–8*

Elijah went a day's journey into the desert, until he came to a broom tree and sat beneath it. He prayed for death, saying: "This is enough, O LORD! Take my life, for I am no better than my fathers." He lay down and fell asleep under the broom tree, but then an angel touched him and ordered him to get up and eat. Elijah looked and there at his head was a hearth cake and a jug of water. After he ate and drank, he lay down again, but the angel of the LORD came back a second time, touched him, and ordered, "Get up and eat, else the journey will be too long for you!" He got up, ate, and drank; then strengthened by that food, he walked forty days and forty nights to the mountain of God, Horeb.

RESPONSORIAL PSALM
Psalm 34:2–3, 4–5, 6–7, 8–9 (9a)

R. Taste and see the goodness of the Lord.

I will bless the LORD at all times;
　　his praise shall be ever in my mouth.
Let my soul glory in the LORD;
　　the lowly will hear me and be glad. R.

Glorify the LORD with me,
　　let us together extol his name.
I sought the LORD, and he answered me
　　and delivered me from all my fears. R.

Look to him that you may be radiant with joy,
　　and your faces may not blush with shame.
When the afflicted man called out,
　　　　the LORD heard,
　　and from all his distress he saved him. R.

The angel of the LORD encamps
　　around those who fear him and delivers them.
Taste and see how good the LORD is;
　　blessed the man who takes refuge in him. R.

READING II *Ephesians 4:30—5:2*

Brothers and sisters: Do not grieve the Holy Spirit of God, with which you were sealed for the day of redemption. All bitterness, fury, anger, shouting, and reviling must be removed from you, along with all malice. And be kind to one another, compassionate, forgiving one another as God has forgiven you in Christ.

So be imitators of God, as beloved children, and live in love, as Christ loved us and handed himself over for us as a sacrificial offering to God for a fragrant aroma.

GOSPEL *John 6:41–51*

The Jews murmured about Jesus because he said, "I am the bread that came down from heaven," and they said, "Is this not Jesus, the son of Joseph? Do we not know his father and mother? Then how can he say, 'I have come down from heaven'?" Jesus answered and said to them, "Stop murmuring among yourselves. No one can come to me unless the Father who sent me draw him, and I will raise him on the last day. It is written in the prophets: *They shall all be taught by God.* Everyone who listens to my Father and learns from him comes to me. Not that anyone has seen the Father except the one who is from God; he has seen the Father. Amen, amen, I say to you, whoever believes has eternal life. I am the bread of life. Your ancestors ate the manna in the desert, but they died; this is the bread that comes down from heaven so that one may eat it and not die. I am the living bread that came down from heaven; whoever eats this bread will live forever; and the bread that I will give is my flesh for the life of the world."

Practice of Faith

Family meals are sacred moments, even between couples. Meals in common signify unity, but also are a time to thank God for blessings of food, both physical and spiritual. As with Elijah, meals strengthen us for mission—so does community life. ◆ If your mealtime prayers have lapsed, or if you just want to give life to an old practice, go to Xavier University's resource guide: http://www.xavier.edu/jesuitresource/online-resources/Mealtime-Prayers.cfm or call 513-745-3777. There are dozens of prayers and prayer cards that can be downloaded. ◆ Assign a different family member as prayer leader each night. Let him or her choose a prayer from the list, or come up with an original. ◆ Before praying over the food, light a candle as a concrete sign of the sacredness of the meal. The prayer leader can do the lighting, provided that would be safe.

Download more questions and activities for families, Christian initiation groups, and other adult groups at http://www.ltp.org/t-productsupplements.aspx.

Scripture Insights

All three readings have examples of people complaining in different ways. Paul contrasts two ways of life. One way, a complaining and dissatisfied life, results in "bitterness, fury, anger . . . " In the other path, the life of the Spirit, others are treated with love and compassion and everyone strives to be "imitators of God, as beloved children who live in love."

In the First Reading, the prophet Elijah is despondent. The king and queen of Israel seek to kill him because he had destroyed the prophets of Baal. Afraid, Elijah calls upon the Lord to end his life, saying that he has suffered enough. In the midst of his complaint, the Lord strengthens Elijah with food. This food renews Elijah and he sets out to "the mountain of God, Horeb," where the Ten Commandments were given to Moses (Deuteronomy 5:2).

The people of Israel also complain against Jesus in John's Gospel today as the "Bread of Life Discourse" continues. Jesus contrasts the bread that he is to give with the bread that their ancestors ate. Their ancestors ate the bread and died. On the other hand, Jesus, the true living bread, guarantees eternal life for all who eat of it. John goes on to explain that "the bread that I will give is my flesh for the life of the world." The idiom "flesh and blood" is a Hebrew way of referring to the "whole person." Here John deliberately connects the Death of Jesus and the Eucharist. By eating of his body, the bread of life, Jesus promises the fruits of his Death and Resurrection: eternal life and a living relationship with God.

As God sustained and renewed Elijah's life, so Jesus now sustains his followers through himself, "the living bread that came down from heaven." The Eucharist is the true food for our life's journey.

◆ Why do "the Jews" complain in today's Gospel?

◆ How would you explain the connection between the Eucharist and Jesus' Death and Resurrection to a newcomer?

◆ In your own experience how does the Eucharist renew you and give you a new sense of strength for your life's journey?

READING I   *Proverbs 9:1–6*

Wisdom has built her house,
    she has set up her seven columns;
she has dressed her meat, mixed her wine,
    yes, she has spread her table.
She has sent out her maidens; she calls
    from the heights out over the city:
"Let whoever is simple turn in here;
    to the one who lacks understanding,
        she says,
Come, eat of my food,
    and drink of the wine I have mixed!
Forsake foolishness that you may live;
    advance in the way of understanding."

RESPONSORIAL PSALM
Psalm 34:2–3, 4–5, 6–7 (9a)

R. Taste and see the goodness of the Lord.

I will bless the LORD at all times;
    his praise shall be ever in my mouth.
Let my soul glory in the LORD;
    the lowly will hear me and be glad. R.

Glorify the LORD with me,
    let us together extol his name.
I sought the LORD, and he answered me
    and delivered me from all my fears. R.

Look to him that you may be radiant with joy,
    and your faces may not blush with shame.
When the poor one called out, the LORD heard,
    and from all his distress he saved him. R.

READING II   *Ephesians 5:15–20*

Brothers and sisters: Watch carefully how you live, not as foolish persons but as wise, making the most of the opportunity, because the days are evil. Therefore, do not continue in ignorance, but try to understand what is the will of the Lord. And do not get drunk on wine, in which lies debauchery, but be filled with the Spirit, addressing one another in psalms and hymns and spiritual songs, singing and playing to the Lord in your hearts, giving thanks always and for everything in the name of our Lord Jesus Christ to God the Father.

GOSPEL   *John 6:51–58*

Jesus said to the crowds: "I am the living bread that came down from heaven; whoever eats this bread will live forever; and the bread that I will give is my flesh for the life of the world."

The Jews quarreled among themselves, saying, "How can this man give us his flesh to eat?" Jesus said to them, "Amen, amen, I say to you, unless you eat the flesh of the Son of Man and drink his blood, you do not have life within you. Whoever eats my flesh and drinks my blood has eternal life, and I will raise him on the last day. For my flesh is true food, and my blood is true drink. Whoever eats my flesh and drinks my blood remains in me and I in him. Just as the living Father sent me and I have life because of the Father, so also the one who feeds on me will have life because of me. This is the bread that came down from heaven. Unlike your ancestors who ate and still died, whoever eats this bread will live forever."

Practice of Faith

Taking part in Eucharist is our unparalleled way to closer unity with Jesus. The more fully we get involved, the more we advance toward the promised eternal life. The Second Vatican Council called us to "fully conscious and active participation" in liturgy. ◆ Read paragraphs 47 and 48 of *Sacrosanctum Concilium*, the Second Vatican Council's *Constitution on the Sacred Liturgy*, available at http://www.vatican.va/archive/hist_coun cils/ii_vatican_council/documents/vat-ii _const_19631204_sacrosanctum-concilium_en. html. ◆ Arrive at Mass at least ten minutes early so you can quietly prepare, perhaps by reading the Scriptures ahead of time or reflecting silently on the meaning of what is about to happen. ◆ During Mass, open yourself to a new kind of awareness, receiving the words, sights, sounds, and smells of the liturgy. Be in the sacred moment instead of thinking about the past or the future.

Download more questions and activities for families, Christian initiation groups, and other adult groups at http://www.ltp.org/t-productsupplements.aspx.

Scripture Insights

Proverbs opens the Liturgy of the Word with the image of Woman Wisdom calling us to share in her banquet. Begotten by God and helper at creation (8:22–31), Woman Wisdom promises to feed us with insight and knowledge. For Christians, her banquet foreshadows the gift of the Eucharist

Today's Gospel continues the Bread of Life discourse with some of the deepest theological and sacramental insights in the Gospel of John. With Jesus' statement that "the bread that I will give is my flesh for the life of the world" John connects the Incarnation with the events of salvation: "The Word became flesh" (John 1:14) for the purpose of giving his life for the salvation of the world.

This is also is a reminder of the words of the Institution of the Eucharist: "Then he took the bread, said the blessing, broke it, and gave it to them, saying, 'This is my body, which will be given for you . . .'" (Luke 22:19). The connection between the Eucharist and Jesus' Death is further strengthened by the words "unless you drink his blood." As Jesus is "the living water" (John 4:11–14), he is also the "living bread." As the Sacrament of Baptism confers the life of God, the Sacrament of the Eucharist nourishes this life. For John, the purpose of the Incarnation of the Word was more than becoming flesh to take on our human nature. The Incarnation also embraced Jesus' Death and Resurrection—the Paschal Mystery—whose life-giving effects would nourish believers in the celebration of the Eucharist.

Jesus' words culminate by saying that "the one who feeds on me will have life because of me." Unequivocally Jesus tells us that in the Eucharist we share in the very life of God.

◆ In what ways have you been a seeker of Wisdom?

◆ How does John show that the Incarnation also had in mind Jesus' Death for our salvation?

◆ In what way might today's Responsorial Psalm be a prayer of thanksgiving for the Eucharist?

READING I *Joshua 24:1–2a, 15–17, 18b*

Joshua gathered together all the tribes of Israel at Shechem, summoning their elders, their leaders, their judges, and their officers. When they stood in ranks before God, Joshua addressed all the people: "If it does not please you to serve the Lord, decide today whom you will serve, the gods your fathers served beyond the River or the gods of the Amorites in whose country you are now dwelling. As for me and my household, we will serve the Lord."

But the people answered, "Far be it from us to forsake the Lord for the service of other gods. For it was the Lord, our God, who brought us and our fathers up out of the land of Egypt, out of a state of slavery. He performed those great miracles before our very eyes and protected us along our entire journey and among the peoples through whom we passed. Therefore we also will serve the Lord, for he is our God."

RESPONSORIAL PSALM *Psalm 34:2–3, 16–17, 18–19, 20–21 (9a)*

R. Taste and see the goodness of the Lord.

I will bless the Lord at all times;
   his praise shall be ever in my mouth.
Let my soul glory in the Lord;
   the lowly will hear me and be glad. R.

The Lord has eyes for the just,
   and ears for their cry.
The Lord confronts the evildoers,
   to destroy remembrance
      of them from the earth. R.

When the just cry out, the Lord hears them,
   and from all their distress
      he rescues them.
The Lord is close to the brokenhearted;
   and those who are crushed
      in spirit he saves. R.

Many are the troubles of the just one,
   but out of them all the Lord delivers him;
he watches over all his bones;
   not one of them shall be broken. R.

READING II *Ephesians 5:21–32*

Shorter: Ephesians 5:2a, 25–32

Brothers and sisters: Be subordinate to one another out of reverence for Christ. Wives should be subordinate to their husbands as to the Lord. For the husband is head of his wife just as Christ is head of the church, he himself the savior of the body. As the church is subordinate to Christ, so wives should be subordinate to their husbands in everything. Husbands, love your wives, even as Christ loved the church and handed himself over for her to sanctify her, cleansing her by the bath of water with the word, that he might present to himself the church in splendor, without spot or wrinkle or any such thing, that she might be holy and without blemish. So also husbands should love their wives as their own bodies. He who loves his wife loves himself. For no one hates his own flesh but rather nourishes and cherishes it, even as Christ does the church, because we are members of his body.

For this reason a man shall leave his father
    and his mother
   and be joined to his wife,
   and the two shall become one flesh.

This is a great mystery, but I speak in reference to Christ and the church.

GOSPEL *John 6:60–69*

Many of Jesus' disciples who were listening said, "This saying is hard; who can accept it?" Since Jesus knew that his disciples were murmuring about this, he said to them, "Does this shock you? What if you were to see the Son of Man ascending to where he was before? It is the spirit that gives life, while the flesh is of no avail. The words I have spoken to you are Spirit and life. But there are some of you who do not believe." Jesus knew from the beginning the ones who would not believe and the one who would betray him. And he said, "For this reason I have told you that no one can come to me unless it is granted him by my Father."

As a result of this, many of his disciples returned to their former way of life and no longer accompanied him. Jesus then said to the Twelve, "Do you also want to leave?" Simon Peter answered him, "Master, to whom shall we go? You have the words of eternal life. We have come to believe and are convinced that you are the Holy One of God."

Practice of Hope

We cannot deny it; many young people step away from practicing their faith—at least temporarily. Like some of the disciples in today's Gospel, they find the ways of Jesus and the Church hard to accept. What is our response? Scripture makes it clear that Jesus and the Lord of Israel never forced adherence, but instead invited, urged, and appealed. That is still how God works. ◆ Read section 3 of Pope Francis' message for World Youth Day 2016: https://w2.vatican.va/content/francesco /en/messages/youth/documents/papa-fran cesco_20150815_messaggio-giovani_2016.html. ◆ Look up the Catholic campus ministry at the nearest college or university; volunteer, send a donation, or write a note of support. ◆ Pick one young person in your life, someone who has set aside faith life. Pray for that person and if it feels appropriate, send a note that is encouraging, but not condemning.

Download more questions and activities for families, Christian initiation groups, and other adult groups at http://www.ltp.org/t-productsupplements.aspx.

Scripture Insights

In life we face many important choices, and today's readings illustrate some of them. In the Letter to the Ephesians, Paul speaks about the foundational choice man and woman make when they commit themselves totally to each other: "and the two shall become one flesh." In their self-sacrificing love for each other in marriage, we glimpse the depths of Christ's self-sacrificing love for the Church.

The Book of Joshua presents the foundational choice the people of Israel face on entering the Promised Land: "Decide today whom you will serve, the gods your fathers served beyond the River or the gods of the Amorites?" Memories of God's faithful love, mercy, and care influence their decision. "Therefore, we also will serve the LORD, for he is our God." The people renew themselves to the covenant relationship with God.

At the conclusion to the Bread of Life discourse, Jesus asks his followers to make their foundational choice for or against him. So many were shocked by Jesus' words and walked away when he identified himself as the "Bread that came down from heaven" and then went further by adding "unless you eat the flesh of the Son of Man and drink his blood you have no life in you." So Jesus asked his own disciples if they too wished to leave. As usual, Peter replies on behalf of the others, "Master, to whom shall we go? You have the words of eternal life."

As God committed himself to his people, Jesus committed himself to us, the new people of God, through his Death and Resurrection. The self-sacrificing love in Christian Marriage witnesses to God's love for us in Christ Jesus.

◆ How does Paul's call to love in marriage show that husband and wife are equal partners?

◆ What in the Gospel narrative shows that Peter's commitment to Jesus is a response to the gift of faith he has received?

◆ Reflect on your own relationship and commitment to the Lord. In what ways are you able to confess with Peter: "Master, to whom shall we go? You have the words of eternal life."

Prayer before Reading the Word

O strong and faithful God,
in Jesus we have found the path to wisdom.

Pierce our inmost heart with the two-edged
     sword of your Word.
Open our eyes to your presence everywhere.
Unstop our ears to hear the challenge of
     your Word.
Loose our tongues in songs of praise
and fearless witness to your justice.

We ask this through our Lord Jesus Christ,
your Son, who lives and reigns with you
in the unity of the Holy Spirit,
one God, for ever and ever. Amen.

Prayer after Reading the Word

Lord our God,
whose voice we have heard in our midst,
whose face we have seen in Christ Jesus,
and whose Spirit dwells within us:

Enlightened by your wisdom,
may we value aright the things of time and
     of eternity
and, freed from preoccupation with this
     world's wealth,
be poor enough to welcome the incomparable
     treasure of your Kingdom.

Teach us to use well the riches of nature and grace,
to care generously for those in need,
and to look carefully to our own conduct.

We ask this through our Lord Jesus Christ,
your Son, who lives and reigns with you
in the unity of the Holy Spirit,
one God, for ever and ever. Amen.

Weekday Readings

September 3: *1 Corinthians 2:1–5; Luke 4:16–30*
September 4: *1 Corinthians 2:10b–16; Luke 4:31–37*
September 5: *1 Corinthians 3:1–9; Luke 4:38–44*
September 6: *1 Corinthians 3:18–23; Luke 5:1–11*
September 7: *1 Corinthians 4:1–5; Luke 5:33–39*
September 8: Feast of the Nativity of the
    Blessed Virgin Mary
    Micah 5:1–4a or Romans 8:28–30; Matthew 1:1–16,
    18–23 or 1:18–23

September 10: *1 Corinthians 5:1–8; Luke 6:6–11*
September 11: *1 Corinthians 6:1–11; Luke 6:12–19*
September 12: *1 Corinthians 7:25–31; Luke 6:20–26*
September 13: *1 Corinthians 8:1b–7, 11–13; Luke 6:27–38*
September 14: Feast of the Exaltation of the Holy Cross
    Numbers 21:4b–9; Philippians 2:6–11; John 3:13–17
September 15: *1 Corinthians 10:14–22; John 19:25–27 or*
    Luke 2:33–35

September 17: *1 Corinthians 11:17–26, 33; Luke 7:1–10*
September 18: *1 Corinthians 12:12–14, 27–31a; Luke 7:11–17*
September 19: *1 Corinthians 12:31—13:13; Luke 7:31–35*
September 20: *1 Corinthians 15:1–11; Luke 7:36–50*
September 21: Feast of St. Matthew
    Ephesians 4:1–7, 11–13; Matthew 9:9–13
September 22: *1 Corinthians 15:35–37, 42–49; Luke 8:4–15*

September 24: *Proverbs 3:27–34; Luke 8:16–18*
September 25: *Proverbs 21:1–6, 10–13; Luke 8:19–21*
September 26: *Proverbs 30:5–9; Luke 9:1–6*
September 27: *Ecclesiastes 1:2–11; Luke 9:7–9*
September 28: *Ecclesiastes 3:1–11; Luke 9:18–22*
September 29: Feast of St. Michael, St. Gabriel,
    and St. Raphael
    Daniel 7:9–10, 13–14 or Revelation 12:7–12a;
    John 1:47– 51

October 1: *Job 1:6–22; Luke 9:46–50*
October 2: *Job 3:1–3, 11–17, 20–23; Matthew 18:1–5, 10*
October 3: *Job 9:1–12, 14–16; Luke 9:57–62*
October 4: *Job 19:21–27; Luke 10:1–12*
October 5: *Job 38:1, 12–21; 40:3–5; Luke 10:13–16*
October 6: *Job 42:1–3, 5–6, 12–17; Luke 10:17–24*

October 8: *Galatians 1:6–12; Luke 10:25–37*
October 9: *Galatians 1:13–24; Luke 10:38–42*
October 10: *Galatians 2:1–2, 7–14; Luke 11:1–4*
October 11: *Galatians 3:1–5; Luke 11:5–13*
October 12: *Galatians 3:7–14; Luke 11:15–26*
October 13: *Galatians 3:22–29; Luke 11:27–28*

October 15: *Galatians 4:22–24, 26–27, 31—5:1; Luke 11:29–32*
October 16: *Galatians 5:1–6; Luke 11:37–41*
October 17: *Galatians 5:18–25; Luke 11:42–46*
October 18: Feast of St. Luke
    2 Timothy 4:10–17b; Luke 10:1–9
October 19: *Ephesians 1:11–14; Luke 12:1–7*
October 20: *Ephesians 1:15–23; Luke 12:8–12*

October 22: *Ephesians 2:1–10; Luke 12:13–21*
October 23: *Ephesians 2:12–22; Luke 12:35–38*
October 24: *Ephesians 3:2–12; Luke 12:39–48*
October 25: *Ephesians 3:14–21; Luke 12:49–53*
October 26: *Ephesians 4:1–6; Luke 12:54–59*
October 27: *Ephesians 4:7–16; Luke 13:1–9*

October 29: *Ephesians 4:32—5:8; Luke 13:10–17*
October 30: *Ephesians 5:21–33 or 5:2a, 25–32; Luke 13:18–21*
October 31: *Ephesians 6:1–9; Luke 13:22–30*
November 1: Solemnity of All Saints
    Revelation 7:2–4, 9–14; 1 John 3:1– 3; Matthew 5:1–12a
November 2: Commemoration of all the Faithful Departed
    Wisdom 3:1–9; Romans 5:5–11; John 6:37–40
November 3: *Philippians 1:18b–26; Luke 14:1, 7–11*

November 5: *Philippians 2:1–4; Luke 14:12–14*
November 6: *Philippians 2:5–11; Luke 14:15–24*
November 7: *Philippians 2:12–18; Luke 14:25–33*
November 8: *Philippians 3:3–8a; Luke 15:1–10*
November 9: Feast of the Dedication of the Lateran Basilica
    Ezekiel 47:1–2, 8–9, 12; 1 Corinthians 3:9c–11, 16–17;
    John 2:13–22
November 10: *Philippians 4:10–19; Luke 16:9–15*

November 12: *Titus 1:1–9; Luke 17:1–6*
November 13: *Titus 2:1–8, 11–14; Luke 17:7–10*
November 14: *Titus 3:1–7; Luke 17:11–19*
November 15: *Philemon 7–20; Luke 17:20–25*
November 16: *2 John 4–9; Luke 17:26–37*
November 17: *3 John 5–8; Luke 18:1–8*

November 19: *Revelation 1:1–4; 2:1–5; Luke 18:35–43*
November 20: *Revelation 3:1–6, 14–22; Luke 19:1–10*
November 21: *Revelation 4:1–11; Luke 19:11–28*
November 22: *Revelation 5:1–10; Luke 19:41–44*
November 23: *Revelation 10:8–11; Luke 19:45–48*
November 24: *Revelation 11:4–12; Luke 20:27–40*

November 26: *Revelation 14:1–3, 4b–5; Luke 21:1–4*
November 27: *Revelation 14:14–19; Luke 21:5–11*
November 28: *Revelation 15:1–4; Luke 21:12–19*
November 29: *Revelation 18:1–2, 21–23; 19:1–3, 9a;*
    Luke 21:20–28
November 30: Feast of St. Andrew
    Romans 10:9–18; Matthew 4:18–22
December 1: *Revelation 22:1–7; Luke 21:34–36*

READING I *Deuteronomy 4:1–2, 6–8*

Moses said to the people: "Now, Israel, hear the statutes and decrees which I am teaching you to observe, that you may live, and may enter in and take possession of the land which the LORD, the God of your fathers, is giving you. In your observance of the commandments of the LORD, your God, which I enjoin upon you, you shall not add to what I command you nor subtract from it. Observe them carefully, for thus will you give evidence of your wisdom and intelligence to the nations, who will hear of all these statutes and say, 'This great nation is truly a wise and intelligent people.' For what great nation is there that has gods so close to it as the LORD, our God, is to us whenever we call upon him? Or what great nation has statutes and decrees that are as just as this whole law which I am setting before you today?"

RESPONSORIAL PSALM
Psalm 15:2–3, 3–4, 4–5 (1a)

R. The one who does justice will live in the presence of the Lord.

Whoever walks blamelessly and does justice;
   who thinks the truth in his heart
   and slanders not with his tongue. R.

Who harms not his fellow man,
   nor takes up a reproach against his neighbor;
by whom the reprobate is despised,
   while he honors those who fear the LORD. R.

Who lends not his money at usury
   and accepts no bribe against the innocent.
Whoever does these things
   shall never be disturbed. R.

READING II
James 1:17–18, 21b–22, 27

Dearest brothers and sisters: All good giving and every perfect gift is from above, coming down from the Father of lights, with whom there is no alteration or shadow caused by change. He willed to give us birth by the word of truth that we may be a kind of firstfruits of his creatures.

Humbly welcome the word that has been planted in you and is able to save your souls.

Be doers of the word and not hearers only, deluding yourselves.

Religion that is pure and undefiled before God and the Father is this: to care for orphans and widows in their affliction and to keep oneself unstained by the world.

GOSPEL *Mark 7:1–8, 14–15, 21–23*

When the Pharisees with some scribes who had come from Jerusalem gathered around Jesus, they observed that some of his disciples ate their meals with unclean, that is, unwashed, hands.—For the Pharisees and, in fact, all Jews, do not eat without carefully washing their hands, keeping the tradition of the elders. And on coming from the marketplace they do not eat without purifying themselves. And there are many other things that they have traditionally observed, the purification of cups and jugs and kettles and beds.—So the Pharisees and scribes questioned him, "Why do your disciples not follow the tradition of the elders but instead eat a meal with unclean hands?" He responded, "Well did Isaiah prophesy about you hypocrites, as it is written:

This people honors me with their lips,
   but their hearts are far from me;
in vain do they worship me,
   teaching as doctrines human precepts.

You disregard God's commandment but cling to human tradition."

He summoned the crowd again and said to them, "Hear me, all of you, and understand. Nothing that enters one from outside can defile that person; but the things that come out from within are what defile.

"From within people, from their hearts, come evil thoughts, unchastity, theft, murder, adultery, greed, malice, deceit, licentiousness, envy, blasphemy, arrogance, folly. All these evils come from within and they defile."

Practice of Charity

"I die the king's faithful servant, but God's first." Those were some of the final words of St. Thomas More, the chancellor of England beheaded in 1535 for abiding by his Catholic faith and refusing to assent to King Henry VIII's divorce. The price for our integrity might not be so high, but living our beliefs does call for sacrifice sometimes. ◆ Rent the 1966 film *A Man for All Seasons*—the story of St. Thomas More—or read the play by Robert Bolt. ◆ St. James says faith needs action to be pure. He mentions orphans and widows. Today, take one action that follows from your beliefs: for example, you could sponsor a child or elderly person overseas through the Catholic organization Unbound (www.unbound.org). ◆ In your private prayer today, imagine ways you might live out your faith in the days ahead.

Download more questions and activities for families, Christian initiation groups, and other adult groups at http://www.ltp.org/t-productsupplements.aspx.

Scripture Insights

Today's readings challenge us to think about the motivations for our actions, reminding us that God calls us to lead lives of integrity. The Book of Deuteronomy calls the Israelites to keep the commandments of the Lord so that all the nations will consider Israel's laws as a true gift: "This great nation is truly a wise and intelligent people." Wisdom in the ancient world embraced practical insight and knowledge about how to act and how to make the right decisions in difficult situations. Think of the great King Solomon who was celebrated as the wisest of kings. The commandments are God's ultimate gift of wisdom, inspiring his people to decide according to God's will.

Today we begin reading from the Letter of James for the next four weeks. This letter is a true wisdom writing in that it offers practical advice on how to lead one's life. The source of this wisdom is divine: "All good giving and every perfect gift is from above, coming down from the Father of lights." Living a good life, James insists, must also include caring for "widows and orphans"—truly the most vulnerable members of society.

In the Gospel, Jesus takes on the scribes and Pharisees, who have forgotten that the laws and commandments are a source of wisdom and insight for leading their lives. They have come to see them legalistically as ends in themselves rather than as guidance for actions. The Pharisees were concentrating on externals, but unless one's interior dispositions are guided by God's Word and laws, one's actions will tend toward selfish and evil interests. Wise decisions and good actions come from hearts that have steeped themselves in God's wisdom.

◆ How does the Letter of James define "religion"? Why do you think he defines it in this way?

◆ What connection can you find between today's Responsorial Psalm and Jesus' point in the Gospel about the connection between the disposition of our hearts and our actions?

◆ How might the understanding of God's laws as a gift of God's wisdom help us in leading a good Christian life?

READING I *Isaiah 35:4–7a*

Thus says the LORD:
  Say to those whose hearts are frightened:
    Be strong, fear not!
  Here is your God,
    he comes with vindication;
  with divine recompense
    he comes to save you.
  Then will the eyes of the blind be opened,
    the ears of the deaf be cleared;
  then will the lame leap like a stag,
    then the tongue of the mute will sing.
  Streams will burst forth in the desert,
    and rivers in the steppe.
  The burning sands will become pools,
    and the thirsty ground, springs of water.

RESPONSORIAL PSALM
Psalm 146:6–7, 8–9, 9–10 (1b)

R. Praise the Lord, my soul!
  or: Alleluia.

The God of Jacob keeps faith forever,
  secures justice for the oppressed,
  gives food to the hungry.
The LORD sets captives free. R.

The LORD gives sight to the blind;
  the LORD raises up those who were
    bowed down.
The LORD loves the just;
  the LORD protects strangers. R.

The fatherless and the widow the LORD sustains,
  but the way of the wicked he thwarts.
The LORD shall reign forever;
  your God, O Zion, through all generations.
    Alleluia. R.

READING II *James 2:1–5*

My brothers and sisters, show no partiality as you adhere to the faith in our glorious Lord Jesus Christ. For if a man with gold rings and fine clothes comes into your assembly, and a poor person in shabby clothes also comes in, and you pay attention to the one wearing the fine clothes and say, "Sit here, please," while you say to the poor one, "Stand there," or "Sit at my feet," have you not made distinctions among yourselves and become judges with evil designs?

Listen, my beloved brothers and sisters. Did not God choose those who are poor in the world to be rich in faith and heirs of the kingdom that he promised to those who love him?

GOSPEL *Mark 7:31–37*

Again Jesus left the district of Tyre and went by way of Sidon to the Sea of Galilee, into the district of the Decapolis. And people brought to him a deaf man who had a speech impediment and begged him to lay his hand on him. He took him off by himself away from the crowd. He put his finger into the man's ears and, spitting, touched his tongue; then he looked up to heaven and groaned, and said to him, *"Ephphatha!"*—that is, "Be opened!"—And immediately the man's ears were opened, his speech impediment was removed, and he spoke plainly. He ordered them not to tell anyone. But the more he ordered them not to, the more they proclaimed it. They were exceedingly astonished and they said, "He has done all things well. He makes the deaf hear and the mute speak."

Practice of Hope

"Be opened!" Those words of Jesus, uttered before the ears of a deaf man, have meaning for us now. Are we closed to God? Do we not hear the life-saving Word? In the twenty-first century, the "noise" of consumerism, entertainment, and our own ambition can make us deaf to our brothers and sisters in need, and it is through them that we can encounter Jesus. ◆ Read paragraph 2 of *Evangelii Gaudium*, Pope Francis' 2013 apostolic exhortation: http://w2.vatican.va/content/francesco/en/apost _exhortations/documents/papa-francesco_esor tazione-ap_20131124_evangelii-gaudium.html. To order a paper copy, call the United States Conference of Catholic Bishops at 202-541-3000. ◆ Try to eliminate what blocks you from hearing God's Word—take a day off from television and the internet—including leisure and shopping— and instead arrange a face-to-face visit with some-one. ◆ As school begins, pray that young people won't be deafened by material desires and self-glorification, fueled by the over-use of social media.

Download more questions and activities for families, Christian initiation groups, and other adult groups at http://www.ltp.org/t-productsupplements.aspx.

Scripture Insights

Isaiah presents a reassuring vision of God's heal-ing and restorative powers. Those marginalized by suffering will receive new life: the blind, deaf, lame, and mute. Even creation will be renewed and the desert overflow with life-giving water.

The Gospel shows us the fulfillment of Isaiah's vision in Jesus' ministry with the healing of the deaf and mute man. Mark's account describes Jesus performing the miracle in realistic detail. Jesus treats the man with respect by taking him aside from the crowd and showing him special concern. Looking up to heaven as he performs the healing, Jesus demonstrates his unity with the Father. Putting his fingers into the man's ears and touching his tongue with spittle, Jesus utters his command, "Be opened," and the man is healed of his disabilities. These actions of Jesus have been incorporated into the Church's baptismal ritual. Before the Baptism of adults and after the Baptism of children, the priest touches the person's mouth and ears, asking the Lord to open their ears to receive the Word of the Lord and to open the mouth to proclaim their faith. This is the Ephphetha, named after the words Jesus spoke. Mark reports that the people acknowledge what Jesus has done by saying: "He has done all things well"—a reminder of God's words at the creation of the world (Genesis 1:31).

James' letter offers a vignette that challenges us to emulate Jesus, who treated every person with dignity. No distinctions should be made among Jesus' followers. Rich and poor must be embraced equally without discrimination. James shows how Jesus' teaching should be carried out in the lives of the worshipping community.

◆ What words or images do you find in common in the First Reading, Responsorial Psalm, and Gospel?

◆ What do the explicit details of Jesus' miracle and the baptismal liturgy tell us about the role of bod-ies in our God-given personhood?

◆ Does the passage from the Letter of James feel to you like a challenge or an affirmation?

READING I   *Isaiah 50:4c–9a*

The Lord GOD opens my ear that I may hear;
  and I have not rebelled,
    have not turned back.
I gave my back to those who beat me,
  my cheeks to those who
      plucked my beard;
my face I did not shield
  from buffets and spitting.

The Lord GOD is my help,
  therefore I am not disgraced;
I have set my face like flint,
  knowing that I shall not be put to shame.
He is near who upholds my right;
  if anyone wishes to oppose me,
  let us appear together.
Who disputes my right?
  Let that man confront me.
See, the Lord GOD is my help;
  who will prove me wrong?

RESPONSORIAL PSALM
Psalm 116:1–2, 3–4, 5–6, 8–9 (9)

R. I will walk before the Lord,
      in the land of the living.
  or: Alleluia.

I love the LORD because he has heard
  my voice in supplication,
because he has inclined his ear to me
  the day I called. R.

The cords of death encompassed me;
  the snares of the netherworld seized upon me;
  I fell into distress and sorrow,
and I called upon the name of the LORD,
  "O LORD, save my life!" R.

Gracious is the LORD and just;
  yes, our God is merciful.
The LORD keeps the little ones;
  I was brought low, and he saved me. R.

For he has freed my soul from death,
  my eyes from tears, my feet from stumbling.
I shall walk before the LORD
  in the land of the living. R.

READING II   *James 2:14–18*

What good is it, my brothers and sisters, if someone says he has faith but does not have works? Can that faith save him? If a brother or sister has nothing to wear and has no food for the day, and one of you says to them, "Go in peace, keep warm, and eat well," but you do not give them the necessities of the body, what good is it? So also faith of itself, if it does not have works, is dead.

Indeed someone might say, "You have faith and I have works." Demonstrate your faith to me without works, and I will demonstrate my faith to you from my works.

GOSPEL   *Mark 8:27–35*

Jesus and his disciples set out for the villages of Caesarea Philippi. Along the way he asked his disciples, "Who do people say that I am?" They said in reply, "John the Baptist, others Elijah, still others one of the prophets." And he asked them, "But who do you say that I am?" Peter said to him in reply, "You are the Christ." Then he warned them not to tell anyone about him.

He began to teach them that the Son of Man must suffer greatly and be rejected by the elders, the chief priests, and the scribes, and be killed, and rise after three days. He spoke this openly. Then Peter took him aside and began to rebuke him. At this he turned around and, looking at his disciples, rebuked Peter and said, "Get behind me, Satan. You are thinking not as God does, but as human beings do."

He summoned the crowd with his disciples and said to them, "Whoever wishes to come after me must deny himself, take up his cross, and follow me. For whoever wishes to save his life will lose it, but whoever loses his life for my sake and that of the gospel will save it."

Practice of Faith

Jesus was widely misunderstood in his day, even by his closest followers. For many, he was not the kind of messiah they were expecting. Instead of leading a revolution he actually said, "Take up your cross!" It's still easy to misread Jesus. ◆ To help ensure you are embracing the authentic Jesus, seek out Scripture. Join a Bible study at your parish led by a trustworthy teacher. ◆ Watch the PBS Frontline Special, *From Jesus to Christ: The First Christians*: http://www.pbs.org/wgbh/pages/front line/shows/religion/watch/. It may challenge some assumptions, but in the end your faith will be well informed and can deepen on that basis. ◆ An encounter with the Holy Land is an important spiritual experience. If you cannot go to a place like Israel or Jordan, read passages of Scripture using your imagination, picturing Jesus in a particular place and time in history.

Download more questions and activities for families, Christian initiation groups, and other adult groups at http://www.ltp.org/t-productsupplements.aspx.

Scripture Insights

"Who do people say that I am?" Jesus poses this question to his disciples on his journey through Caesarea Philippi. It elicits Peter's acknowledgment that Jesus is the Messiah. For centuries Israel had looked forward to God fulfilling his promise to King David by raising up another great leader to restore Israel's kingdom (2 Samuel 7). These hopes had become clouded in political and earthly expectations.

Peter's response, in unambiguous terms, "You are the Christ (or the Messiah)," gives Jesus the opportunity to offer a different understanding. Jesus says that he has come not to establish an earthly kingdom in power, but rather a spiritual kingdom in weakness. God's Kingdom will be established through Jesus' Death and Resurrection.

The First Reading, from the third of Isaiah's "Servant Songs," belongs to another tradition pointing to the Messiah's coming in humiliation and suffering. Jesus draws upon this tradition in referring to his own ministry of suffering and death on behalf of God's people.

Peter fails to take this tradition into account when he tells Jesus not to talk about suffering and death. He is utterly perplexed and alarmed, for Peter believed that the Messiah would come in power and glory. When Jesus says to Peter, "Get behind me, Satan," he is referring to Satan in the Book of Job, where Satan, as the name actually means, is God's adversary. Jesus reinforces this by saying that Peter's thoughts are human ways of thinking, not God's way.

A further challenge emerges for Jesus' followers from his revelation that he is going to suffer and die. His followers' lives will embrace the same path of suffering, Death, and Resurrection. As true Christians, our lives too will share in Jesus' redemptive suffering.

◆ From these readings, how would you explain the meaning of the word "Messiah (Christ)"?

◆ What would be your answer to Jesus' question, "Who do you say that I am?"

◆ Have you experienced the reality of Jesus' words, "Take up your cross and follow me"?

READING I *Wisdom 2:12, 17–20*

The wicked say:
Let us beset the just one, because
    he is obnoxious to us;
  he sets himself against our doings,
reproaches us for transgressions of the law
  and charges us with violations
    of our training.
Let us see whether his words be true;
  let us find out what will happen to him.
For if the just one be the son
    of God, God will defend him
  and deliver him from the hand of his foes.
With revilement and torture let us put the
    just one to the test
  that we may have proof of his gentleness
  and try his patience.
Let us condemn him to a shameful death;
  for according to his own words,
    God will take care of him.

RESPONSORIAL PSALM
Psalm 54:3–4, 5, 6–8 (6b)

R. The Lord upholds my life.

O God, by your name save me,
  and by your might defend my cause.
O God, hear my prayer;
  hearken to the words of my mouth. R.

For the haughty have risen up against me,
  the ruthless seek my life;
  they set not God before their eyes. R.

Behold, God is my helper;
  the Lord sustains my life.
Freely will I offer you sacrifice;
  I will praise your name, O LORD, for its
    goodness. R.

READING II *James 3:16—4:3*

Beloved: Where jealousy and selfish ambition exist, there is disorder and every foul practice. But the wisdom from above is first of all pure, then peaceable, gentle, compliant, full of mercy and good fruits, without inconstancy or insincerity. And the fruit of righteousness is sown in peace for those who cultivate peace.

Where do the wars and where do the conflicts among you come from? Is it not from your passions that make war within your members? You covet but do not possess. You kill and envy but you cannot obtain; you fight and wage war. You do not possess because you do not ask. You ask but do not receive, because you ask wrongly, to spend it on your passions.

GOSPEL *Mark 9:30–37*

Jesus and his disciples left from there and began a journey through Galilee, but he did not wish anyone to know about it. He was teaching his disciples and telling them, "The Son of Man is to be handed over to men and they will kill him, and three days after his death the Son of Man will rise." But they did not understand the saying, and they were afraid to question him.

They came to Capernaum and, once inside the house, he began to ask them, "What were you arguing about on the way?" But they remained silent. They had been discussing among themselves on the way who was the greatest. Then he sat down, called the Twelve, and said to them, "If anyone wishes to be first, he shall be the last of all and the servant of all." Taking a child, he placed it in their midst, and putting his arms around it, he said to them, "Whoever receives one child such as this in my name, receives me; and whoever receives me, receives not me but the One who sent me."

Practice of Charity

Jesus says that those who receive a child receive him. Today, the scourge of human trafficking continues to make the lives of some children a hellish slavery. They are laborers and often sex objects. ✦ Read paragraph 4 of Pope Francis' statement for World Day of Peace, 2015: "No Longer Slaves, but Brothers and Sisters," https://w2.vatican.va/content/francesco/en/messages/peace/documents/papa-francesco_20141208_messaggio-xlviii-giornata-mondiale-pace-2015.html. ✦ The United States Conference of Catholic Bishops operates an anti-trafficking program that includes the Amistad Movement, named after the *Amistad* slave ship, site of an 1839 revolt that eventually resulted in freedom for the Africans who had been seized. The movement offers awareness programs and training to immigrants to help them avoid becoming trafficking victims. To schedule training in your area, go to http://www.usccb.org/about/anti-trafficking-program/amistad.cfm or call 202-541-3021. ✦ Pray for the intercession of St. Josephine Bakhita for the victims of human trafficking. She was a nineteenth-century Sudanese slave who later became a woman religious in Italy.

Download more questions and activities for families, Christian initiation groups, and other adult groups at http://www.ltp.org/t-productsupplements.aspx.

Scripture Insights

What is authentic, selfless ambition? Today's liturgy issues God's call to avoid jealousy and selfish ambition, and to cultivate sincerity, humility, and peace (James 3:13–18). The Gospel illustrates this message especially clearly. As Jesus continues to journey toward Jerusalem, he makes a second prediction that his journey will end in his Death and Resurrection.

As with the prediction last Sunday, the disciples fail to understand its meaning. They are so preoccupied with their own ambitions that they have failed to confront Jesus' reality—so in conflict with their expectations: "They had been discussing who was the greatest." Jesus uses this opportunity to illustrate true discipleship: "If anyone wishes to be first, he shall be the last of all and the servant of all." True leadership, says Jesus, is servant leadership!

Taking a little child, Jesus draws everyone's attention to this child. A child is vulnerable and powerless with no influence at all. Especially in the society of Jesus' day, a child was considered to be at the lowest level of society's hierarchy. Children are dependent and need things done for them. In this way Jesus shows that his kingdom values are very different. Instead of promoting one's own prestige, the focus must be on the other, on the most vulnerable members of society—the poor, those who have no wealth or power, those who need things done for them—like little children.

In reaching out and caring for the most vulnerable members of society (like children), one is, in reality, receiving Jesus himself and ultimately welcoming God. Jesus repeats this same message later in his final sermon in Matthew's Gospel on the judgment of the nations where he says: "Whatever you did for one of these least brothers [and sisters] of mine, you did for me" (Matthew 25:40).

✦ How does today's Responsorial Psalm add to the meaning of today's readings?

✦ What does the disciples' self-centeredness and lack of empathy teach you about the importance of listening to the one who is speaking?

✦ How can you, or do you exercise servant leadership in your own life?

READING I *Numbers 11:25–29*

The LORD came down in the cloud and spoke to Moses. Taking some of the spirit that was on Moses, the LORD bestowed it on the seventy elders; and as the spirit came to rest on them, they prophesied.

Now two men, one named Eldad and the other Medad, were not in the gathering but had been left in the camp. They too had been on the list, but had not gone out to the tent; yet the spirit came to rest on them also, and they prophesied in the camp. So, when a young man quickly told Moses, "Eldad and Medad are prophesying in the camp," Joshua, son of Nun, who from his youth had been Moses' aide, said, "Moses, my lord, stop them." But Moses answered him, "Are you jealous for my sake? Would that all the people of the LORD were prophets! Would that the LORD might bestow his spirit on them all!"

RESPONSORIAL PSALM
Psalm 19:8, 10, 12–13, 14 (9a)

R   The precepts of the Lord give joy to the heart.

The law of the LORD is perfect,
  refreshing the soul;
the decree of the LORD is trustworthy,
  giving wisdom to the simple. R.

The fear of the LORD is pure,
  enduring forever;
the ordinances of the LORD are true,
  all of them just. R.

Though your servant is careful of them,
  very diligent in keeping them,
yet who can detect failings?
  Cleanse me from my unknown faults! R.

From wanton sin especially, restrain your servant;
  let it not rule over me.
Then shall I be blameless and innocent
  of serious sin. R.

READING II *James 5:1–6*

Come now, you rich, weep and wail over your impending miseries. Your wealth has rotted away, your clothes have become moth-eaten, your gold and silver have corroded, and that corrosion will be a testimony against you; it will devour your flesh like a fire. You have stored up treasure for the last days. Behold, the wages you withheld from the workers who harvested your fields are crying aloud; and the cries of the harvesters have reached the ears of the Lord of hosts. You have lived on earth in luxury and pleasure; you have fattened your hearts for the day of slaughter. You have condemned; you have murdered the righteous one; he offers you no resistance.

GOSPEL *Mark 9:38–43, 45, 47–48*

At that time, John said to Jesus, "Teacher, we saw someone driving out demons in your name, and we tried to prevent him because he does not follow us." Jesus replied, "Do not prevent him. There is no one who performs a mighty deed in my name who can at the same time speak ill of me. For whoever is not against us is for us. Anyone who gives you a cup of water to drink because you belong to Christ, amen, I say to you, will surely not lose his reward.

"Whoever causes one of these little ones who believe in me to sin, it would be better for him if a great millstone were put around his neck and he were thrown into the sea. If your hand causes you to sin, cut it off. It is better for you to enter into life maimed than with two hands to go into Gehenna, into the unquenchable fire. And if your foot causes you to sin, cut it off. It is better for you to enter into life crippled than with two feet to be thrown into Gehenna. And if your eye causes you to sin, pluck it out. Better for you to enter into the kingdom of God with one eye than with two eyes to be thrown into Gehenna, where 'their worm does not die, and the fire is not quenched.'"

Practice of Hope

We humans naturally tend toward tribalism and pride. We resent someone moving onto our turf, even if he or she is doing good. Christians can attest to this, as almost every parish has examples of choir members, benefit dinner chiefs, and even food bank operators who grumpily scare off fresh helpers and their newfangled ideas. ◆ Watch the 1944 Catholic film *Going My Way*, with Bing Crosby as a young priest trying to breathe some life into a parish, including its veteran pastor. Imagine yourself as the older priest. ◆ Involved in your parish St. Vincent de Paul Society? Sing in the choir? Coach a team? Loosen the reins and try to find a young person to assist you. At the very least, ask the young adult or teen for some advice to keep the ministry fresh. ◆ Meditate on the scene of Jesus before the Sanhedrin, Luke 22:66—23:25. Put yourself in the room and take the role of the leaders. Realize how painful it is to accept fresh ideas and vision.

Download more questions and activities for families, Christian initiation groups, and other adult groups at http://www.ltp.org/t-productsupplements.aspx.

Scripture Insights

God's work in the world cannot be the exclusive domain of only one group of people. The reading from the Book of Numbers relates that some Israelites wanted Moses to stop outsiders from prophesying. Similarly, the disciples in today's Gospel ask Jesus to stop an outsider from driving out demons. Both Moses and Jesus, however, welcome the good actions of these outsiders. As Jesus says, "Whoever is not against us is for us!" It is not for us to decide where and how God works. We are called to embrace the good no matter its origin!

When evil is perpetrated, however, we must identify it. Speaking like the Old Testament prophets, James condemns the uncaring rich. He does not, however, rail against the wealthy as such. Rather, James condemns those who live in luxury with no thought for the poor; he condemns those who profit at the expense of the poor, those who refuse to pay their laborers. (Workers were paid daily, so their families were dependent on that wage.)

The Gospel reading continues to offer significant wisdom advice for avoiding the destructive power of sin. Speaking metaphorically, Jesus says that whatever becomes an obstacle to following God's will must be eliminated—"If your hand causes you to sin, cut it off." And anyone who causes a new, vulnerable Christian to sin deserves the worst punishment. *Gehenna*, to which Jesus refers, has become for Christians a traditional symbol for hell. The word comes from the Valley of *Hinnom* outside Jerusalem where the city refuse was thrown and burned. This foul smelling and smoldering valley became a symbol for a place of punishment for those who do not live according to God's will. Good and evil are realities in our world. The readings in the liturgy call us to stand united with those who are on the side of goodness.

◆ How would you describe the tone of James' condemnation of the rich?

◆ Where do you see God working in the world around you, even if not through your group?

◆ Which group experiencing economic discrimination weighs heaviest on your heart?

READING I   *Genesis 2:18–24*

The LORD God said: "It is not good for the man to be alone. I will make a suitable partner for him." So the LORD God formed out of the ground various wild animals and various birds of the air, and he brought them to the man to see what he would call them; whatever the man called each of them would be its name. The man gave names to all the cattle, all the birds of the air, and all wild animals; but none proved to be the suitable partner for the man.

So the LORD God cast a deep sleep on the man, and while he was asleep, he took out one of his ribs and closed up its place with flesh. The LORD God then built up into a woman the rib that he had taken from the man. When he brought her to the man, the man said:

"This one, at last, is bone of my bones
    and flesh of my flesh;
this one shall be called 'woman,'
    for out of 'her man' this one
        has been taken."

That is why a man leaves his father and mother and clings to his wife, and the two of them become one flesh.

RESPONSORIAL PSALM
Psalm 128:1–2, 3, 4–5, 6 (see 5)

R. May the Lord bless us all the days of our lives.

Blessed are you who fear the LORD,
    who walk in his ways!
For you shall eat the fruit of your handiwork;
    blessed shall you be, and favored. R.

Your wife shall be like a fruitful vine
    in the recesses of your home;
your children like olive plants
    around your table. R.

Behold, thus is the man blessed
    who fears the LORD.
The LORD bless you from Zion:
    may you see the prosperity of Jerusalem
    all the days of your life. R.

May you see your children's children.
    Peace be upon Israel! R.

READING II   *Hebrews 2:9–11*

Brothers and sisters: He "for a little while" was made "lower than the angels," that by the grace of God he might taste death for everyone.

For it was fitting that he, for whom and through whom all things exist, in bringing many children to glory, should make the leader to their salvation perfect through suffering. He who consecrates and those who are being consecrated all have one origin. Therefore, he is not ashamed to call them "brothers."

GOSPEL   *Mark 10:2–16*

Shorter: Mark 10:2–12

The Pharisees approached Jesus and asked, "Is it lawful for a husband to divorce his wife?" They were testing him. He said to them in reply, "What did Moses command you?" They replied, "Moses permitted a husband to write a bill of divorce and dismiss her." But Jesus told them, "Because of the hardness of your hearts he wrote you this commandment. But from the beginning of creation, *God made them male and female. For this reason a man shall leave his father and mother and be joined to his wife, and the two shall become one flesh.* So they are no longer two but one flesh. Therefore what God has joined together, no human being must separate." In the house the disciples again questioned Jesus about this. He said to them, "Whoever divorces his wife and marries another commits adultery against her; and if she divorces her husband and marries another, she commits adultery."

And people were bringing children to him that he might touch them, but the disciples rebuked them. When Jesus saw this he became indignant and said to them, "Let the children come to me; do not prevent them, for the kingdom of God belongs to such as these. Amen, I say to you, whoever does not accept the kingdom of God like a child will not enter it." Then he embraced them and blessed them, placing his hands on them.

Practice of Charity

"It is not good for the man to be alone." In the original plan of creation, which Jesus seeks to restore, marriage is an unbreakable covenant bond, like the relationship between God and his people. We are meant to be closely united with others, not alone. But many people, especially those elders who have lost a spouse, deal with great loneliness. ✦ Read section 13 of St. John Paul's 1999 "Letter to the Elderly": http://w2.vatican.va/content /john-paul-ii/en/letters/1999/documents/hf_jp-ii _let_01101999_elderly.html. The pope, himself feeling the effects of old age, pours compassion on those who are alone. ✦ Chances are, your parish or diocese has programs for outreach to elderly people. For example, the Archdiocese of Boston Elder Services provides visits to the homebound, pastoral support, counseling, and services to people raising their grandchildren. Volunteer with your local organization. ✦ Ask an elderly friend at your parish to become a prayer partner; visit to pray, pray over the phone, or just keep each other's intentions in mind.

Download more questions and activities for families, Christian initiation groups, and other adult groups at http://www.ltp.org/t-productsupplements.aspx.

Scripture Insights

Marriage was part of God's plan from the very beginning of creation. Today's First Reading from the Book of Genesis opens with a religious reflection on the creation of woman. The context for her creation is the simple proclamation that "It is not good for the man to be alone. I will make a suitable partner for him." Through the specific body imagery of this story, a clear message emerges that man and woman complement each other. Through the bond that joins them together they "become one body": "This is why a man leaves his father and mother and clings to his wife, and the two of them become one flesh."

In the Gospel, Jesus continues journeying toward Jerusalem. Some scholars of the Jewish Law pose a question to Jesus about divorce. In the Book of Deuteronomy 24:1, Moses allowed a man to divorce his wife if "he is later displeased with her and finds in her something indecent." Legal scholars of that time argued passionately over what concrete circumstances would permit such a decision.

Without entering into the disputes, Jesus returns to God's original intent in creating man and woman by quoting the passage in the First Reading. God intends "the two to become one flesh." In effect Jesus says that from the creation of the world marriage is meant to establish absolute permanency and a deep unity. This bond is never to be broken. In doing so Jesus makes a commitment to the equality of man and woman. While his own Jewish tradition allowed a man to divorce his wife, by returning to God's original plan for man and woman to become "one flesh," Jesus rejects divorce and raises the status of the woman, who is an equal partner to the man.

✦ What does the First Reading regard as the purpose for marriage?

✦ Find specific words that illustrate how today's readings celebrate the equality of man and woman.

✦ What issues in today's culture challenge Jesus' vision of marriage? How might one find that God's grace enables one to overcome these challenges? What wisdom from these readings might inform other relationships besides marriage?

READING I   *Wisdom 7:7–11*

I prayed, and prudence was given me;
    I pleaded, and the spirit of wisdom came
        to me.
I preferred her to scepter and throne,
and deemed riches nothing in comparison
        with her,
    nor did I liken any priceless gem to her;
because all gold, in view of her, is a little sand,
    and before her, silver is to be accounted mire.
Beyond health and comeliness I loved her,
and I chose to have her rather than the light,
    because the splendor of her
        never yields to sleep.
Yet all good things together came
        to me in her company,
    and countless riches at her hands.

RESPONSORIAL PSALM
Psalm 90:12–13, 14–15, 16–17 (14)

R. Fill us with your love, O Lord, and we will
        sing for joy!

Teach us to number our days aright,
    that we may gain wisdom of heart.
Return, O LORD! How long?
    Have pity on your servants! R.

Fill us at daybreak with your kindness,
    that we may shout for joy
        and gladness all our days.
Make us glad, for the days when you afflicted us,
    for the years when we saw evil. R.

Let your work be seen by your servants
    and your glory by their children;
and may the gracious care of the Lord our
        God be ours;
    prosper the work of our hands for us!
    Prosper the work of our hands! R.

READING II   *Hebrews 4:12–13*

Brothers and sisters: Indeed the word of God is living and effective, sharper than any two-edged sword, penetrating even between soul and spirit, joints and marrow, and able to discern reflections and thoughts of the heart. No creature is concealed from him, but everything is naked and exposed to the eyes of him to whom we must render an account.

GOSPEL   *Mark 10:17–30*

Shorter: Mark 10:17–27

As Jesus was setting out on a journey, a man ran up, knelt down before him, and asked him, "Good teacher, what must I do to inherit eternal life?" Jesus answered him, "Why do you call me good? No one is good but God alone. You know the commandments: *You shall not kill; you shall not commit adultery; you shall not steal; you shall not bear false witness; you shall not defraud; honor your father and your mother.*" He replied and said to him, "Teacher, all of these I have observed from my youth." Jesus, looking at him, loved him and said to him, "You are lacking in one thing. Go, sell what you have, and give to the poor and you will have treasure in heaven; then come, follow me." At that statement his face fell, and he went away sad, for he had many possessions.

    Jesus looked around and said to his disciples, "How hard it is for those who have wealth to enter the kingdom of God!" The disciples were amazed at his words. So Jesus again said to them in reply, "Children, how hard it is to enter the kingdom of God! It is easier for a camel to pass through the eye of a needle than for one who is rich to enter the kingdom of God." They were exceedingly astonished and said among themselves, "Then who can be saved?" Jesus looked at them and said, "For human beings it is impossible, but not for God. All things are possible for God." Peter began to say to him, "We have given up everything and followed you." Jesus said, "Amen, I say to you, there is no one who has given up house or brothers or sisters or mother or father or children or lands for my sake and for the sake of the gospel who will not receive a hundred times more now in this present age: houses and brothers and sisters and mothers and children and lands, with persecutions, and eternal life in the age to come."

Practice of Faith

The Reign of God demands that we be all-in. "Sell what you have . . . [and] follow me." Elsewhere, Jesus says that the one who puts hand to the plow and looks back is not fit for service in the Kingdom. He even tells a mourner to come along and let the dead bury the dead. ◆ St. Maximilian Kolbe is an example of a modern person who made a full commitment, dying in place of another man at Auschwitz. Read more of his story at http://www.fatherkolbe.com. ◆ We will not all be martyrs. But we can still stay alert to what keeps us from total engagement in God's kingdom—Desire for comfort? Fear of what friends and family will think? Pride in what we've earned and saved? Make a list of things that hold you back. ◆ Pray for the strength to have an authentic desire for God's reign.

Download more questions and activities for families, Christian initiation groups, and other adult groups at http://www.ltp.org/t-productsupplements.aspx.

Scripture Insights

What are your priorities in life? Today's readings reflect on this challenging question. In the Book of Wisdom, the writer prays to God for the spirit of wisdom to be given him. Wisdom is God's greatest gift, since it provides true insight into how to lead life with integrity—a gift far more precious than gold, silver, or even health!

Today's Gospel offers us a concrete example of a man discerning his priorities in life. He comes running to Jesus with enthusiasm, eagerly asking: "What must I do to inherit eternal life?" Jesus tries to curb his enthusiasm and deepen his understanding by challenging him to consider exactly what his priorities are. The Lord focuses on those commandments that involve how we lead our lives and treat our neighbor. They all reflect a common thread: "I have never done anything to harm anyone!" But, Jesus implies something more is needed: "What have you done to help another person?"

Looking into this man's heart, Jesus says in effect: "You consider that leading a good life entails not harming others. Instead, spend your resources in doing good for others." Unfortunately, the eager young man could not accept Jesus' challenge, and he walked away.

Notice that Jesus is not stating that riches are evil and we all have to give everything away. This rich man was presented with the challenge of accepting the real priorities in his life: using his gifts and talents to help others. We discover true happiness in serving others. This challenge is presented to us as well: to discover our true priorities and scale of values and to implement them in our lives.

◆ In what specific ways does the Responsorial Psalm offer wisdom that harmonizes with the Gospel?

◆ Jesus challenges the young man to reform his way of thinking from doing no harm to doing positive good to others. How might this question spur us to discern our relationship with Christ and others in a different way?

◆ The Second Reading teaches that the Word of God has power to help us align ourselves with God's wisdom. How has it helped you?

October 21, 2018

READING I *Isaiah 53:10–11*

The LORD was pleased
    to crush him in infirmity.

If he gives his life as an offering for sin,
    he shall see his descendants in a long life,
    and the will of the LORD shall
        be accomplished through him.

Because of his affliction
    he shall see the light in fullness of days;
through his suffering, my servant
        shall justify many,
    and their guilt he shall bear.

RESPONSORIAL PSALM
Psalm 33:4–5, 18–19, 20, 22 (22)

R. Lord, let your mercy be on us, as we place
    our trust in you.

Upright is the word of the LORD,
    and all his works are trustworthy.
He loves justice and right;
    of the kindness of the LORD
        the earth is full. R.

See, the eyes of the LORD are upon those who
        fear him,
    upon those who hope for his kindness;
to deliver them from death
    and preserve them in spite of famine. R.

Our soul waits for the LORD,
    who is our help and our shield.
May your kindness, O LORD, be upon us
    who have put our hope in you. R.

READING II *Hebrews 4:14–16*

Brothers and sisters: Since we have a great high priest who has passed through the heavens, Jesus, the Son of God, let us hold fast to our confession. For we do not have a high priest who is unable to sympathize with our weaknesses, but one who has similarly been tested in every way, yet without sin. So let us confidently approach the throne of grace to receive mercy and to find grace for timely help.

GOSPEL *Mark 10:35–45*
Shorter: Mark 10:42–45

James and John, the sons of Zebedee, came to Jesus and said to him, "Teacher, we want you to do for us whatever we ask of you." He replied, "What do you wish me to do for you?" They answered him, "Grant that in your glory we may sit one at your right and the other at your left." Jesus said to them, "You do not know what you are asking. Can you drink the cup that I drink or be baptized with the baptism with which I am baptized?" They said to him, "We can." Jesus said to them, "The cup that I drink, you will drink, and with the baptism with which I am baptized, you will be baptized; but to sit at my right or at my left is not mine to give but is for those for whom it has been prepared." When the ten heard this, they became indignant at James and John. Jesus summoned them and said to them, "You know that those who are recognized as rulers over the Gentiles lord it over them, and their great ones make their authority over them felt. But it shall not be so among you. Rather, whoever wishes to be great among you will be your servant; whoever wishes to be first among you will be the slave of all. For the Son of Man did not come to be served but to serve and to give his life as a ransom for many."

Practice of Faith

At every Mass, we arrive at the heart of a mystery. Jesus Christ, the Son of God, saves humanity not through power, but through service and weakness and pain. We hold that our Eucharist makes this saving act real for us here, now. ◆ Abbot Jeremy Driscoll of Mount Angel Abbey in Oregon has taught at high levels in seminaries in the United States and in Rome. But his simple book, *What Happens at Mass*, removes the blinders of familiarity and makes the reader realize how Christ shakes the earth. "God is acting! He acts to save us," Abbot Jeremy writes. "It is a huge event. In fact, there is nothing bigger." To order a copy, go to http://www.ltp.org/p-2365-what-happens-at-mass-revised-edition.aspx or call 1-800-933-1800. ◆ Before you attend Mass next, consider a way you can serve. ◆ Take that idea to prayer, especially during the Eucharist.

Download more questions and activities for families, Christian initiation groups, and other adult groups at http://www.ltp.org/t-productsupplements.aspx.

Scripture Insights

In embracing our human nature completely, Jesus, the Son of God, also had to experience suffering and death. Our First Reading, from the most well-known of the four servant songs of Isaiah, looks to the servant's future suffering when he will take our guilt on himself for the sake of our salvation. Today's Gospel reading shows that Jesus, the Son of Man, fulfills this servant song. In its context in Mark's Gospel account, Jesus is approaching Jerusalem. Immediately prior to today's reading, Jesus spoke for the third and final time in great detail about his upcoming Death and Resurrection. The Gospel opens with two of Jesus' closest disciples, James and John, responding to what Jesus had said by asking him: "Grant that in your glory we may sit one at your right and the other at your left." They are thinking in human terms and are looking for glory. Jesus instructs them that they have misunderstood his whole message. Discipleship entails embracing suffering and service just as he is doing. The hallmark of a disciple is humble service: "Whoever wishes to be first among you will be the servant of all."

Speaking about himself, Jesus demonstrates that his life's mission embraces giving his life in service, "as a ransom for many." In a metaphorical way, Jesus states very simply and clearly that the salvation of humanity comes at the cost of his life. Out of love for humanity and at the cost of his life, Jesus brought humanity from sin into a bond of love with his Father. Humanity's salvation cost him his life. Jesus teaches us a new path to greatness: humble service. True discipleship means following the model of Jesus' own path of suffering and service.

◆ It's no wonder that the other ten disciples in today's Gospel are "indignant at James and John." Self-centeredness often stimulates the same in others—even in church groups. How could today's Responsorial Psalm serve as an antidote?

◆ When have you experienced something that cost you dearly when you stayed true to your faith?

◆ In what ways have you been able to serve others instead of self?

READING I *Jeremiah 31:7–9*

Thus says the LORD:
Shout with joy for Jacob,
    exult at the head of the nations;
    proclaim your praise and say:
The LORD has delivered his people,
    the remnant of Israel.
Behold, I will bring them back
    from the land of the north;
I will gather them from the ends of the world,
    with the blind and the lame in their midst,
the mothers and those with child;
    they shall return as an immense throng.
They departed in tears,
    but I will console them and guide them;
I will lead them to brooks of water,
    on a level road, so that none shall stumble.
For I am a father to Israel,
    Ephraim is my first-born.

RESPONSORIAL PSALM
Psalm 126:1–2, 2–3, 4–5, 6 (3)

R. The Lord has done great things for us; we are
    filled with joy.

When the LORD brought back the captives of Zion,
    we were like men dreaming.
Then our mouth was filled with laughter,
    and our tongue with rejoicing. R.

Then they said among the nations,
    "The LORD has done great things for them."
The LORD has done great things for us;
    we are glad indeed. R.

Restore our fortunes, O LORD,
    like the torrents in the southern desert.
Those that sow in tears
    shall reap rejoicing. R.

Although they go forth weeping,
    carrying the seed to be sown,
they shall come back rejoicing,
    carrying their sheaves. R.

READING II *Hebrews 5:1–6*

Brothers and sisters: Every high priest is taken from among men and made their representative before God, to offer gifts and sacrifices for sins. He is able to deal patiently with the ignorant and erring, for he himself is beset by weakness and so, for this reason, must make sin offerings for himself as well as for the people. No one takes this honor upon himself but only when called by God, just as Aaron was. In the same way, it was not Christ who glorified himself in becoming high priest, but rather the one who said to him:

    You are my son:
        this day I have begotten you;
just as he says in another place:
    You are a priest forever
        according to the order of Melchizedek.

GOSPEL *Mark 10:46–52*

As Jesus was leaving Jericho with his disciples and a sizable crowd, Bartimaeus, a blind man, the son of Timaeus, sat by the roadside begging. On hearing that it was Jesus of Nazareth, he began to cry out and say, "Jesus, son of David, have pity on me." And many rebuked him, telling him to be silent. But he kept calling out all the more, "Son of David, have pity on me." Jesus stopped and said, "Call him." So they called the blind man, saying to him, "Take courage; get up, Jesus is calling you." He threw aside his cloak, sprang up, and came to Jesus. Jesus said to him in reply, "What do you want me to do for you?" The blind man replied to him, "Master, I want to see." Jesus told him, "Go your way; your faith has saved you." Immediately he received his sight and followed him on the way.

Practice of Charity

At every time in our life, God is trying to bring us back from exile to guide us to wholeness. But as with the blind man Bartimaeus, a key to our healing is a faithful response to God's loving presence. ◆ For ideas about how you or someone you love might respond to God's personal offer of healing to you, go to www.vocationnetwork.org. There, take the Vocation Match survey, which is for those who are single, married, widowed, and divorced. The survey will suggest organizations you can contact for a possible life of service. ◆ This time of year, many parishes have people in the process of responding to God's call through the process of Christian initiation. They are discerning, praying, and being formed by the community to take their place in the Body of Christ through the Roman Catholic Church. ◆ Pray for those in this process and prayerfully let their search inspire your ongoing response to God.

Download more questions and activities for families, Christian initiation groups, and other adult groups at http://www.ltp.org/t-productsupplements.aspx.

Scripture Insights

In the midst of devastating wars and deportation among the nations, the prophet Jeremiah offers his people God's vision for the future. God promises to unite his people from the places to which they have been scattered. And in particular, God shows special concern for the most vulnerable of society by "gathering them from the ends of the world, with the blind and the lame in their midst, the mothers and those with child."

Today's Gospel reading shows Jeremiah's vision being realized. By healing the blind man, Jesus fulfills Jeremiah's prophecy: "The blind and the lame in their midst" follow Jesus into Jerusalem where he will establish God's Kingdom.

As Jesus passes through Jericho (some fifteen miles from Jerusalem), Bartimaeus, who is blind, is among the crowd lining the street. He shouts out: "Jesus, son of David, have pity on me." The scene is vivid and contains significant aspects. Bartimaeus is *persistent*—he is desperate and knows that Jesus can help him. Jesus calls Bartimaeus over, and the man's *response is immediate*—he rushes over to Jesus. Jesus asks him simply: "What do you want me to do for you?" His reply is direct: "Master, I want to see." Jesus sends him away telling him, "Your faith has saved you." Bartimaeus regains his sight and *follows Jesus*. Bartimaeus demonstrates the characteristics of a true disciple: *persistent request, immediate response, faith, and dedication.*

In last Sunday's Gospel the disciples' ambitions prevented them from seeing and understanding: they were spiritually blind to Jesus' message. Today's account of the blind beggar, Bartimaeus, offers a contrasting picture of the qualities of authentic discipleship. The true disciple sees more clearly, appeals to Christ for help, places faith in Christ as the only source of life and light, and is dedicated to following Christ.

◆ How does the Gospel's portrait of Bartimaeus as a true disciple echo your discipleship? How does it offer you encouragement?

◆ How might today's Responsorial Psalm be a fitting prayer for Bartimaeus after Jesus' healed him? How might it touch you in your current circumstances?

◆ What insights does the Second Reading offer about Jesus?

READING I *Deuteronomy 6:2–6*

Moses spoke to the people, saying: "Fear the LORD, your God, and keep, throughout the days of your lives, all his statutes and commandments which I enjoin on you, and thus have long life. Hear then, Israel, and be careful to observe them, that you may grow and prosper the more, in keeping with the promise of the LORD, the God of your fathers, to give you a land flowing with milk and honey.

"Hear, O Israel! The LORD is our God, the LORD alone! Therefore, you shall love the LORD, your God, with all your heart, and with all your soul, and with all your strength. Take to heart these words which I enjoin on you today."

RESPONSORIAL PSALM *Psalm 18:2–3, 3–4, 47, 51 (2)*

R. I love you, Lord, my strength.

I love you, O LORD, my strength,
    O LORD, my rock, my fortress,
        my deliverer. R.

My God, my rock of refuge,
    my shield, the horn of my salvation,
        my stronghold!
Praised be the LORD, I exclaim,
    and I am safe from my enemies. R.

The LORD lives! And blessed be my rock!
    Extolled be God my savior,
you who gave great victories to your king
    and showed kindness to your anointed. R.

READING II *Hebrews 7:23–28*

Brothers and sisters: The levitical priests were many because they were prevented by death from remaining in office, but Jesus, because he remains forever, has a priesthood that does not pass away. Therefore, he is always able to save those who approach God through him, since he lives forever to make intercession for them.

It was fitting that we should have such a high priest: holy, innocent, undefiled, separated from sinners, higher than the heavens. He has no need, as did the high priests, to offer sacrifice day after day, first for his own sins and then for those of the people; he did that once for all when he offered himself. For the law appoints men subject to weakness to be high priests, but the word of the oath, which was taken after the law, appoints a son, who has been made perfect forever.

GOSPEL *Mark 12:28b–34*

One of the scribes came to Jesus and asked him, "Which is the first of all the commandments?" Jesus replied, "The first is this: *Hear, O Israel! The Lord our God is Lord alone! You shall love the Lord your God with all your heart, with all your soul, with all your mind, and with all your strength.* The second is this: *You shall love your neighbor as yourself.* There is no other commandment greater than these." The scribe said to him, "Well said, teacher. You are right in saying, 'He is One and there is no other than he.' And 'to love him with all your heart, with all your understanding, with all your strength, and to love your neighbor as yourself' is worth more than all burnt offerings and sacrifices." And when Jesus saw that he answered with understanding, he said to him, "You are not far from the kingdom of God." And no one dared to ask him any more questions.

Practice of Hope

Some people asked Jesus questions to trap him. Others asked because they wanted to know how to believe and live. It's midterm election time in the United States, and we have all heard the pointed questions candidates fire at each other. By contrast, Catholics are called to ask questions aimed at the common good. ◆ For tips on a good approach to public life and voting, read the United States Conference of Catholic Bishops' document "Forming Consciences for Faithful Citizenship," available at http://www.usccb.org/issues-and -action/faithful-citizenship/upload/forming-co nsciences-for-faithful-citizenship.pdf or by calling 202-541-3000. The document says in part, "Without the proper ordering of relationships of persons with each other, with creation, and ultimately with God himself, sin takes hold." The Canadian Conference of Catholic Bishops publishes similar material on their website: http:// www.cccb.ca/. ◆ As you vote, consider the common good. Cast ballots as an informed Catholic, not someone in lockstep with a party. ◆ Pray for elected officials and for the country.

Download more questions and activities for families, Christian initiation groups, and other adult groups at http://www.ltp.org/t-productsupplements.aspx.

Scripture Insights

"Love God and love your neighbor" captures the essence of Jesus' message. Today's First Reading contains a passage known as the Shema Israel ("Hear, O Israel," Deuteronomy 6:4), the central statement of belief of the Jewish people. A high point in the synagogue service still today is the recitation of these words. There is only one God, and God alone is Israel's God. This belief calls forth a total dedication to God with "your heart, your soul, and your strength"—God must be loved with our entire being.

A scribe (someone well trained in interpreting the Jewish Law) comes to Jesus in today's Gospel with a question: "Which is the first of all the commandments?" This was a much discussed question in Israel at that time with two main schools of thought: Rabbi Shammai was very strict, while Rabbi Hillel was more pastoral and taught that the whole law is summed up in the words "What you hate for yourself, do not do to your neighbor."

Against this background the scribe wishes to see where Jesus stands. Jesus quotes the words of the Shema Israel, but goes even farther by adding a second part: "You shall love your neighbor as yourself" (from Leviticus 19:19). By bringing together these two commandments, Jesus makes an important point. While he upholds the Old Testament, he also offers a clear way of interpreting the numerous laws—through the lens of love: love God and love your neighbor as yourself.

Jesus offers us today a path to follow in life: love of God and love of neighbor should direct every action. When faced with decisions in life, our first question must always be: How does the law of love of God and neighbor influence this situation?

◆ Looking carefully at the First Reading and Gospel, find specific words that reveal the bonds of affection between God and humanity rather than simply dutiful or even fearful obedience from the people.

◆ What helpful insights about the love of God does today's Responsorial Psalm offer you?

◆ How do you live the commandment of love in your private life and in your public life?

READING I *1 Kings 17:10–16*

In those days, Elijah the prophet went to Zarephath. As he arrived at the entrance of the city, a widow was gathering sticks there; he called out to her, "Please bring me a small cupful of water to drink." She left to get it, and he called out after her, "Please bring along a bit of bread." She answered, "As the LORD, your God, lives, I have nothing baked; there is only a handful of flour in my jar and a little oil in my jug. Just now I was collecting a couple of sticks, to go in and prepare something for myself and my son; when we have eaten it, we shall die." Elijah said to her, "Do not be afraid. Go and do as you propose. But first make me a little cake and bring it to me. Then you can prepare something for yourself and your son. For the LORD, the God of Israel, says, 'The jar of flour shall not go empty, nor the jug of oil run dry, until the day when the LORD sends rain upon the earth.'" She left and did as Elijah had said. She was able to eat for a year, and he and her son as well; the jar of flour did not go empty, nor the jug of oil run dry, as the LORD had foretold through Elijah.

RESPONSORIAL PSALM
Psalm 146:7, 8–9, 9–10 (1b)

R. Praise the Lord, my soul!
   or: Alleluia.

The LORD keeps faith forever,
   secures justice for the oppressed,
   gives food to the hungry.
The LORD sets captives free. R.

The LORD gives sight to the blind;
   the LORD raises up those
       who were bowed down.
The LORD loves the just;
   the LORD protects strangers. R.

The fatherless and the widow he sustains,
   but the way of the wicked he thwarts.
The LORD shall reign forever;
   your God, O Zion, through all generations.
       Alleluia. R.

READING II *Hebrews 9:24–28*

Christ did not enter into a sanctuary made by hands, a copy of the true one, but heaven itself, that he might now appear before God on our behalf. Not that he might offer himself repeatedly, as the high priest enters each year into the sanctuary with blood that is not his own; if that were so, he would have had to suffer repeatedly from the foundation of the world. But now once for all he has appeared at the end of the ages to take away sin by his sacrifice. Just as it is appointed that human beings die once, and after this the judgment, so also Christ, offered once to take away the sins of many, will appear a second time, not to take away sin but to bring salvation to those who eagerly await him.

GOSPEL *Mark 12:38–44*

Shorter: Mark 12:41–44

In the course of his teaching Jesus said to the crowds, "Beware of the scribes, who like to go around in long robes and accept greetings in the marketplaces, seats of honor in synagogues, and places of honor at banquets. They devour the houses of widows and, as a pretext recite lengthy prayers. They will receive a very severe condemnation."

He sat down opposite the treasury and observed how the crowd put money into the treasury. Many rich people put in large sums. A poor widow also came and put in two small coins worth a few cents. Calling his disciples to himself, he said to them, "Amen, I say to you, this poor widow put in more than all the other contributors to the treasury. For they have all contributed from their surplus wealth, but she, from her poverty, has contributed all she had, her whole livelihood."

Practice of Charity

The widow who fed Elijah with the last food she had and the widow who contributed her whole livelihood to the Temple treasury inspire us: "If they can do that, I can at least do something!" Heroes have that effect on us because they are not centered on themselves. ◆ The Church has reemphasized stewardship as an approach to life, not just a matter of giving money. It is centered on living out of gratitude. When we receive gifts, we naturally want to respond. Read a summary of the United States Conference of Catholic Bishops' document on stewardship at http://www.usccb.org/beliefs-and-teachings/what-we-believe/stewardship/index.cfm or call 202-541-3000 to obtain a copy. ◆ Take a look at your giving practices—in terms of money, time, and talent. Does what you are doing fit your values? ◆ Meditate on the gifts God has given you and consider a fitting response.

Download more questions and activities for families, Christian initiation groups, and other adult groups at http://www.ltp.org/t-productsupplements.aspx.

Scripture Insights

"The widow's mite" would be a suitable headline for today's readings. True generosity is portrayed through the lives of two widows, the most vulnerable people in society. In the First Reading a widow, in the middle of a great famine, shares the last of her resources with the prophet Elijah. Elijah's trust and encouragement ("Do not be afraid.") strengthen her trust in God and her generosity in sharing her last meal with Elijah is rewarded with a supply of food that lasts throughout the famine.

Today's Gospel reading opens with Jesus' remarks about the scribes, and these provide the context for what follows. He is criticizing the Jewish scribes, the legal experts, for being more interested in receiving honor from people than serving them. Jesus singles out the way "they devour the houses of widows"—a devastating criticism!

In contrast to their selfishness, Jesus observes a widow in the Temple who provides an authentic example of sacrificial giving. Jesus draws attention to her putting "two small coins worth a few cents" into one of the thirteen collection boxes. Sadly, this translation has lost the beauty of a long English tradition! Literally, the translation should read: *"a poor widow came and threw in two mites that make up half a farthing!"* The coin referred to here as "a mite" (Greek *lepton*) is the lowest denomination of a coin that has ever been struck by any nation in history! And yet she is giving to the treasury what in fact she could not afford.

Both readings illustrate the genuine self-sacrificing nature of giving. The widows gave to the extent of hurting! These acts of self-sacrifice by the poorest and most vulnerable offer a beautiful foreshadowing of the genuine self-sacrifice of Jesus whereby he gave his very life for our salvation.

◆ Have you had an experience (as donor or recipient) in which generosity was truly an act of self-sacrifice?

◆ How does the Second Reading enhance our understanding of the First Reading and Gospel?

◆ Is there some part of your life where you hold back and do not put all you are at Christ's disposal?

November 18, 2018

READING I *Daniel 12:1–3*

In those days, I, Daniel,
>   heard this word of the Lord:
"At that time there shall arise
>   Michael, the great prince,
>   guardian of your people;
it shall be a time unsurpassed in distress
>   since nations began until that time.
At that time your people shall escape,
>   everyone who is found written in the book.

"Many of those who sleep in the dust of the
>   earth shall awake;
some shall live forever,
>   others shall be an everlasting horror
>   and disgrace.

"But the wise shall shine brightly
>   like the splendor of the firmament,
and those who lead the many to justice
>   shall be like the stars forever."

RESPONSORIAL PSALM
Psalm 16:5, 8, 9–10, 11 (1)

R. You are my inheritance, O Lord!

O LORD, my allotted portion and my cup,
>   you it is who hold fast my lot.
I set the LORD ever before me;
>   with him at my right hand
>   I shall not be disturbed. R.

Therefore my heart is glad and my soul rejoices,
>   my body, too, abides in confidence;
because you will not abandon my soul to the
>   netherworld,
>   nor will you suffer your faithful one to
>   undergo corruption. R.

You will show me the path to life,
>   fullness of joys in your presence,
>   the delights at your right hand forever. R.

READING II *Hebrews 10:11–14, 18*

Brothers and sisters: Every priest stands daily at his ministry, offering frequently those same sacrifices that can never take away sins. But this one offered one sacrifice for sins, and took his seat forever at the right hand of God; now he waits until his enemies are made his footstool. For by one offering he has made perfect forever those who are being consecrated.

Where there is forgiveness of these, there is no longer offering for sin.

GOSPEL *Mark 13:24–32*

Jesus said to his disciples: "In those days after
>   that tribulation
>   the sun will be darkened,
>   and the moon will not give its light,
and the stars will be falling from the sky,
>   and the powers in the heavens will
>   be shaken.

"And then they will see 'the Son of Man coming in the clouds' with great power and glory, and then he will send out the angels and gather his elect from the four winds, from the end of the earth to the end of the sky.

"Learn a lesson from the fig tree. When its branch becomes tender and sprouts leaves, you know that summer is near. In the same way, when you see these things happening, know that he is near, at the gates. Amen, I say to you, this generation will not pass away until all these things have taken place. Heaven and earth will pass away, but my words will not pass away.

"But of that day or hour, no one knows, neither the angels in heaven, nor the Son, but only the Father."

Practice of Hope

When the liturgical year reaches a close, the readings urge us to remember that the cycle won't always continue, not for individuals, not for the Church, not for the universe. Right before the end time, it won't be pretty, but the pain will conclude in a long-awaited reunion with Christ. ◆ For a good reflection on trials and tribulations, listen to this podcast from Fr. Charles Gordon at the Garaventa Center for Catholic Intellectual Life and American Culture: https://sites.up.edu/garaventa/33rd-sunday-in-ordinary-time-cycle-b-november-15-2015. ◆ Reach out to someone you know who is in the middle of a crisis or a hard time. It's best not to say, "Everything will be alright," but your presence and willingness to listen to their story will lead toward that conclusion. ◆ If you are in the middle of your own trials—as a young person discerning your life, as a parent, or as an ailing elder, pray over the apocalyptic pattern—bad things happen and lead the way to advances and deeper glory.

Download more questions and activities for families, Christian initiation groups, and other adult groups at http://www.ltp.org/t-productsupplements.aspx.

Scripture Insights

Reading the signs of the times! The tone and words of today's readings appear dark and troubling, but they are intended to offer us hope and expectation. Our First Reading, from the prophet Daniel, looks forward to an afterlife where those faithful to God will rise to an eternal life. This passage is the earliest reference in the Scriptures to hope in an individual resurrection.

Today's Gospel passage comes from a chapter in Mark's Gospel in which Jesus speaks, for the entire chapter, about his Second Coming at the end of time. Jesus uses images, pictures, and the imagination of the Jewish people to describe this event. He is not giving a blueprint for exactly what is going to take place in the future. Instead, by means of the images, he conveys a simple truth that he will return at the end of time. We proclaim this truth in the Apostles Creed: "I believe in the resurrection of the dead and the life of the world to come."

Jesus' words are not meant to be terrifying. The apocalyptic imagery at least partly reflects the suffering and evil that people were already experiencing. This evil will surely be vanquished when Christ returns, and this vanquishing of evil will surely entail some chaos before the dawn of peace. As part of the Gospel, the Good News, Jesus' words offer us the hope that we are destined for eternal life. The Gospel calls on us to be watchful and to lead our lives in expectation of the master's return. *When* he will come is not important; what is important is that we lead our daily lives prepared to meet him when in fact he does return, as we pray daily in the Our Father, "Thy Kingdom come!"

We can be sure that the world as we know it will pass away, but one thing remains steadfast: "My words will not pass away!"

◆ How does today's Responsorial Psalm resonate with the Gospel?

◆ Which words or images in these readings give hope?

◆ How does the realization that all things are transitory help you know how to lead your daily life?

November 25, 2018

READING I *Daniel 7:13–14*

As the visions during the night continued, I saw
  one like a son of man coming,
    on the clouds of heaven;
  when he reached the Ancient One
    and was presented before him,
  the one like a Son of man received dominion,
      glory, and kingship;
  all peoples, nations,
      and languages serve him.
His dominion is an everlasting dominion
    that shall not be taken away,
  his kingship shall not be destroyed.

RESPONSORIAL PSALM
Psalm 93:1, 1–2, 5 (1a)

R. The Lord is king; he is robed in majesty.

The LORD is king, in splendor robed;
  robed is the LORD and girt about with
      strength. R.

And he has made the world firm,
  not to be moved.
Your throne stands firm from of old;
  from everlasting you are, O LORD. R.

Your decrees are worthy of trust indeed;
  holiness befits your house,
  O LORD, for length of days. R.

READING II *Revelation 1:5–8*

Jesus Christ is the faithful witness, the firstborn
of the dead and ruler of the kings of the earth. To
him who loves us and has freed us from our sins
by his blood, who has made us into a kingdom,
priests for his God and Father, to him be glory and
power forever and ever. Amen.

Behold, he is coming amid the clouds,
  and every eye will see him,
  even those who pierced him.
All the peoples of the earth will lament him.
  Yes. Amen.

"I am the Alpha and the Omega," says the
Lord God, "the one who is and who was and who
is to come, the almighty."

GOSPEL *John 18:33b–37*

Pilate said to Jesus, "Are you the King of the Jews?"
Jesus answered, "Do you say this on your own or
have others told you about me?" Pilate answered,
"I am not a Jew, am I? Your own nation and the
chief priests handed you over to me. What have
you done?" Jesus answered, "My kingdom does
not belong to this world. If my kingdom did belong
to this world, my attendants would be fighting to
keep me from being handed over to the Jews. But
as it is, my kingdom is not here." So Pilate said to
him, "Then you are a king?" Jesus answered, "You
say I am a king. For this I was born and for this I
came into the world, to testify to the truth. Everyone who belongs to the truth listens to my voice."

Practice of Faith

The liturgical year has ended again, with a reminder that Jesus is King. We Americans have a tricky relationship with royalty. We don't like to defer to authority. We like to control our own destinies. But as Alcoholics Anonymous reminds all of us, the first step in any spiritual progress is utter surrender. ◆ Whether or not you have an addiction, read the first three steps of AA, a process formed with the help of a Catholic priest. ◆ Today, find a concrete way to give up control of someone or something not well served by your zealous intentions. ◆ Soon, subjects as we are, we begin Advent, a time of waiting that is such a key part of the Christian life. Pray over this from Cardinal John Henry Newman: "They, then, watch and wait for their Lord, who are tender and sensitive in their devotion towards Him; who feed on the thought of Him, hang on His words; live in His smile, and thrive and grow under His hand" (Sermon 3).

Download more questions and activities for families, Christian initiation groups, and other adult groups at http://www.ltp.org/t-productsupplements.aspx.

Scripture Insights

On this final Sunday of the liturgical year, we celebrate Jesus Christ as ruler over ourselves and the universe. In the opening words of Mark's Gospel, Jesus calls us to accept the Kingdom: "The Kingdom of God is at hand. Repent, and believe in the gospel" (Mark 1:15). Christians believe that God's rule took a leap forward when the Son of God became human, but it will only reach fulfillment at the end of time. Today's readings celebrate the culmination of God's plan. When Christ returns, everything, even death itself, will be subjected to him.

The First Reading gives a striking picture of Daniel's vision: "one like a Son of Man coming on the clouds of heaven." All nations will serve him, and he will bring everything under "his Kingship that shall not be destroyed." The Book of Revelation offers insight into what Christ's kingship means for us. He has freed us from our sins by his blood and has made us "into a kingdom, priests for his God and Father." The kingdom is not a place! Christ made us into a kingdom of priests who worship God by our lives. He rules over our hearts, making his kingdom within us.

Finally in the Gospel Jesus stands before an earthly ruler who asks if he is King of the Jews. Jesus explains that his kingdom is not of this world. By acknowledging the rule of Christ over us, we ask him to rule us with the power of his love. As St. Augustine wrote: to "pray that His kingdom may come, is . . . to wish of Him, that He would make us worthy of His kingdom . . . for then to us will His kingdom come" (Sermon 8 on the New Testament).

◆ What do the images in the first and second readings have in common? What impression do they give you of the Second Coming?

◆ What words in the Responsorial Psalm speak to you of kingship?

◆ In the Gospel, Jesus says his kingdom is not earthly, and that he came into the world to testify to the truth. What could he mean?